THE ROLE OF EMPLOYER ASSOCIATIONS AND LABOUR UNIONS IN THE EMU

The Role of Employer Associations and Labour Unions in the EMU

Institutional requirements for European economic policies

Edited by
GERHARD HUEMER
MICHAEL MESCH
FRANZ TRAXLER

Ashgate

Aldershot • Brookfield USA • Singapore • Sydney

Published by
Ashgate Publishing Ltd
Gower House
Croft Road
Aldershot
Hants GU11 3HR
England

HD
6948
.E85
R 65
1999

Ashgate Publishing Company
Old Post Road
Brookfield
Vermont 05036
USA

British Library Cataloguing in Publication Data
The role of employer associations and labour unions in the
    EMU : institutional requirements for European economic
    policies
    1. Trade-unions - European Union countries - Congresses
    2. European Union countries - economic conditions - 20th
    century - Congresses
    I. Huemer, Gerhard II. Mesch, Michael III. Traxler, Franz
    331.8'8'094

Library of Congress Catalog Card Number: 99-73477

ISBN 0 7546 1076 4

Printed in Great Britain by
Antony Rowe Ltd, Chippenham, Wiltshire

Contents

List of Figures

List of Tables

List of Graphs

List of Contributors

Colin Crouch, Professor of Sociology, Department of Political and Social Sciences, European University Institute, San Domenico di Fiesole, Italy.

Bernhard Ebbinghaus, Max Planck Institute for the Study of Societies, Cologne, Germany.

Ulrich Fritsche, German Institute for Economic Research (DIW), Berlin, Germany.

Justin Greenwood, Professor of European Public Policy, School of Public Administration and Law, Faculty of Management, Robert Gordon University, Aberdeen, United Kingdom.

Gustav A. Horn, German Institute for Economic Research (DIW), Berlin, Germany.

Wolfgang Scheremet, German Institute for Economic Research (DIW), Berlin, Germany.

Philippe C. Schmitter, Professor of Political Science, Department of Political and Social Sciences, European University Institute, San Domenico di Fiesole, Italy.

Ludwig Schubert, Director, European Commission, DG II, Brussels.

Franz Traxler, Professor of Sociology, Institute of Sociology, University of Vienna, Austria.

Jelle Visser, Professor of Empirical Sociology, Amsterdam Institute for Advanced Labour Studies, University of Amsterdam, Netherlands.

Rudolf Zwiener, German Institute for Economic Research (DIW), Berlin, Germany.

Preface

The present volume is based on the proceedings of an international symposium organised by the *"Arbeitskreis für ökonomische und soziologische Studien"* (Working Group for Economic and Social Studies) entitled "Institutional Requirements for European Economic Policies". The conference was held in Vienna on September 5th and 6th, 1998.

The Arbeitskreis is comprised of representatives of the Austrian Federal Economic Chamber, the Austrian Federal Chamber of Labour, the Austrian Federation of Trade Unions, and the Federation of Austrian Industry. Its goal is to carry out scientific research on issues that are of long-term importance to the Austrian economy and that relate to the activities of the organisations mentioned.[1]

With the start of European Economic and Monetary Union, the year 1999 marks the beginning of a new stage of integration in Europe. A common currency for 11 EU member states substantially changes the conditions under which economic transactions take place and it establishes a new framework for macro-economic policy in Europe.

By "European economic policies" we do not mean "European" in a geographical sense, but in the sense that certain essential characteristics of Europe's economy and society are shared by all—or at least by many— member states of the EU and are therefore also elements of a common European identity. The symposium was intended to analyse and discuss in depth how these characteristics will or could be affected by the recent institutional changes brought about by the integration process and in addition also by intensifying global competition.

The main focus was on those aspects of change in institutional and other framework conditions in which social partners are involved as actors in policy-making and therefore share responsibilities for outcomes: for successes as well as for failures. Contributions were grouped around three basic subjects: What constitutes the European economic and social model? What are the consequences of EMU for macro-economic policy, especially monetary policy and wage formation? Finally, what are the institutional and other requirements for policy co-ordination at the European level?

It was the intention of the organisers of this symposium to bring together social scientists and practitioners of the Social Partnership for a fruitful debate.

The Arbeitskreis expresses its thanks to all contributors and also to the editors on whose shoulders not only rested the main responsibility for preparation and organisation of the symposium but also for making this publication possible within one year after the event. Finally, we should like to express our appreciation for editorial assistance by Marjorie Fiebinger (language editing), Lina Zehetner (Zehetner GesmbH, formatting), and the publisher.

Günther Chaloupek
Chairman of the *Arbeitskreis für ökonomische und soziologische Studien*

Vienna, March 1999

Note

1   To mention only the most recent one: Michael Mesch (ed.), Sozialpartnerschaft und Arbeitsbeziehungen in Europa (MANZ: Vienna 1995).

1 Does a European Social Model Exist and Can It Survive?

BERNHARD EBBINGHAUS

Introduction

More than ten years ago, when the project of the Single European Market was on the European political agenda, Michael Emerson—on leave from the European Commission— wrote a small monograph entitled *What Model for Europe?* (1988). He begins his book with an anecdote from a conference at which an American economist criticised Europeans for their employment problem and recommended the adoption of the American model of an unregulated labour market. This provoked the sharp reply of a European politician: "You do not understand that Europe operates on a different model" (Emerson, 1988, p. 1). A decade later, we still quest for a European social model as a base for transnational co-operation and cohesion, in particular, in the debate on EU social policy. An answer to the query might depend on the lens we use: From afar, when we compare the European welfare states with the advanced market economies of North America and Asia, we can recognise Europe's shared distinctiveness, whereas, when we look closer, we perceive intra-European, cross-national diversity. If there is—or should be—a model that takes the lead in European integration, this blue-print would have to portrait as much about Europe's unity of shared social values, institutions and structure as it would about how to manage historically-entrenched cross-national diversity.

The quest for a European social model is not merely an academic endeavour but also an issue of political relevance for European integration. An analysis of the congruence of European societies helps us to understand the sources and potential for political and economic transnational co-operation. The European Commission has made explicit reference to the "European social model" in order to advance a common social policy agenda and to include social partners in the process. An analysis of the European socio-economic model is also of importance for understanding its

1

comparative advantages and the continued viability of this model, given global competition. Thus, we might ask whether European market societies distinguish themselves from other leading industrial world regions, in particular from North America and the Asia-Pacific region. In a comparison of the triad of "global players"—to borrow from the jargon of international business—we can indeed detect some distinct European features vis-à-vis the USA and Japan, and some trends towards convergence within Europe (Boyer, 1996; Kaelble, 1987; Therborn, 1995).

When we look more closely, we find that there is not one European model, but that Europe is built on a "variable geometry" not only of political membership but also of partially overlapping social institutions and sets of national models that co-exist across Europe (Ebbinghaus and Kraus, 1997). There are significant cross-national variations among the major components of *the* European model that have been entrenched in national social institutions over centuries. Moreover, because national modes of regulation, in particular social policy and industrial relations, serve an important integrative function for nation-states, they are reluctant to transfer competencies to the European level. The scope of EU redistributive social policies and transnational regulation in labour relations is rather limited, particularly in such matters as social insurance, strike laws, or workplace representation (Leibfried and Pierson, 1995; Marks et al., 1996; Ulman, Eichengreen, and Dickens, 1993).

But even if European unity has been built on a distinct mix of national socio-economic models, the question remains whether these socio-economic institutions and social practices are still viable under on-going globalisation pressures and further steps toward European integration. With the Single European Market and European Monetary Union (EMU), European economies are increasingly facing "regime competition" (Streeck, 1995) vis-à-vis the other OECD countries and developing markets. For instance, Swedish neo-corporatism and the German "social market" economy, hailed in the past for their successful combination of competitive export-oriented market economies and advanced welfare states, have become heavily undermined in the 1990s (Pontusson, 1997; Streeck, 1997b). As these are prime examples, the debate on the "end of corporatism" (Lash and Urry, 1987) or the German "Standort" (Immerfall and Franz, 1998) is disclosing cases of the multiple threats to the viability of Europe's model. But even if the malaise of these two important economies may not be the fate of their smaller neighbours, their economic problems will have repercussions on the whole European Economic Area.

Certainly, transnational pressures cannot be denied—external competition and internal challenges will require the adaptation of both national and European-level socio-economic institutions (Grahl and Teague, 1997). The question remains whether Europe's only possible response is to follow the Anglo-American liberal deregulatory path on which at least Britain has set her course. Whether regime competition will undermine the present models or lead to downward spirals of deregulation and fragmentation is hotly debated, yet thus far the issues remain largely unresolved (Abrahamson, 1991, Streeck, 1995, Scharpf, 1996). The public and academic debate is swayed by examples of national economies both within Europe and outside Europe that fare better than others, and these are seen as possible "models" for adaptation. Most recently, such show-cases include the US job-machine, the radical welfare state reforms of New Zealand, the Dutch employment "miracle", the Irish economic growth record, and the Danish turn-around in unemployment.

While the term "model" as used in public debate often implies a masterplan, it is used here as shorthand for the way in which specific combinations of institutions and social practices govern marketsociety relations in a particular nation-specific combination. This conception of socio-economic models goes beyond a narrow focus on the governance of markets, macro-economic policy, and production systems, to include the employment relations, labour market organisation and social policies. In fact, one would expect that different models arise more from the non-economic spheres than from the mode of economic governance.

In the brief comparative analysis presented here, the focus will be on the main aspects of economic governance, industrial relations employment regimes, and the welfare state. In this chapter, we will first analyse the main trends and cross-national differences in these areas, comparing the European Economic Area with the USA and Japan. While there has been some convergence in macro-economic development, especially in inflation rates and economic growth, there are still important cross-national differences in the degree of internationalisation between the "global players" and within Europe. With the help of some main indicators, I will map the cross-national differences in labour relations, labour market trends, and welfare state policies. This supports the thesis that there are still marked differences throughout Europe. In a second step, four different European models will be described. Each model represents a particular combination of economic governance, industrial relations, employment regimes, and welfare state policies. Finally, at the end of this chapter, I consider the repercussions of the

Table 1.1   Socio-Economic Indicators, Europe, USA and Japan, 1990s

Model	Country	Trade (%GDP) 1995	Bargaining coverage 1990	Wage spread (males) 1994/3	Employment ratio 1995	Unemployment rate 1990–6	Taxation (%GDP) 1995	Social exp. (%GDP) 1993
		(1)	(2)	(3)	(4)	(5)	(6)	(7)
Nordic	Sweden	62.7	83	1.36	77.9	6.0	49.7	38.0
	Denmark	54.8	..	*1.38	72.9	8.4	51.3	31.0
	Finland	58.3	95	1.46	71.0	13.3	46.5	35.4
	Norway	59.1	75	*1.32	72.4	5.4	41.5	29.3
Centre	Germany	41.2	90	1.37	64.9	7.4	39.2	28.3
	Austria	62.7	98	1.67	63.0	4.0	42.4	25.8
	Belgium	82.4	90	1.38	56.6	10.1	46.5	*27.0
	Netherlands	76.7	71	1.56	65.2	6.8	44.0	30.2
Southern	France	40.0	92	1.60	59.0	10.9	44.5	27.3
	Italy	45.2	..	1.65	51.2	11.4	41.3	25.0
	Portugal	58.5	79	1.72	65.3	20.1	33.8	16.3
	Spain	41.5	68	..	55.8	5.8	34.0	22.5
	Greece	36.8	..	..	54.9	9.0	41.4	17.2
Anglo-Saxon	UK	49.3	47	1.74	68.3	8.5	35.3	23.4
	Ireland	92.4	..	..	55.3	14.2	33.8	20.1
	USA	22.5	18	2.13	73.3	6.2	27.9	15.6
Japanese	Japan	16.7	23	1.60	74.1	2.6	28.5	12.4

Source: (1, 4–5) OECD Historical Statistics, 1997,(2) OECD Employment Outlook 1994, (3) OECD Employment Outlook 1996. Notes: (*) 1990/91, (6–7) OECD in Figures, 1997.

coexistence of different models for European integration as well as the particular problems involved and their viability. Indeed, since national adaptations of the particular models are needed, the main task of bringing the collective actors together to co-ordinate the reform of the given institutional arrangements remains largely a national affair, in spite of whatever we might be able to learn from other models.

Global Convergence or Cross-National Diversity?

Does the European Economic Area resemble the American and Japanese economies, and have Europe's economies become more like their global competitors? Or can we still speak of a distinct European way? The globalisation debate has led to a revival of the convergence thesis (Boyer, 1996), though at the same time many comparative institutional studies point to persistent cross-national diversity (Berger and Dore, 1996, Crouch and Streeck, 1997). A brief comparative analysis of some major aspects of the socio-economic development with the help of a number of selected indicators (see Table 1.1) provides an overview of the main patterns and trends. In order to show convergence or divergence, we have described four aspects that are different in Europe than in the USA and Japan, though these are areas in which we can also find *intra*-European variations. These aspects are:

(1) *economic performance:* Europe has, by and large, a lower growth performance but higher trade dependency than Japan or the USA;
(2) *industrial relations*: Europe is marked by a higher degree of interest organisation and co-ordinated bargaining as well as a more equal wage structure;
(3) *labour market:* Europe suffers more from severe unemployment and a less flexible labour market;
(4) *welfare state*: Europe differs in its larger public budget and deficits, which finance more advanced social protection.

Economic Performance

Sustained economic growth, which in turn fosters welfare and employment, is a paramount indicator of economic performance. With the oil price shocks, the post-war golden age of record economic growth ended: Average growth rates declined to post-war lows in the early 1980s, affecting all parts of

Graph 1.1   GDP growth rates (in %), 1975–96

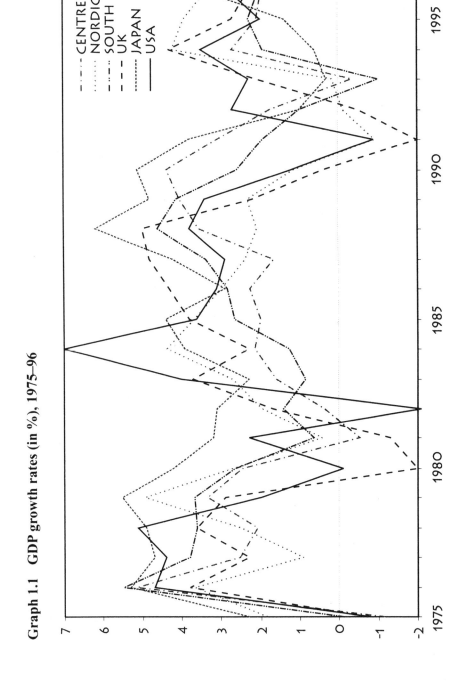

Europe, North America and even Asia. However, despite high dependency on oil, Japan fared far better than any other economy in the 1970s and 1980s and the USA was not hit as hard by the economic downturn as many European countries were. While the European economies followed a similar downward cycle, some were more severely hit by the recession of the mid-1970s and early 1980s: The UK and continental countries had growth rates of less than 2% in the first half of the 1980s, while the Scandinavians, the USA, and Japan did somewhat better. Note that Japan and the modernising Southern economies had higher growth rates until recently, due to the late-comer catching-up effect, and the fact that in contrast to the Nordic and continental European countries, the USA and UK oscillate through more pronounced up-and-downs. Yet by the early 1990s, recession had set in again and now all advanced economies, including Japan, the USA and UK seem to be converging around modest growth rates between 2% and 4% (Graph 1.1).

This convergence in economic growth, together with a narrowing of inflation rates, indicates how close European economies have grown with the Single European Market and the preparation for EMU. Today, the European Union is the largest "single market" in terms of consumers (373 million in 1996), compared with the US domestic market (265 million), which is one-third smaller and Japanese home market (126 million), which is much smaller, but more protected. However, in terms of economic strength (whether measured in GDP per head in US dollars or purchasing power parity), the US and Japanese economies still perform better than the Single European Market, and even most national economies in Europe. Yet today Japan faces a severe economic crisis, while the USA has good growth prospects. Also, some European countries share this good fortune, in particular, Ireland's now booming economy stands out for attracting foreign investment.

Europe is remarkable, however, in terms of its trade dependency (measured as combined export and import in percentage of GDP): The European single market countries, in particular the smaller economies were always more internationalised than the large domestic markets of the USA or Japan. While the two other "global players" are much less dependent on imports and exports, each national economy in Europe is at least twice as internationalised. Some smaller countries, such as Belgium, Ireland and, of course, Luxembourg, import and export nearly as much as their national gross domestic products. It should be noted, however, that the largest share of this trade dependency is due to the internal European market and not to world-wide trading. In the past, the European export economies were relatively dependent on the US dollar and Japanese yen exchange rates. The euro will provide better conditions for intra-European trade and might bring some advantages to the world market in the future, if it is able to become the second most important international currency after the US dollar.

Industrial Relations

The relations between organised capital and labour assume an important role in modern economies: They shape the environment for economic growth and social welfare. In Europe industrial relations at the national as well as the workplace level differ from those in North America and Japan, though there are also pronounced differences within Europe. In some countries with corporatist labour relations, especially in Scandinavia and continental Europe, trade union movements have gained an institutionalised role in national politics and economy (Crouch, 1993), while the two other "global players" have traditions of business or enterprise unionism. In the Nordic countries, unions have negotiated representative rights at the workplace level, while in some continental European countries, the state has legislated "dual" workplace representative structures with participation rights for employees. Such participation rights are unknown in North America and Japan (Rogers and Streeck, 1995).

In terms of membership strength, union density (measured as the share of the dependent labour force that is unionised) is higher on the average in Europe than in the USA and Japan (Visser, 1991). The American and Japanese union movements have suffered from severe declines in membership. But there are large cross-national differences in membership levels and trends across Europe (Ebbinghaus and Visser, 1999): The Nordic countries with union-led unemployment funds have gained in membership during the last decades, while most other countries have lost members. In particular, membership in France and the UK declined most dramatically, followed by Italy and Ireland, but also more gradually by the Netherlands and Austria. Instead of convergence, we find persistent—if not growing—divergence in the level and composition of union membership across Europe and vis-à-vis North America and Japan (Graph 1.2).

Employers associations— at least in the countries with neo-corporatist or social partnership traditions— are more centralised, more representative, and more co-operative than American employers, who often choose an anti-union strategy. The most important difference is the high coverage rate of collective agreements in Europe (ranging from 67% to 98% in 1990), compared to the USA (18%) and Japan (23%), although the UK (47%) and

Switzerland (53%) are moderately low (Traxler, 1994). In addition to the "social net" provided by the welfare states and stricter employment legislation in Europe, a larger section of the dependent workforce is collectively protected, thanks to a higher degree of union and employer organisation, and, where those are weak, *erga omnes* extension of collective agreements by the state.

As a consequence of the more co-ordinated bargaining structures and strategies, Europe (but also Japan) have less wage dispersion than the USA, which is free-market-oriented. Whereas American unskilled workers (those at the lowest decile of the income distribution) earn only around 40% of the median income, the lowest wage group ranges from around 60% in southern Europe and Japan to around 70% and more in Germany and Scandinavia (Traxler, 1994). Progressive taxation and social transfers may reduce these market induced income inequalities, yet again this holds true less for the US and Southern Europe. As a consequence of the residual welfare state, relative poverty levels are highest in the USA (17% after tax and transfers), followed by southern European countries (Italy, 14%), whereas Germany,

Graph 1.2   Net union density (in %), 1970–95

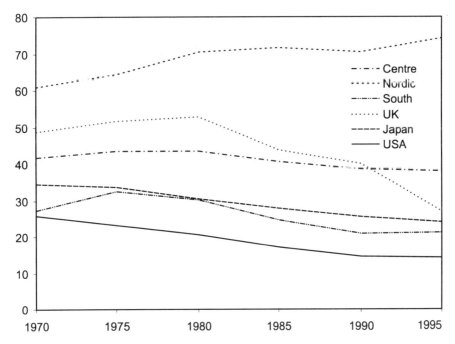

France, the Netherlands and the Nordic countries range below 10% (Esping-Andersen, 1990; Esping-Andersen, 1996a).With their more egalitarian wage structure and the lower post-tax / post-transfer income inequality, most European countries show a different conception of "fair share" in the value and profits gained from work. However, international competition, higher wages and non-wage labour costs tax the economic growth potential in the less productive sectors, such as private services, and hamper job creation, particularly for the less skilled.

Employment Trends

Large differences among the three "global players" can also be detected in respect to the structure of unemployment and the changes in it. One telling measure of the level of activity is employment ratios—that is, the share of the working population (15–64) with gainful employment. Both the US and Japanese labour markets have reached levels beyond 70% since the late 1970s and early 1980s respectively, whereas the European average has been below 65% ever since the first oil price shock in 1973. However, the Nordic countries (also Luxembourg and Switzerland) stand out with employment levels that are higher than those in the USA or Japan, despite their better welfare provision in case of non-work. Unlike the Nordic countries, the UK or the USA, the continental European societies still show a relatively low participation rate for women. They also use early retirement as an "exit" route to reduce labour supply during periods of mass unemployment. While labour market rigidities, through strict employment rights and practices, provide an obstacle to job growth, some of the high-value production systems in Europe profited from job tenure rules and internal labour markets. As in Japanese firms, these rules provide an institutional incentive for skill investment (vocational training), peaceful employment relations, and social acceptance of new technologies.

While for Japan with its tradition of life-long employment, and the USA with its relatively flexible labour market and wages, unemployment is less of a political concern, it has become the most urgent political problem in Europe. In the mid-1990s, the EU has about 20 million unemployed (11%), compared to only 8 million in the USA (6%) and 2 million in Japan (3%) (OECD 1997). Again, there are considerable intra-European variations: Spain stands out with a jobless rate of more than 20% followed by Finland, Ireland, France and Italy. Persistent unemployment in these countries goes together with high youth and long-term unemployment, indicating major problems of structural unemployment and labour market rigidities. Also noteworthy is the increase in unemployment in the 1990s of the previously unaffected full employment economies Austria, Finland and Sweden. The reduction of high unemployment in the USA, the Netherlands, and more recently in Denmark is remarkable: They all have become "models" over the last few years and are being discussed on an international basis. The American job machine and Dutch "(half) employment miracle" indicate the importance of the creation of service, part-time and temporary employment for a successful reduction of mass unemployment (Graph 1.3).

The Welfare State

The welfare state assumes a larger role in Europe than in the USA or Japan, requiring a much larger share of economic resources, though it has also reached its limits. European states tax their citizens more than other states: The EU member states receive on average over 40% of GPD in the form of taxes and social contributions, compared to less than 30% in Japan and the

Graph 1.3   Unemployment rates (in %), 1970–96

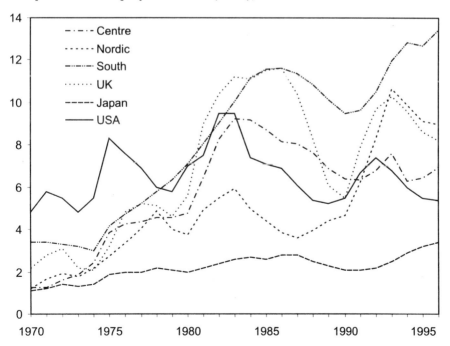

USA (see Table 1.1). However, there are also marked intra-European differences between high-tax welfare states such as Denmark and Sweden and those EU member states like Portugal, Spain and Britain, which tax less. In the past, some European welfare states expanded their public services without increasing the general and payroll taxes, thus running growing public deficits (most prominently: Italy and Belgium). Given the convergence criteria and the stability pact of the EMU, such fiscal policies have been stalled and countries with large public deficits have been forced to cut welfare expenses over the last few years. As in the USA, and followed most prominently by Thatcher's Britain, governments have started to downsize the public sector by means of employment cuts, privatisation, and marketisation, though European countries were much slower and less radical in following the Anglo-American example (Wright, 1994).

As in taxation and public spending, Europe stands out for its highly developed social transfer programmes. Public social spending (in percentage of GDP) of the six founding members of the Common Market vary between 25% and 30% (see Table 1.1). With the entry of Britain, the South and the Nordic countries, these differences in the "social dimension" became even larger within united Europe: The Nordic universalistic welfare states are leading the ranks (above 30%), followed by the continental conservative welfare states plus France and Italy, and then by the more residual, liberal British and Irish welfare states and the welfare laggards Greece, Spain, and Portugal (less than 25%). Nevertheless, all European welfare states compare favourably to the liberal US welfare state (15%) as well as the welfare laggard Japan (12%). However, outside the welfare state, US firms and larger Japanese corporations provide—partly mandated, partly voluntary—company benefits to their workers. Remarkably, there is a correlation among OECD countries between trade openness and social expenditure (albeit also with country size): Small states with open economies tend to spend more on social programmes, suggesting that they use social policy as a buffer for the vagaries of world market dependency (Rieger and Leibfried, 1997).

Two Varieties of Capitalism

Most prominently, Michel Albert has juxtaposed the Atlantic (Anglo-American) capitalism from Rhenish (German) capitalism (Albert, 1991).[1] Free market capitalism relies on short-term investment capital and thus seeks high profits for shareholders. It also rests on competition by means of low-wage mass production, which in turn requires a flexible labour market and wage structure. Due to a fragmented, uncoordinated, and decentralised system of industrial relations, "free riding" the institutional benefits without contributing to them is possible, while the production of collective goods such as non-firm-specific vocational training is rare, given lacking state support and weak associational capacity. Following voluntarist and pluralist traditions, the trade union movement is weak and fragmented. Moreover, it pays for companies to be "non-union" workplaces or to weaken trade union rights as was evident under the Reagan and Thatcher administrations.

"Rhenish" capitalism, on the other hand, profits come from patient long-term investment capital, "good" employment relations and stable producer-supplier ties. This is not only the case for Germany, but also for the Japanese model (Dore, 1997), though the Japanese labour relations at the national level and state social policy are less developed. Patient capital and life-long employment have provided, at least until today, the backbone of the Japanese model of diversified production. In contrast to Europe, the Japanese export-oriented economy remained relatively closed to international competition, thus protecting its own home market. Moreover, the future of the Japanese system is questionable, given the recent crisis in its financial system, the rising cost pressures of an ageing society, and the need for reform of its relatively rigid institutions.

These social institutions have not emerged by themselves but are the result of historical legacies and past collective decisions made by collective actors, the state and social partners. "Rhenish" capitalism, instead of relying merely on market mechanisms, enforces collectively-imposed "beneficial constraints" (Streeck, 1997a), such as high wages, which compel employers to seek cost-saving technological advances. In order to keep wages out of competition between firms and allow higher wages than the market-rate, a high degree of organisation and compliance is needed among employers and unions. For the success of a high-value growth strategy, encompassing interest organisation (Olson, 1982) is also important in providing other public goods, for instance, long-term investment in vocational training and upskilling of the workforce. Thus firms, especially small-scale handicraft employers and workers, have to be convinced by their associations to invest in contributing to a collective good, such as vocational training, since it is in everyone's interest. Also for workers, some social institutions, such as life-long employment, high wages, transferability of skills, career perspectives, and further training in case of technical change are important motivations for an upgrading of skills.

How many European Models?

Given these two varieties of capitalism, can we speak of "one" European model or should we specify several socio-economic models that coexist within the European Economic Area? The past and present reluctance of some countries—in particular Britain—to endorse European harmonisation beyond a mere free market project, has led to a "variable geometry" of Europeanisation. While a liberal uncoordinated market-economy is the undisputed model in Britain, the rest of Europe has not achieved the opposite form of coordinated capitalism everywhere. The role of the state and organised interests in providing such co-ordination varies considerably across Europe since individual states have deviating traditions of governing markets. Indeed, we can claim the coexistence of different models of socio-economic governance within the European Economic Area. While some countries come close to either pole of the two varieties of capitalism, others fall between (or more or less outside) these ideal-type opposite modes. Each model combines particular features and also faces specific problems of adaptation today. What we refer to as a "model" here is the way in which particular economic and social institutions fit together. Patterns will become clearer when we analyse the particular institutional mixes.

The four institutional complexes that we outlined in the descriptive tableau of major socio-economic trends constitute supportive "pillars" of the respective national models. In the core of the model lies the economic governance system (Hall, 1997; Lane, 1995; Soskice, 1990): an economic growth strategy that relies on a particular production regime and a supporting financial system that determines the scope of investment decisions. The particular economic governance model is coupled with specific national forms of industrial relations, employment regimes, and welfare states. These three institutional complexes provide an important supportive function for economic development. Thus the production regime is dependent on the nature of the relations between unions and employers and the way in which the collective bargaining system is organised. In addition, the employment regime defines the employment opportunities and regulation of the labour market. Further, the welfare state taxes economic resources but also provides social protection against social risks, which helps to maintain a skilled labour force.

All of these social institutions emerged during the post-war period as particular national combinations; they are deeply rooted in institutional legacies, national values and social cleavage structures. While the four

Table 1.2 The European Socio-Economic Models

	Nordic	Centre	Southern	Anglo-Saxon
Economic governance:				
financial governance	long-term, patient capital from banks	long-term, patient capital from banks	nationalised banks, state intervention	short-term, financial markets (share holders)
production regime	export dependent high-quality, high-skill flexible specialisation	export dependent, high-quality, high-skill flexible specialisation	(ex)nationalised mass production / flexible small firms	low-skill mass production, privatisation
Industrial relations:				
organised interests	centralised organisations, high union density, workplace representation	centralised organisations, membership declining, works councils	weak, fragmented labour, intransigent employers, strike propensity	fragmented unions, membership crisis, no-union strategy
bargaining system	Nordic neo-corporatism co-ordinated bargaining but decentralisation trend	"social partnership" co-ordinated bargaining but exit threat	decentralised bargaining, ad hoc state intervention, state-union crisis pacts	decentralised bargaining, voluntarism, lobbyism
Employment regime:				
employment	high employment rate (also female, part-time) recent unemployment	medium employment rate, mass unemployment and early retirement route	low employment rate, large public sector, mass (youth) unemployment	high employment rate (also female, part-time) cyclical unemployment
labour market	regulated labour market, life-long employment, skilled workforce	regulated labour market, life-long employment, skilled workforce	regulated labour market but flexible atypical work in SME/informal sector	flexible deregulated labour market
Welfare state:				
financing	high public expenditure, largely tax financed	medium expenditure, largely wage tax	medium expenditure, public debt, wage tax	medium expenditure, tax and private funded
social security	universalist welfare state, social service oriented	social insurance state, transfer oriented	residual, familist, transfer oriented welfare state	liberal welfare state, increased privatisation

described socio-economic "pillars" are often separately governed, we should not underestimate the ways in which they are interlinked: They are mutually-supporting and dependent of each other. Therefore, changes in one realm have consequences in others, as each set of institutions might have to rely on others for its functioning. Most importantly, a particular production regime, be it a low-wage mass production or high-value quality production strategy, requires a supporting "institutional infrastructure" (Soskice, 1991) in the realm of collective bargaining and workplace relations, labour market, and social protection. For instance, employment regulation guaranteeing life-long employment, a high-wage structure provided by centralised, co-ordinated bargaining, and social insurance against unemployment may all add to the institutional incentives for long-term skill investment by employers and workers that is crucial for the success of a high-value-added production strategy. This strategy will, in turn, finance and legitimate these non-market social institutions. Looking at the map of cross-national variations (see Table 1.2), I will argue that the European social landscape is built upon four distinct models.

Anglo-Saxon Model

The British model, particularly since the "Thatcher revolution", has followed the American "free market" model in applying supply-side macro-economic policies. The financial markets, concentrated in London's City, had always played a larger role in Britain (and in the USA), than on the Continent or in Japan. The privatisation of post-war nationalised industry and the public-service sector in the 1980s added to the dominance of short-term shareholder values, seeking immediate returns on invested capital. Ever since the late nineteenth century, a debate on the "industrial decline" of Britain has pointed to some of the shortcomings of such values: the lack of long-term and infrastructure investment, the low financing of research and development, a skill-deficit in the labour force, and relatively low levels of productivity. While the Conservative governments were able to attract some foreign capital and help industry by deregulation, they bet on a low-wage mass production strategy.

In order to make British industry more cost-competitive, the state intervened in the traditionally voluntarist system of industrial relations, restricting union immunities, strike rights, and closed shop practices. Collective bargaining became further decentralised as the union movement was not only fragmented, but also suffered a severe membership decline, while the employers lacked any interest in strong national organisation, except for lobbying purposes. Thus the low-wage mass production strategy finds institutional support by decentralised voluntarist labour relations, unregulated employment that allows "hiring and firing", and a liberal welfare state with low social benefits. Employment levels are relatively high, especially for women, compared to the continent, partly due to the lower social benefits, which are granted for a shorter period of time, and the more flexible labour market. The competitiveness problem has been tackled by further labour market deregulation, decentralisation of wage bargaining, lowering of the reservation wage, and further privatisation of public services and welfare provisions. After more than a year in office, the new Labour government does not appear to be reversing these prior measures or departing from this route.

Nordic Model

Not long ago, the Nordic model had been hailed for its "universalist" welfare state and full employment commitment of Sweden and its Nordic neighbours (Esping-Andersen, 1990). This was a remarkable achievement given the relatively high trade dependency of these small economies, the relatively well-developed employment rights, and high wages. The export dependent, high-quality, high-skill industrial sector was sustained by means of a financial system with neo-Keynesian macro-economic steering and long-term patient capital through state-financed co-operative loans, at least until the entry in the European currency system and recent liberalisation of capital controls (Stephens, 1996). Moreover, a system of centralised bargaining between encompassing and well-organised unions and employer associations had provided relatively high and equalising "solidaristic" wage structures that encouraged companies to restructure in order to become more productive (Pontusson, 1997). The social partners were also involved in nation-wide corporatist interest intermediation that went beyond income policies and included active employment and social policies. However, following the employment growth in the public sector and wage push by this sector, as well as state intervention into management prerogatives, private employers are seeking to further decentralise wage bargaining and are calling for labour market deregulation, undermining the post-war neo-corporatist system (Kjellberg, 1992; Lash and Urry, 1987).

With an exceptional record in maintaining full employment in the

1970s and 1980s, Sweden, Finland and Norway faced rising unemployment in the 1990s, while Denmark, a Common Market member, had always higher unemployment. Nevertheless, all Nordic countries still have remarkably high employment rates, thanks to high female labour force participation, widespread part-time work, a large public employment sector, and a relatively late actual retirement age (Esping-Andersen, 1990). Employment law and collective agreements have also provided nearly full-career life-long job security, providing the incentives to invest in skills needed by an export-oriented industry. The universalist welfare state also supported both the skilled workforce for the private sector and employment opportunities for women in social services. However, high public expenditures had driven taxation and social contributions to the highest level in Europe, lowering the competitiveness of the Nordic welfare states. Tax revolts like in Denmark, the entry in the EU by Sweden and Finland, and the financial crisis in the 1990s added to the problems of public financing and the need for retrenchment in welfare spending. Many observers see an end to the Nordic model, though these recent reforms, while breaking with some time-tested principles, have not been radical changes in course and were the outcome of relatively broad consensus building.

Europe's Centre Model

In Europe's Centre (Germany, and its neighbours, Austria, Belgium, and the Netherlands), the governance structure is traditionally different from the Anglo-American free market model (Soskice, 1991). Here long-term patient capital provided by "Hausbanken" has played a much larger role, as has the state in providing the needed infrastructure and social protection. These "social market" economies are all export-oriented, even Germany, which has a much larger home market than her smaller neighbours. Due to relatively high wages, companies can only compete on today's world markets with high-quality products and flexible specialisation, thus requiring highly-skilled labour and a high degree of technological innovation (Streeck, 1997b). However, given the relatively high wage levels, tailored to support the skilled industrial male breadwinner, there has been structural mass and long-term unemployment since the mid-1970s. Female, part-time and service employment all have been traditionally less frequent than in the Anglo-American or Nordic countries, yet some countries like the Netherlands have increased part-time and female employment in recent years (Visser and Hemerijck, 1997).

The "Social Partnership" between well-organised unions and employer associations plays a role beyond subsidiaristic self-regulation and co-ordinated wage bargaining—organised interests also play a role in social policy administration. Even at the workplace level statutory works councils have institutionalised forms of worker participation (on German management boards even co-determination). Worker representatives can secure employment rights, mediate in case of grievances and codetermine technological change. Moreover, due to the consensual style and strike-ban until the termination of a collective agreement, firms profit from the absence of industrial unrest, which would be particularly harmful to a just-in-time quality production strategy.

However, the model of Social Partnership has come under heavy pressure due to recent calls of employers to make the bargaining system more flexible and decentralised, but also due to the ongoing losses in membership and legitimisation on both sides. The continental employment dilemma (Scharpf, 1998) is rooted in the fact that social transfer-oriented welfare states are largely financed by social contributions that increase non-wage labour costs, thus taxing the competitiveness of export-oriented firms. In the past, social benefits have been used to support the unemployed and allow a reduction in labour supply through early retirement measures. The "social market" model has relied largely on a "welfare without work" strategy (Esping-Andersen, 1996b), thereby reinforcing the employment problem. In order to pay for the welfare of the non-active population, social contributions have to be raised and thus the rising non-wage labour costs are putting even more people out of work, leading to a vicious circle.

Southern Model

The Southern model shares many features of the Centre model (especially France and Italy), but it has some distinct features that show a different weight of state intervention and—in the case of Greece, Portugal and Spain—also late democratisation and opening towards Europe (Castles, 1995; Ferrera, 1996). These Southern economies are marked by a legacy of belated or incomplete transition from agrarian society to industrialisation, a large small-to-medium-sized firm sector, and a larger state role via nationalised banks, state-controlled conglomerates or public subsidies that substitute for lacking private capital (Lane, 1995; Schmidt, 1996). Recent privatisation efforts have increased market pressures, but the dualism between relatively monopolistic national industrial champions and a more or less flexible small-scale sector remains. State intervention was also necessary in the realm of labour relations, collective bargaining and employment regulation, because of the politically-fragmented union movement and intransigence of employers in the private sector. Large politically-motivated and wildcat sectionalist strikes are still common, particularly in the public sector. National social pacts and co-operative workplace relations have been difficult to institutionalise, although recent efforts in Italy, Spain and Portugal have shown some success.

These Southern economies are facing a severe employment problem: high unemployment, in particular for the young and foreign-born population, widespread early retirement, and low female participation rates. While part of the labour market is relatively well protected by seniority rights and employment law, those with atypical work contracts, younger job-seekers, or those in the informal sector are not enjoying the social protection of their fellow workers. With the exception of France and to some extent Italy, the Southern welfare states were relative latecomers and incompletely developed, public spending tended to follow a political clienteles motivation, but also remained residual due to still familistic and subsidiaristic principles of self-support (Ferrera, 1996). To meet the EMU convergence criteria, all Southern welfare states have faced severe financial limits of public spending, putting social policy reform and public sector downsizing high on the agenda of government-union-employer talks.

Strength and Weaknesses Reconsidered

These important intra-European variations have made European integration more difficult and led to a "variable geometry" of political, economic and social integration. While economic integration with the help of liberalisation has integrated all countries of the European Economic Area, EMU will not include all EU members (and the consequences of EMU for wage bargaining are still unknown). The future Eastern enlargement of the European Union will add considerable variation in economic governance, industrial relations and social protection, not to speak of the large differences in economic development. Moreover, the European "Social Dimension" remains underdeveloped, given the large variation across Europe and the concern for subsidiarity in the fields of social and labour policies (see Leibfried and Pierson, 1995; Marks et al., 1996). Since the latter are one of the last constituent national policy fields, national governments have and will be reluctant to transfer too much regulatory authority and redistributive resources to the European level, instead relying partially on the European Social Partners to come to a voluntary agreement in the European Social Dialogue.

The sources of strength of the co-ordinated social market models are — or at least have been—manifold. By and large, these social models allow a more socially-acceptable and peaceful adaptation to economic imperatives and global pressures, thanks to the more developed welfare state and better employment relations. Despite all rigidities, national and European-level concertation strategies provide opportunities and means for co-ordinated adaptation, while keeping negative social consequences at a minimum. In those European economies with established practices of co-ordinated capitalism, the high-skill, value-added, long-term strategies have provided a positive growth perspective. These economies did not follow the pronounced cyclical up-and-downs of the American or British market economies. The role of organised interests through institutionalised co-ordination procedures has been important for the support of these social models. Their viability rest on the "beneficial constraints" and institutional incentives that foster the provision of quasi public goods: negotiated wage moderation, avoidance of social dumping and harmful inequalities, collective provision of vocational training.

Although these socio-economic models have benefits or at least beneficial constraints, they also suffer from important disadvantages. The institutional logic of each model creates its own particular problems, and thus calls for specific national responses. For instance, the reliance of continental welfare states on early retirement measures, which allowed firms to shed well-protected older workers, has transferred the unemployment problem to the social insurance system, increasing social costs and payroll taxes (Esping-Andersen, 1996b; Scharpf, 1997). Today, the European models are under considerable pressure, not only due to global competition, but also for particular internal reasons. Four problems are of special concern as they undermine the "European social model" of combining market and social welfare principles that the continental and Nordic models share:

(1) The European welfare states have grown to their limits and are under severe pressure to be thoroughly reformed. These social policy reforms will have to take into account the contingency of increasing age dependency, changing employment and family patterns, the need to lower social costs, and limited public resources for social services. Yet, those in

favour of the "European social model", including the European Commission, want to emphasise its comparative advantages: avoiding large inequalities, allowing long-term skill investment, and granting protection against major social risks.

(2) In order to lower labour costs and increase competitiveness, European welfare states are under pressure to reduce social contributions, corporate taxes and income taxes. The proposed reforms suggest a partial shift from contribution-finances schemes to tax-financed schemes, from pay-as-you-go schemes to funded schemes, and from mandatory public insurance to voluntary private forms of savings. On the side of the collective bargaining parties, this will also entail an acceptance of wage moderation in return for jobs and social benefits and a reconsideration of the wage schemes, especially at the lower end.

(3) The reduction of labour cost strategy will by itself not suffice to alleviate mass unemployment, thus new policies to create employment and bring the unemployed back into work have been part of the recent successes of the Dutch and Danish reforms. In order to allow for the more differentiated work profiles and diversified production systems, regulation of collective contracts and employment laws is overdue. Here some of the rigidities of employment protection have to be reconsidered by the collective bargaining partners and the state, as the regulator of employment law. Moreover, more flexible regulations for service, part-time and temporary work have been proposed, but would require fine tuning of social policy instruments to take account of the new employment forms.

(4) The co-ordination capacity of organised interests, both labour and employers, has become increasingly undermined by declining membership, a crisis of legitimacy, increased "exits" from associational regulations, mobilisation of sectionalist interests and the pressures towards decentralisation in collective bargaining. Yet co-ordination is crucial to the success of negotiated "social pacts", which help to adapt the social model. Thus, instead of unilateral state intervention or mere reliance on market-mechanisms, as has been the case in the past for the Southern states and Anglo-Saxon models, the government and social partners are now seeking to co-ordinate welfare state reform, employment activities and wage bargaining policies in several European countries, but not in the UK (Hassel, 1998).

This brings us to our final questions: Can we learn from national models overseas or within Europe, which have apparently been successful? Is it possible, and—if so—preferable, to transplant social institutions and "best practices" from one economic, political and social context to another?

To what degree are national models and the Europeanisation process the intended outcome of public policies as implied by the idea of a "model"? Or were these models more the result of historical contingencies, unintended consequences and ungoverned processes? History teaches us at least one lesson: Learning from other nations has always included a translation and adaptation of foreign "best" practices to the national set of values, institutions and structures.

Given Europe's laboratory of diverse national policies, it might be more advisable to look for "best practices" within Europe as *Leitbilder* than copying the models from other "global players", in particular the USA and Japan. For instance, the Dutch "miracle" (Visser and Hemerijck, 1997) was constituted by the remarkable turn around from its past "welfare without work" problem: job growth thanks to wage moderation, part-time and new forms of employment, and more reliance on active rather than passive employment measures. However, the Dutch reform process was a long and unplanned sequence of measures, though they resulted from a step-by-step negotiated consensus between the main collective actorsthe government and the social partners. What we can learn from the Dutch case is that co-ordination at a national level is helpful in finding specific responses that take into account the institutions in place and the domestic situation. Yet it also requires a willingness of the collective actors to overcome sectionalist interests, seek a common solution and comply to the agreement which has been signed.

At the European level, the European Union has gained more competencies with the Maastricht Social Protocol, and the EU is now more active in shaping a common agenda on employment policies. This has opened up new routes for self-regulation (and tripartite concertation) by the European Social Partners and for a co-operation among European governments in matters of social and employment policies. Thus the European Commission's Social Action Programme 1998 2000 "provides a framework within which the process of social policy renewal will be taken forward, with the aim of reinforcing the core values of the European social model while ensuring that the Union is well placed to respond to new and emerging challenges in a fast changing world (Com(98)259: v)." Yet we should note that the EU mainly sets common policy aims, exchanges information on possible "best practices" and regulates by some selected framework agreements and directives. Moreover, the main reforms in economic governance, industrial relations, and welfare state and employment policies remain national prerogatives. Even after the Single

European Market and a possible future European company law, economic governance will have a national imprint. Similarly, wage bargaining will by and large remain a national affair despite EMU, though again, transnational co-ordination of national bargaining by unions has started to become a possible response to increased interdependency.

Despite globalization and Europeanisation, the discussed cross-national trends and patterns indicate that "the complex set of contradictory forces that are pushing simultaneously toward convergence and divergence are far from moving toward a single best institutional design" (Boyer, 1996, p. 59). Thus, while cross-national diversity provides some obstacles to Europeanisation, it also contributes to the richness and plurality of Europe. Indeed unity and diversity mark Europe, and this might provide the needed variety and experimental ground for generating and testing multiple adaptation strategies. How could we otherwise learn from "best practices" if there were no policy variations across Europe? Hence, Europe still has a long way to go until we can speak of "one" European model that is more than the "variable geometry" of different national practices that become increasingly interdependent.

Note

1   There is now a great deal of institutionalist literature in the field of comparative political economy (led by works of P Hall and D Soskice). This literature distinguishes between liberal uncoordinated market economies and co-ordinated "social" market economies (see Hall, 1997 and Rhodes and van Apeldoorn, 1997 for a literature review).

References

Abrahamson, P E (1991), "Welfare and progress in the Europe of the 1990s: Social progress or social dumping?", *International Journal of Health Services*, 21(2): 237–64.

Albert, M (1991), *Capitalisme contre Capitalisme*. Paris: Le Seuil.

Berger, S and R Dore, eds. (1996), *National Diversity and Global Capitalism*. Ithaca, NY: Cornell University.

Boyer, R (1996), "The Convergence Hypothesis Revisited: Globalization but Still the Century of Nations?", in S Berger and R Dore, eds., *National Diversity and Global Capitalism*. Ithaca, NY: Cornell University, 29–59.

Castles, F G (1995), "Welfare State Development in Southern Europe". *West European Politics*, 18(2): 291–313.

Crouch, C (1993), *Industrial Relations and European State Traditions*. Oxford: Clarendon Press.

Crouch, C and W Streeck, eds. (1997), *Political Economy of Modern Capitalism. Mapping Convergence and Diversity*. London: Sage.

Dore, R (1997), "The Distinctiveness of Japan", in C Crouch and W Streeck, eds., *Political Economy of Modern Capitalism. Mapping Convergence and Diversity*. London: Sage, 19–32.

Ebbinghaus, B and P A Kraus (1997), "Die variable Geometrie der Subsidiarität: Zur Problematik territorialer und funktionaler Integration in Europa", in T König, E Rieger, and H Schmitt, eds., *Europäische Institutionenpolitik*. Frankfurt: Campus, 335–58.

Ebbinghaus, B and J Visser (1999), "When Institutions Matter: Union Growth and Decline in Western Europe, 1950–95". *European Sociological Review*, 15(2): forthcoming.

Emerson, M (1988), *What Model for Europe?* Cambridge, MA: MIT Press.

Esping-Andersen, G (1990), *Three Worlds of Welfare Capitalism*. Princeton: Princeton University Press.

Esping-Andersen, G, ed. (1996a), *Welfare States in Transition. National Adaptations in Global Economies*. London: Sage.

Esping-Andersen, G (1996b), "Welfare States without Work: the Impasse of Labour Shedding and Familialism in Continental European", in G Esping-Andersen, ed., *Welfare States in Transition. National Adaptations in Global Economies*. London: Sage, 66–87.

Ferrera, M (1996), "The 'Southern Model' of Welfare in Social Europe". *Journal of European Social Policy*, 6(1): 17–37.

Grahl, J and P Teague (1997), "Is the European Social Model Fragmenting?" *New Political Economy*, 2(3): 405–26.

Hall, P A (1997), "The Role of Interests, Institutions, and Ideas in the Comparative Political Economy of the Industrialized Nations", in M I Lichbach and A S Zuckerman, eds., *Comparative Politics. Rationality, Culture, and Structure*. New York: Cambridge University Press, 174–207.

Hassel, A (1998), "Soziale Pakte in Europa", *Gewerkschaftliche Monatshefte*, 10/1998, 617–628.

Immerfall, S and P Franz (1998), *Standort Deutschland. Stärken und Schwächen im weltweiten Strukturwandel*. Opladen: Leske + Budrich.

Kaelble, H (1987), *Auf dem Weg zu einer europäischen Gesellschaft. Eine Sozialgeschichte Westeuropas 1880–1980*. München: Verlag C. H. Beck.

Kjellberg, A (1992), "Sweden: Can the Model Survive?", in A Ferner and R Hyman, eds., *Industrial Relations in the New Europe*. Oxford: Blackwell, 88–142.

Lane, C (1995), *Industry and Society in Europe. Stability and Change in Britain, Germany and France*. Aldershot: Edgar Elgar.

Lash, S and J Urry (1987), *The End of Organized Capitalism*. Cambridge: Polity Press.

Leibfried, S and P Pierson, eds. (1995), *European Social Policy: Between Fragmentation and Integration*. Washington, DC: Brookings Institution.

Marks, G et al., eds. (1996), *Governance in the European Union*. London: Sage.

Olson, M (1982), *The Rise and Decline of Nations*. New Haven, London: Yale University Press.

Pontusson, J (1997), "Between Neo-Liberalism and the German Model: Swedish Capitalism in Transition", in C Crouch and W Streeck, eds., *Political Economy of Modern Capitalism. Mapping Convergence and Diversity*. London: Sage, 55–70.

Rhodes, M and B van Apeldoorn (1997), "Capitalism versus Capitalism in Western Europe", in M Rhodes, P Heywood, and V Wright, eds., *Developments in West European Politics*. London: Macmillan, 171–89.

Rieger, E and S Leibfried (1997), "Die sozialpolitischen Grenzen der Globalisierung". *Politische Vierteljahresschrift*, 38(4): 771–96.

Rogers, J and W Streeck, eds. (1995), *Works Councils. Consultation, Representation, and Cooperation in Industrial Relations*. Chicago: University of Chicago.

Scharpf, F W (1996), "Negative and Positive Integration in the Political Economy of European Welfare States", in G Marks et al., eds., *Governance in the European Union*. London: Sage, 15–39.

Scharpf, F W (1997), "Employment and the Welfare State: A Contiental Dilemma". *MPIfG, Cologne, Working Paper*, 7.

Scharpf, F W (1998), "Employment and the Welfare State: A Contiental Dilemma", in GAAC, ed., *Labour Markets in the USA and Germany*. Bonn: GAAC, 387–404.

Schmidt, V A (1996), "Industrial Policy and Policies of Industry in Advanced Industrialized Nations (Review Article)". *Comparative Politics*, 28: 225–48.

Soskice, D. (1990), "Reinterpreting Corporatism and Explaining Unemployment: Co-ordinated and Non-co-ordinated Market Economies", in R Brunetta and C Dell'Aringa, eds., *Labour Relations and Economic Performance*. New York: New York University Press, 170–211.

Soskice, D (1991), "The Institutional Infrastructure for International Competitiveness: A Comparative Analysis of the UK and Germany", in A B Atkinson and B. Renato, eds., *Economics for the New Europe*. London: Macmillan.

Stephens, J D (1996), "The Scandinavian Welfare States: Achievements, Crisis and Prospects", in G Esping-Andersen, ed., *Welfare States in Transition. National Adaptations in Global Economies*. London: Sage, 32–65.

Streeck, W (1995), "From Market-Making to State-Building? Reflections on the Political Economy of European Social Policy", in S Leibfried and P Pierson, eds., *European Social Policy: Between Fragmentation and Integration*. Washington, DC: Brookings Institution, 389–431.

Streeck, W (1997a), "Beneficial Constraints: On the Economic Limits of Rational Voluntarism", in J R Hollingsworth and R Boyer, eds., *Contemporary Capitalism. The Embeddedness of Institutions*. New York: Cambridge University Press, 197–219.

Streeck, W (1997b), "German Capitalism: Does it Exist? Can it Survive?", in C Crouch and W Streeck, eds., *Political Economy of Modern Capitalism. Mapping Convergence and Diversity*. London: Sage, 33–54.

Therborn, G (1995), *European Modernity and Beyond: The Trajectory of European Societies, 1945–2000*. London: Sage.

Traxler, F (1994), "Collective Bargaining: Levels and Coverage". *OECD Employment Outlook*, 167–94.

Ulman, L, B Eichengreen, and W T Dickens, eds. (1993), *Labor and an Integrated Europe*. Washington: Brookings Institute.

Visser, J (1991), "Trends in Trade Union Membership", *OECD Employment Outlook 1991*. Paris: OECD, 97–134.

Visser, J and A Hemerijck (1997), *'A Dutch Miracle': Job Growth, Welfare Reform, and Corporatism in the Netherlands*. Amsterdam: Amsterdam University Press.

Wright, V, ed. (1994), *Privatization in Western Europe: Pressures, Problems and Paradoxes*. London: Pinter.

2 Adapting the European Model: the Role of Employers' Associations and Trade Unions

COLIN CROUCH

According to neo-liberal theory, economic interest associations act solely as obstacles to economic change, and as rent-seeking cartels. Many substantiating examples can be found. Lobbies of producer organizations persuade governments to subsidize industries which have no real hope of long-term survival; unions bargain for the tenure rights of the existing workforce, producing youth unemployment; collective bargaining maintains wages at levels too high to enable the labour market to clear. By the mid-1970s three decades of peaceful institutional development in most advanced economies had left a complex web of policies, deals, agreements designed to mollify and modify the impact of the raw labour market, a situation which had been quite manageable during its years of growth in the context of stable expansion of those first post-war decades, but which began to appear very different. With the return on economic turbulence the web seemed more like an incoherent tangle inhibiting change and adjustment, creating inflation, slowing technological innovation, creating unemployment. The abstract arguments of neo-classical economics fed the political doctrine of neo-liberalism: if only the tangle could be ripped apart, market forces could flow again and economies would adjust.

And yet we know both in theory and in practice that economic interest associations do not always act simply as lobbies and cartels. Where they are so organized that they are unable to avoid responsibility for the economic consequences of their actions, they can facilitate the pursuit of collective competition goods, reducing problems of free-riding and resolving prisoner's dilemmas, in a number of ways.

Various forms of organization can achieve this. Olson (1982) developed the concept to deal with cases where, the members of an association comprising such a large proportion of a particular population, the association

27

could not externalize costs on to that population without obviously harming the interests of its members as also members of that population. Associations representing firms or workers in industries strongly exposed to external trade are also unable to engage in much rent-seeking, as they can usually influence only their local national government, not the rest of the trading world (Crouch, 1993).

A major example for the provision of public goods has been income restraint and the pursuit of favourable trade-offs between inflation and unemployment. This was an issue which lost prominence during the deflationary years of the 1980s and 1990s, but that was a conjunctural rather than a long-term change. More positively, where a capacity to act collectively exists, the provision of collective goods can be sought. An important example here is vocational education and training, where associative action can be fundamental in ensuring that all firms contribute to a good from which all benefit but where free-riders can make unfair gains, eventually destroying the basis for co-operation.

Given that the capacity of different economies to generate institutional structures capable of behaving in this way, maximizing collective goods, they can serve in ways very similar to natural resource endowments. Just as an economy with ready access to certain mineral deposits has initial advantages in production industries using those minerals, so one with a capacity for institutional governance is better equipped to tackle tasks for which co-operation and collective action produce important gains.

The legacy of both social and economic theory and recent economic history therefore give us two very different perspectives on the role of economic interest organizations, leading to directly opposed but equally clear sets of policy recommendations. According to the logic of neo-classicism and neo-liberalism, these institutions should be weakened and marginalized as much as possible—assuming that democratic principles of free association inhibit the ideal choice of abolishing them altogether. According to the logic of institutionalist theories,[1] these organizations should be encouraged and enabled to play neo-corporatist governance roles—that is, where they are constrained to share responsibility for developing collective goods for maximizing economic gains and have significant negative and political incentives not to use their strength largely for lobbying and rent-seeking. Given that in most societies social and political forces seeking neo-liberal outcomes and those seeking institutional solutions are both strong, a very likely outcome of this confrontation is some kind of compromise. This is likely to mean economic interest organizations which retain some strength but which are kept away from playing a governance role. This amounts to the lobbying, rent-seeking role which, all theories would agree, is the worst of all worlds. The policy dilemma is therefore severe, and compromise is difficult to achieve.

The matter cannot be resolved by ruling one of the rival perspectives on organizations as somehow in error; there is too much evidence on either side for that. While they produce opposed policy prescriptions, they are not mutually incompatible as accounts of how institutions may work. The analogy with natural resource endowments is very relevant here, as these too can be both sources of competitive gain and traps luring into non-innovative path dependencies. Firms in an industry with ready access to certain minerals are likely to fail to seek out new forms of production, marketing and other aspects of the business, until they are overtaken by firms based in economies with weaker resource endowments and therefore forced to be inventive and enterprising. But what conclusion follows from this for the economy with the resource endowment? It can hardly be to block up all its ore mines. What is likely to happen in practice is that, once the resource-poor competitors begin to overtake firms in the resource-rich economy, the latter suddenly acquire an incentive to innovate and be enterprising; some will fail to do so and will leave the sector, but the survivors are likely eventually to have a double advantage, retaining their natural resources but now combining them with a more creative business approach. But this usually happens in a wasteful way after considerable losses. The role of policy in such a case must be to give positive and negative incentives to the sector to provoke it to anticipate the need for adaptation earlier than the point when the competition has begun to undermine it.

However, within the area of institutional resources the dominant neo-liberal school does not give advice of this kind, but advocates the equivalent of blocking up the ore mines: countries with strong economic interest organizations are advised to weaken and marginalize these, modelling themselves on the United States of America, the United Kingdom and New Zealand, irrespective of the past role of these organizations in sustaining useful models of economic governance.

I want here to argue the opposite, and to propose that the policy challenge is to reshape the environment of associations so that they behave in entrepreneurial and developmental ways rather than protectionist and cartelistic ones, if possible trying to give them incentives to do this before global markets place them under severe pressure. This is the nub of the conflict between neo-liberals and neo-institutionalists: the former insist on the viability of only one way of achieving economic success; the latter see a diversity of solutions. First however it is necessary to understand why the prevailing orthodoxy in the world is taking the opposite path and advocating weakening and marginalization.

Causes of the Neo-liberal Hegemony

In some respects interest associations play only a secondary part in the current giant ideological struggle, which is that between the roles of free markets and of regulation, since it is normally the state which is seen as the key actor in the latter. Since orthodox economic theory has its objections against both states and associations, it tends to roll them together and see them as mutually self-supporting, joint culprits in the crippling of free economies. In particular the state is often seen as the actor which is really behind governance regimes of interest associations. For example, in the recently and widely read attempt by the sociologist Anthony Giddens (1998) to characterize the so-called Third Way politics of the British Labour government, the rejected strategy of corporatism is defined or rather caricatured as the control by the state over civil society, when in most of the actual cases occurring in recent western European history it has been the almost opposite form of the state sharing its power with associations within civil society.

In fact the relationship between state intervention or regulation and the role of neo-corporatist associations is very diverse, leading to the conclusion that they are analytically quite distinct. There have been some cases where the state has been important in imposing or at least encouraging system governance by associations (e. g. from time to time in Belgium and the Netherlands), but there are equally those where state regulation has been diminished because autonomous interest associations have simply done the job by themselves (Denmark, Germany); and even where the associations have at times co-operated in order to prevent the state from acting (Austria, Sweden). There have also been examples where the very strength of state action has inhibited the development of associations (France). In concentrating on associations we are therefore dealing with an issue that has not been central to the debate, though economic theory has its case against associations well prepared: they will always intervene to impede market efficiency.

Gradually, over the past 25 years, the neo-liberal turn in economic policy has spread from being a primarily academic exercise, gradually influencing various governments and major international investors, until by the mid-1990s it had become the dominant orthodoxy of the Organization for Economic Co-Operation and Development (1994a; 1994b) and, eventually, the European Commission (1996). From this perspective, all mechanisms and institutions which interfere with free markets are sources of inefficiency because, by definition, all actors in the market are perfectly rational and rationally anticipate and calculate risks and probabilities. Anything which interferes with this mechanism must, virtually by definition, produce reduced efficiency. In this way the advocates of neo-liberalism, drawing initially on the theoretical advances being made in neo-classical economic thought from the 1960s onwards, were able to replace the more heterogeneous mix of market economics, Keynesian and institutionalism which had previously dominated economic policy thought in the post-war decades.

There has been an element of fashion in all this, in that, theoretical advances having been made in neo-classical economics, nearly everyone working in economic theory wanted to relate their contributions to is, and so it continued to grow while other bodies of economic thought were neglected. Also, it is central to the concept of fashion that particular modes of acting and being become self-justifying. Once significant trend-setters have adopted a certain fashion, it becomes the right thing to do by virtually of that fact alone. Once the International Monetary Fund, the government of the United States of America and the OECD had begun to advocate the deregulation of markets as the only necessary economic policy, this became a sufficient reason for doing so. The process of self-justification moves a stage further when, on *a priori* grounds following the fashion, international investors conclude that, if the more deregulated economies are the most efficient, it must be rational to concentrate investment on them. The deregulated economies are then proved to have been more efficient, because they are able to attract more inward investment. In 1995 the European Roundtable of Industrialists (ERT, 1996) decided to press the EU and member governments to accept as a definition of competitiveness the ability to attract footloose investment. Since by definition such investment is following the principles of rapidly responding free markets, economies which follow such policies become by definition more competitive than those which concentrate on the development of existing capacities—even if the latter might appear more competitive using normal criteria of productivity, capacity to sustain balance of trade surpluses.

However, arguments about pure fashion are unlikely to be the whole story in such an important field as economic performance: the triumph of neo-liberalism has also been aided by both interests and real evidence.

Although it is usually considered impolite to point it out, the pursuit of free market policies tends to favour the personal interests of the owners of capital, senior business managers, and the highly paid consultants they employ. This happens for a number of reasons. Unrestricted markets have low taxation and therefore low levels of welfare-state provision; this is normally associated with a skewed income distribution. Where labour markets in particular are unregulated, the bargaining power of labour is reduced in relation to that of capital and its associated management. In a world of truly pure markets these inegalitarian effects would not be so clear: perfect competition reduces profit rates and restricts the size of firms (and therefore the size of rewards that can go to those at the top). In practice however the maintenance of such conditions of competition requires considerable government regulation, which it is the tendency of deregulation policies to undermine.

It is therefore not surprising that, as the new orthodoxy has grown, so previous tends to reductions of inequality previously thought to be associated with modernization, came to an end and started to be reversed. Further, the more countries adopted the deregulation orthodoxy, the more unequal they became. The UK and the USA led the world in adopting the neo-liberal recipes, and have similarly led the world in increasing inequalities (Atkinson, 1996; OECD, 1997).[2] The causal relationship may be less unilinear than this suggests: it is also possible that it was only where workers' power had been weakened that it was possible to push through the neo-liberal package; but the link between interests and the policies remains.

But of course the publicly proclaimed legitimation for the policies is the assertion that they succeed; that the more deregulated economies are, the better they perform. There is of course a problem here of how performance is to be measured. Given that there is a diversity of these, and different economies are likely to perform differently on different indicators, this ostensible reality test becomes a political task of advancing the cause of those indicators that most suit the case one wishes to argue. At its most extreme this becomes a matter of choosing indicators that measure the policy input as a proxy for the output—as in the case of the ERT competitiveness measure mentioned above. But there are more obvious contenders that cannot be so easily dismissed.

The one which has dominated political debate has been that of unemployment, since the unregulated economy of the USA (and to a lesser extent the UK) seem to have performed better than the regulated European economies. The case is not really that straightforward (Crouch, 1998; Crouch, Finegold and Sako, 1999: ch 2). It involves treating Japan as unregulated. It involves ignoring German unification. It involves treating Denmark as unregulated. It involves ignoring the black economies of southern Europe. However, it has been a powerful case, not least because it challenges the Keynesian and institutionalists on their home territory. It also has some evidence on its side. In several countries previously functioning governance regimes did degenerate into rent-seeking and cartelization during the 1980s. On the other hand, it is possible to understand how and why this malfunctioning developed, and how it might often be conjunctural damage, capable of repair.

The shocks of the past 25 years, first inflationary, then deflationary, placed considerable strain on organizational structures. The depth of the adjustment crisis of the 1980s in particular imposed burdens on such industries as ship-building, steel-making, coal-mining, textiles, that were so severe that protection and rescue were almost inevitably the initial responses; firms, their associations, trade unions all sought them, and governments tried to provide them. This was not a situation limited to neo-corporatist countries. In the USA as much as anywhere in Europe, such calls were made, whether by individual firms or *ad hoc* local groups. And it is not easy to give a general answer for such cases. Often (as with ship-building) these industries did turn out to be in terminal decline, and all that policy could achieve was some slowing down and gentling of that decline. Once genuine rescue and replacement on a competitive footing had been revealed to be impossible, these efforts seemed to have been a waste of effort and money. Even then a more mixed judgement probably has to be offered. On the one hand such a slowing down of change reduced the shock to people's lives; on the other it delayed the eventual transition to new activities. Which is the better solution depends on some difficult equation between the extent and impact of the shock against any long-term losses in making transitions.

Even if the equation can be made, it can be done so only *ex post facto,* and not at the time the decisions have to be made. Economic theory, using the assumption of rational anticipation, will tell us that, left to itself the market will find the most efficient outcome, and that all intervention can do is to distort those anticipations. However, for this to be true markets and in particular knowledge about them, have to be perfect, and this can in no way be guaranteed.

In other cases (such as the motor industry), adaptation was—or has so far been—possible, and those cases where a planned reorganization using negotiated industrial relations was adopted (e. g. Germany) seem to have fared better than those where the market was allowed to have sway (e. g. the UK). Adaptation in this sense differs strongly from both protectionist rent-seeking and pure market adjustment.

Similarly, many neo-corporatist industrial relations systems took a severe battering, first as a result of the strains placed on them by inflation, and then following the reduction of social partnership as managements took advantage of slack labour markets to reassert their authority. However, as several authors have shown (Schmitter and Grote, 1997; Traxler, 1996; 1997; Visser, 1996; contributions by Traxler and by Visser to this volume) have shown, in almost every western European country (with the expectation of the UK) collective industrial relations have made some kind of recovery during the 1990s. This ranges in efficacy from rather radical renewals as discussed above and below (Denmark, Netherlands, Ireland), and more gradual adjustments of existing systems (Austria, Italy), to rather generalized and rhetorical social pacts (e. g. Czech Republic, Poland, Spain), and to systems which remain rather frozen, unable equally to abolish the former compromise or restructure it (Germany, Sweden). What Schmitter and Grote call the neo-corporatist Sisyphus seems to be once again demonstrating the wave-like rather than unilinear motion of industrial relations history.

Neo-corporatist Past, Neo-liberal Future?

Faced with evidence of the achievements of neo-corporatist arrangements, most neo-liberal economists are likely to argue that the success was illusory, or caused by something else, or coincidental. Alternatively, as with the OECD, the role of such institutions might be accepted, but the tension between that and a general policy stance of regarding them as negative is simply not confronted (see, for example, the contradiction between discussions in the OECD *Jobs Study* which commend associational models of vocational training (OECD, 1994b: ch 7), which could not exist if the deregulation advocated in earlier chapters of the Study were accepted.

Less polemical and far more serious are arguments that more regulated (or, separately, neo-corporatist) economies may be more successful at certain tasks and in certain contexts, while free market economies will be more adept at others—and that the former circumstances belong to the past, the latter to the future. This powerful argument can be developed in a number of ways, covering questions of globalization, coping with radical sectoral change, and the importance of individual company autonomy.

Globalization

Arguments about globalization are becoming so familiar that they are virtually a cliché, but they are worth reviewing (for fuller discussions, see the papers collected in Wilthagen 1998). Neo-corporatist and similar institutions relate overwhelmingly to national contexts, while for capital (though not for labour or governments) these are becoming increasingly relevant. At a time when even international corporations depended on the strength of their home base, it was possible to persuade them that it was in their interests to care about the quality of the social and economic infrastructure of that base, and this might well lead them to co-operate in associational arrangements treating that infrastructure as a collective good. A global enterprise ceases to have a home base in any effective sense of the word; it is interested in neither a local infrastructure nor local business associations themselves, and in fact is likely to "regime shop" to find the local environment that imposes fewest obligations on it to be a good corporate citizen.

While this favours discouragement of neo-corporatist initiatives, it is not without problems for neo-classical theory itself, which cannot easily deal with the very existence of such giant firms (Strange, 1988). Despite its many attempts to cope with imperfect competition, neo-classical economics works best if it can assume markets with large numbers of participants, none of which can affect prices or any other behaviour by their individual action. This is particularly important for the political implications of the neo-classical model in the form of neo-liberalism. It is only to the extent that the perfect model obtains that neo-liberal political theory can sustain its position that there is no such thing as economic power, that consumers are sovereign, and that therefore there is no need for political intervention in market processes.

If economic concentration does reach levels where individual firms are able to set the terms of the market, neo-classical theory has its answer:

anti-monopoly or anti-trust legislation must be used to break up such concentrations. However, this does not reliably happen. Global giants are often able to convince regulatory authorities that technical advance and the risks involved in major investment projects require market concentration; giant firms are effective lobbies. It is odd that, while all attention in the neo-liberal literature has been focused on the role of associations and unions in rent-seeking and special pleading, little concern is shown at individual firms' behaviour, or indeed even at associational action if it takes the form of lobbying rather than governance. This can be seen particularly acutely in Sweden, where not only do that country's particularly large supply of transnational firms have no interest in associational membership and lobby government directly, but business associations themselves have—in the name of neo-liberalism—begun to switch from a neo-corporatist to a lobbying model. This is also becoming an issue at the EU level, where large corporations establish their own lobbying offices in Brussels, with the encouragement of the Commission (Coen, 1996). Global firms of course use their lobbying of several governments in order to negotiate the most favourable terms for themselves, including tax breaks on investment.

Strict neo-classical economists disapprove of all this, but neo-liberalism as a *political* strategy is far more ambivalent, since these same large firms are among the principal sources of material and intellectual support of the neo-liberal strategy. Not only are such lobbies likely to be encouraged, but a core part of the neo-liberal interpretation of the message of globalization—that national labour markets must submit to the consequences of competition with low-wage economies—is embodied in them (Du Gay, 1998). It is important to note what is happening here: special-interest lobbying has been identified as one of the characteristics of poorly functioning neo-corporatist interest representation systems, the unavoidability of which is presented as a key argument for pursuing rigorously the neo-liberal turn. However, it can be seen that the neo-liberal turn generates its own problems of lobbying and rent-seeking—and since these are embedded in individual corporations rather than associations, they cannot be reformed in order to make them adopt an encompassing form, as might be achieved through associations. Only a rigorous anti-trust approach can save neo-liberalism from these consequences, but that is a strategy that is inhibited by political realities, and by the very globalization arguments that neo-liberalism itself uses

Globalization is therefore a problem for every approach to economic management. At the same time, however, both neo-liberalism and neo-corporatism can take comfort from the fact that globalization is not the full story of the advanced modern economy. In many sectors the past two decades have seen the revival of the small-firm sector, including in some advanced sectors. While it is true that these firms are often the clients of global enterprises, they are themselves fairly strongly tied to a national—or even more relevant a local—context and might be expected to have a continued interest in its infrastructure, collective goods, and associations. Second, virtually all current employment growth is in the services sectors, where, even where global enterprises are active, arguments about regime shopping do not apply. If a firm wishes to sell holidays, hamburgers, insurance or English-language classes to the population of a particular country, it will need a presence in that country and, almost certainly, will need to employ personnel of that country. This reduces the extent to which it can cut itself off from the local infrastructure.

However, neither these arguments nor the problems posed for neo-liberalism by the role of giant firms abolish the real difficulties brought to neo-corporatism by globalization and the search by large firms for privileged political access. First, if they are not able to attract the attention of global manufacturing firms, associations become deprived of the concerns of some of the most dynamic and least protectionist firms; in some sectors and some countries they run the risk of becoming the haven of purely local, low-technology, unambitious firms.

Coping with Radical Sectoral Change

A further argument which makes sense of the success of both neo-liberal and neo-corporatist strategies, but which also condemns the latter to the past, is that which relates the two to different kinds of economic task. Institutional economies might do best at perfecting and improving existing technologies and methods and therefore at maximizing essentially stable situations, while deregulated ones might be better equipped to deal with radical and frequent change. The initial post-war decades were periods where the first were particularly important. Within markets stabilized by Keynesian demand management, the basic tasks of equipping industrializing Europe with capital goods and spreading mass-production products throughout the newly growing mass markets could be well cared for through the first mode. Now however, the overall macro-economic climate is far less stable, there is a premium on innovation, old sectors are dying or moving to the newly industrializing economies, and entrepreneurs are trying out a diversity of different plans. None of this provides the kind of environment in which associations representing firms in clearly defined sectors can make stable arrangements for the employment of workers. There is a premium on rapid mobility, constant adjustment to changing markets, and a need for enterprises to respond to market signals with a minimum of external constraints—including those resulting from agreements negotiated by the firms' own membership association. These conditions all seem to favour free markets over either neo-corporatist or government regulation.

Similar arguments about finance run alongside this; the Austro-German *Hausbank* model is seen as well adapted to situations where firms require stability and the expectation of continuing financing providing they meet certain criteria of internal monitoring. The more speculative Anglo- American system may be better attuned to situations of high uncertainty and risk (Merrill Lynch, 1998). Similar arguments can also be deployed about state-initiative systems, which may be very well suited to large-scale projects capable of central direction, but less well adapted to making constant adjustments to fluctuating consumer preferences: the French state has unrivalled performance in setting down the high-speed, high-technology TGV railway system; it has not performed well in developing a French computer industry.

There is evidence to support much of this Crouch, Finegold and Sako, 1999: ch 3; OECD, 1996). The USA certainly outperforms Germany (the main European industrial power) in the new innovative technologies—in particular information technology and biotechnology. Here rapid movement in totally new areas, forming skills ad hoc from an untrained but generally educated work force, finance with easily available but untied venture capital, seems to be particularly favoured by the US economic form. Germany and Austria have led in other sectors, where the UK and the USA have lost out: machine tools, machine construction generally, motor vehicles. It is easy to see how here, for the most part, what is needed is the highly skilled application of existing resources to the reworking and permanent improvement of existing technologies.

We cannot be very confident about these institutional suitabilities for particular industries: information technology seems to have been well adapted to the Japanese economy too, which takes a very different form from the US American one and both Japan and Italy have been successful innovators in machine tools. It would be dangerous to assume that particular institutional models match very precisely to outcomes: there might however be strong tendencies for particular kinds of institutional frameworks to be more likely to be associated with certain outcomes than other types.

Such partial answers enable us to resolve as problem otherwise set by the neo-classical arguments. If unregulated economies are systematically superior to regulated ones, this ought to be true for all times and all sectors. We then have great difficulty explaining why US unemployment was higher than that in some key regulated economies (Germany, Sweden) for most of the post-war period; why according to some very important indicators (productivity improvement, export performance, overall performance in certain manufacturing sectors), several of the continental European economies continue to out-perform the USA.

These arguments enable us to pinpoint some of the deficiencies characteristic of the neo-corporatist form of interest organization. At the same time, they also warn against a rapid dismantling of these systems if they have been associated with past success in industries where neo-liberal economies have poor records. Such sectors as machine construction or vehicle manufacture will continue to be important, particularly as further new countries industrialize and require capital goods. Particular significant here for the western European economies are those in central sand eastern Europe. The growth of world trade may therefore favour the institutionally equipped economies. Also, it must be remembered that, as a continental economy, the USA does not have the same relative prominence in global trading as the individual European economies. Although it participates in world trade more than in the past, it can still cope with a performance in just a few key sectors, for which entrepreneurial opportunity-ceasing may serve adequately. The smaller economies of western Europe find themselves deeply involved in open, competitive trade and need to have a wide front of industries performing well.

Company Autonomy

Closely related to the argument about speed of change is the question of corporate autonomy. When new paths have to be found in conditions of uncertainty, it is preferable for many different firms to be free to seek innovative solutions than for a small number to bear all the risks. We do not require any Schumpeterian belief in the magical qualities of entrepreneurs to accept this argument, but a Popperian approach to action in conditions of uncertainty. If many different autonomous attempts are made, some are likely to succeed. Once the successful few have found the way through, others will imitate them. In the process of course many individual firms will not find a way through and will fail, but that is not the point.

This argument favours neo-classical economic approaches, but creates difficulties for practical neo-liberal politics given that monopolistic industries dominated by a small number of corporate giants are often left alone by public policy. Variety among large numbers of players is often simply not available because the costs of entry are too high. In such situations a large-scale government presence is probably necessary to underpin risky investment—as in the essential role of the US government in defence procurement, which has provided vital support for such high-tech industries as advanced information services and the aerospace sector.

However, this does not dispose of the real problem presented by the same questions to neo-corporatist models at a time of continual radical technical change. Firms seek liberation from external constraints, including those of their own associations. They either try to loosen those constraints, reducing the role of the associations, or leave them altogether, weakening them.

The Future of the Associational Economy

Attempts at establishing the future scope for associational economies need to recognize both the reality and the limitations of the threat posed to them by current developments. To deal first with the second, the limitations, it is important to bear in mind that large parts of economies remain dominated by non-global firms in sectors which continue to have a future and where a system of gradual adaptation will work just as well as radical innovation and complete shifts of forms of production. But if associational systems are to recover a role in economic governance they must resolve certain critical problems: to sustain the participation of the global players that do exist, and will probably grow in number; to be able to facilitate moves into new production sectors; and to enable company autonomy within an overall framework of effective governance. They also need in certain cases a reorientation towards true collective goods. Some of the relevant action lies within the scope of associations themselves; others need stimulation from public actors of various kinds.

What are the main factors which might inhibit constructive responses from associations to these challenges?

Path Dependency

It has become popular among social scientists to make pessimistic predictions based on the theory of path dependency, first developed in this context by Douglass North (1990). This theory holds that, once actors learn a particular type of solution to their problems, they go on using it even after it ceases to be able to solve problems, because that is all that they know. The answer is therefore seen to lie in a complete path shift, of which the existing actors are incapable. This argument is currently often used to justify rejection of the associational model, which is seen as having become a path-dependency trap. The free market itself is rarely seen to have similar vulnerabilities because it is deemed to have perfect adaptation capacities provided it is truly free. Therefore the solution advocated for cases of market failure is to intensify the market.

For present purposes we do not need to consider the adequacy of this particular argument, but must appraise the apparent terminal character of path-dependency disease for associative systems, whose actors are not credited with perfect rational adaptation capacity by any theory. Terminal decline can of course become a self-fulfilling prophecy: if key actors do not want a particular path to succeed any more, they can make this come true by refusing to help reform it and thereby demonstrating its inability to be reformed.

We see something of this in current German institutions, relating to both co-determination and VET provision. German businesses are, in general, not interested in adapting *Mitbestimmung* to cope with challenges of quality circles and similar relatively new approaches to worker involvement. Rather, it is being left "frozen" in its present form, not adapting to new forms of company organization or new tasks, while managements experiment with new forms outside that frame. Their motive is partly of course to avoid the union-influenced contributions which works councillors can make, but in so doing they risk wasting accumulated wisdom. Recent bipartite reform proposals (Bertelsmann Stiftung und Hans-Böckler Stiftung, 1998) might lead to moves beyond this impasse, incorporating a considerable decentralization of the model.

Similarly, within vocational training there is increasing need for further, in-service training in addition to initial basic training. The former is organized entirely outside the dual or apprenticeship system, which is being left frozen with its initial role and in danger of not being developed for the cutting edge of new skill developments (Crouch, Finegold and Sako,

1999: ch 5). Instead most political pressure on it is to make it absorb surplus labour-market capacity, with the danger that in the long run it might become a parking lot for the unemployed rather than a dynamic component of the economy (as in part happened during the 1980s to Swedish active labour market policy). The dual system is organized under the auspices of part of the associative system, the *Kammern,* with some participation by trade unions; further training is the province of individual firms. As a result the associative system is losing touch and expertise, justifying firms' complaints about it as incapable of innovation. Many firms are anxious to lose the obligations for compulsory training provision embedded in the dual system, because they claim it gives them a burden that, for example, British firms do not have to bear. They can also point out that frequent up-dating of existing employees' skills is vital to current competitive needs. The associative system seems to have outrun the value of its path.

However, important among present vocational education needs is that for greater interaction between general education and VET. The dual system has been a valuable instrument for this, with employers in several other countries envying their German counterparts [REFS]. The residualizing of apprenticeship would create considerable problems here. Another important trend in current labour markets is for firms to reduce to a small core the number of workers they retain as their own employees, using sub-contractors and self-employed workers for the remainder. A recognized, publicly certificated initial training scheme becomes a valuable guide to the quality of labour for firms in these situations.

Many German employers feel they would have more freedom to innovate if they could break from constraints by levels of government, trade unions, their own associations. Often they are not so much seeking exit as "sulking", leaving institutions in place because it would take too much conflict to abolish them, but refusing to reform them and seeking innovation in different contexts. For this reason the German social compromise is coming to be seen as one of a rigid incapacity, which then becomes seen as a characteristic of an institutional economy *per se,* an example of a path dependency which has run its course. In fact it is a *strategy* being pursued by certain interests within such an economy, and one which runs the risk of destroying capacities.

The danger German businesses face is that, in trying to exchange their own system for, presumably, an Anglo-American one, they are dropping something they understand well and which has produced results in the past, and seeking something which they may not be very good at or which may not be available to them. For example, it is generally assumed in the economics literature that the USA stands as a kind of proxy for the pure market, and that therefore making markets purer makes a country more American. What if, for example, US entrepreneurship results at least in part from the high number of immigrants in the country—immigrants being likely to be entrepreneurs, not just because they lack settled roots, but also because they are nested in their own supportive communities? In that case, merely adopting free markets might not solve the problem unless at the same time Germany admits large numbers of immigrants from a diversity of ethnic sub-cultures.

In applying path-dependency theory to complex social institutions, we must remember two points: first, the internal complexity of systems, which can give them an endogenous capacity for change not foreseen by the simpler stereotyped theoretical models; second, the fact that cases are in any case rarely reducible to models of abstract systems, and that scope for change is often inbuilt in the tension between the two.

The theory tends to accept abstract stereotypes of the ways in which models work and to miss the subtlety often consequent on the complexity of systems. Sometimes, though of course not necessarily, complexity means that systems have managed to acquire (whether deliberately or not) checks against some of their own in-built sources of inefficiency. For example, neo-corporatist systems are usually taken for granted as favouring insiders over outsiders, and therefore likely to reserve work for ageing employees while young, and probably better educated, people are left in unemployment. It is therefore a great surprise to theory to discover that Germany and Austria are the only two countries in the advanced world to have youth unemployment rates lower than the adult rate (OECD, 1997). This phenomenon results of course from the vocational training system, which can therefore be seen as one of the ways in which the associative system has incorporated a correcting mechanism against its tendency to rigidity.

Empirical cases, especially when they are whole nation-state societies, are in any case rarely reducible to coherent models of systems, however elaborate and complex. It must be remembered that the path dependency argument depends on an analogy. North was basing his arguments about economic development upon knowledge of how scientific progress operates. Technical advance tends to proceed through the logical working out of particular paths, offering a limited range of solutions to problems. Eventually a particular path ceases to be able to solve new problems, but the scientists involved have become dependent on their particular path and cannot shift. Innovation therefore depends on newcomers moving along a different path. There is clearly much in here that corresponds to the operation of socio-economic systems, but the analogy does break down at a certain point. Forms of scientific inquiry and technical problem-solving are rigorous mental products. Social organization lacks that characteristic. Actually existing institutional systems are rarely the pure expressions of system logic, but messy compromises, or simply amalgamations of elements that are part of a particular institutional history but not part of any overall logic. (The above observation on the role of ethnic minorities in the USA, preventing that country from being simply a proxy for free markets, is a case in point.)

If a Northian path dependency really is running out, it is often these incongruous or merely coincidental elements that can become the sources of constructive change. Because they are *in* the empirical system though not *of* its logic, actors can make use of them to shift the operation of the logic. We can see this in the Danish case (Due et al., 1994). The fact that this very small, particularly open economy consists primarily of small firms made it difficult for firms to seek an exit from Danish institutions in the way that Swedish multinationals seem to be trying to exit Swedish ones. Forced to realize their dependency on the country, they became committed to reforming its institutions rather than bypassing them (as had been their original intention in the 1980s). Small size of firms is not a component of the theory of neo-corporatist systems, nor built into the logic of their functioning. This was an empirical characteristic that stimulated system reform.

In the Dutch case, a neo-corporatist system which had become stereotyped as sclerotic acquired new life and found an extraordinary capacity for innovation (Visser and Hemerijck, 1997). Here the social actors were deeply experienced in operating structures of this kind; perhaps it may also be that they knew that they were not expert at alternative policy approaches. Also, there was widespread public support for the use of these institutions. Therefore, when faced with a situation where there was no possibility of continuing with former policies, which had produced widespread economic activity, they were simply forced to try to innovate. As Visser and Hemerijck (ibid.) show, they could not do this in all necessary policy areas, but were able to act in those where urgency of the issue and their own legitimacy coincided.

Pressure for System Reform

While it might alleviate some of our pessimism, it might seem that we must draw from the above discussion the not very helpful conclusion that contingency governs the capacity of systems for change. However, I think we can go considerably further than this. The cases we are dealing with are those where two conditions obtain: (i) interest organizations have, or have had, a capacity for strategy; (ii) these systems are now coming under great strain and are faced with a possible loss of function and pressure from either government or their own members to desist from past practices which are no longer functioning. Rather than simply decline, these organizations might demonstrate capacity for radical internal change—provided enough of their active members perceive either abolition of the structure or allowing it to continue in a worn-out fashion as undesirable.

Attempts by external academic observers to produce substantive policy remedies are rarely successful: abstract arguments rarely meet the case in hand; attempts to be more practical by citing examples from elsewhere usually provide models not capable of imitation. Innovation comes from social actors themselves working under pressure to find a way out of difficult dilemmas. The external policy advisor can simply point to the kinds of constraints most likely to produce creative rather than defensive outcomes. The appropriate context for the reform of associative systems is for the association actors to be forced to find solutions (rather than being relieved of responsibility) but finding protectionist and rent-seeking options blocked off by government refusal to respond. In the case of EU countries, competition law usually provides a convenient exogenous Leviathan for blocking off this option. It is this context of pressure to reform the model—neither to stand still nor to overthrow it—which is the central, generalizable lesson the currently much discussed Dutch case, more than any specific policy proposals which emerged from the process.

The late Mancur Olson's (1982) analysis of the role of associations in economic dynamism and decline will long stand as one of the great classics of institutional economics. He was however mistaken in his account of the German and Japanese immediate post-war economies as institutional *tabulae rasae*. An extensive network of powerful associations was rapidly restored to place in these countries soon after the war—in Germany re-establishment of associational structures predated the formation of the Federal Republic itself, just as their establishment had preceded the foundation of the Wilhelmine empire in the 1860s. What the associations in both countries could not do was to be rent-seekers; there were no rents to be had in those societies after the war. In the German case (though not Japan) foreign trade protection was also removed, the country was committed to free trade, and associations as much as individual firms were forced to act entrepreneurially. Industrial relations too had to orient itself to export competitiveness.

Similarly, domestic rent-seeking has historically been of little use to organized actors in the small open economies (Katzenstein, 1985). However much the domestic market might be regulated by government on insiders' behalf, the global context remains highly open, and firms must succeed in it. These cases all demonstrate that the behaviour of associative systems will depend on the structure of incentives to behave either entrepreneurially or defensively that are afforded by their context, a context which can often be articulated and shaped by public policy or indeed by associations themselves if they are determined to improve their own mode of behaviour. If the problem is that firms are exiting from the associational system in order to avoid its obligations, governments have the capacity to make it clear that they will only take note of direct enterprise lobbying by those firms which have reputations as good associational citizens.

We here encounter again a central irony of economic organization already discussed above: the more that an interest organization system reflects the free market ideal subject to the caveat of associations being permitted, the more it is likely to take the form of a pluralistic rent-seeking. The more it has a neo-corporatist architecture of shared governance, the more likely is it to be pushed into constructive roles. The reshaping to Danish and other industrial relations systems to make them more responsive to individual firms' needs, helping overcome firm/association antagonisms, has been an important if surprising aspect of this. On the face of it, accepting a shift of an unprecedented degree of pay bargaining to the firm level seemed to mark a loss of governance capacity for the associative actors. However, once it was accepted that such a shift was necessary, the choice was whether to give up altogether the task of co-ordination (and thus relinquish capacity for governance) or to find means of sustaining a residual but effective steering capacity. It was the latter which was achieved.

As argued above, the need for such autonomy for firms results primarily from the fact that, in conditions of great uncertainty, it is necessary to have many firms searching in various different directions for success, so that some might find it. This produces a difficult situation for organized labour. Workers' prioritization of security becomes particularly important at precisely the moment when it becomes less possible to give it: not only are firms unwilling in their insecure environment to accept burdens of worker security, but the fact that many firms will fail makes the demand for security an urgent one. This argues however, not for the abolition of collective relations, but their enhancement and improved sophistication, since the way in which workers' security can be reconciled with firms' needs has to be a matter for constant experiment. Once workers' security and firms' flexibility are both recognized as necessary, rather than being seen in zero-sum competition, it becomes clear that co-operative approaches of various kinds will be best placed to resolve the dilemma, since workers' security has to be treated as a collective good rather than the responsibility of a single employer.

One way in which this can be achieved is through the role of labour hiring agencies.[3] This is ironic because for many years the labour movement has seen these unequivocally as the source of bad and insecure employment relations, poor levels of training, and attacks on worker solidarity. Recent European legislation preventing the outlawing of such agencies has however forced unions within associative systems to turn to improving these agencies rather than trying to ban them, and this has produced some creative outcomes, bringing these previously "outlaw" organizations into the associative fold. The advantage for workers of agencies at a time of uncertainty and experiment is that they enable them to avoid some of the risks associated with firms' uncertainty. If some firms will succeed and others fail, employees need to be able easily to move from the losers to the more successful. If they work for a hiring agency, they stand a better chance of doing this. They might, dependent on the character of their skills, even avoid dependence on a particular sector.

Admitting hiring agencies into the world of orderly and dialogistic employment relations—as has been done in the Dutch case (Visser and Hemerijck, 1997)—can therefore make a major contribution to squaring the circle of security and flexibility; and properly institutionalized industrial relations can be fundamental to that, by securing understandings between employers in the sectors, the hiring agencies, and unions. Some agencies, like Manpower and Randstad, have shown themselves quite capable of entering the world of collective agreements. A prime requirement for this kind of reorientation of both associative systems and the hiring agencies—as the Dutch case shows—is for government to block off certain traditional forms of security-seeking and then to encourage negotiation of new mechanisms (ibid.).

Cross-sectoral associations are often less likely to be rent-seekers at a time of rapid technological change than single-industry organizations. This might seem odd if the individual firm is becoming more important. However, it follows from an appreciation of the need for flexibility and change, including changes of sector. The problem with an industry-specific association is that it cannot deal with any need to wind down a sector and find alternative activities, and an economy dominated by associations representing the interests of such sectors is unlikely to be able to innovate. The same problems do not apply to general, non-sectoral organizations of the *Kammer* type. These can be particularly useful at local level, where, in the face of a decline of existing industries, their central motivation is to find new activities for their city or area (Voelzkow, 1990). While they cannot solve the problem of not representing sectors that do not yet exist, they are motivated to provide the collective competition goods, the infrastructural facilities, which will attract and be valuable to new kinds of business—especially where local governments and cross-sectoral union organizations are also involved. Again, it is within the capacity of public policy to encourage developments of this kind by involving this kind of association in local economic development strategies.

European Monetary Union

Arguments above concerning the behaviour of associations in open economies dependent on external trade might seem to be diluted as a result of European integration, in particular the Single Market and the Single Currency. In producing one vast internal market, these seem to put European firms in the same position as US ones, able to trade predominantly internally. Given the greater role of associations in most European economies than in the USA, this would seem to strengthen protectionist tendencies. However, national politics remains the most salient level for democratic and trade-union pressure; for a long time national governments will remain the most sensitive to problems of individual industries and regions, and vulnerable to lobbying concerning unemployment and the problems of specific industries. It will be many years before there is any prospect of a European government being the main target of demands for this kind of political action. Meanwhile the maintenance of open competition between member states remains the most well entrenched of all EU rules. Uniquely among the directorates general of the European Commission, that responsible for competition policy (DG II) has powers to act through the courts against firms and countries, without reference to the Council of Ministers. The emerging EU polity remains one where political pressure is concentrated at the nation-state level, while competition rules are organized at the European level beyond the reach of national polities. An attempt by producers in a particular industry in one country to seek protective conditions would meet opposition from other nation states working through the EU's competition directorate—which has powers unlike any other. Then, at global level, the new framework of the World Trade Organization imposes a strongly competitive regime. Whether at national or at European levels, interest organizations have little hope of realizing their goals through rent-seeking. They continue to receive incentives to adapt themselves to competitiveness.

Meanwhile, if we examine the incentives of the main actors involved, we can see that EMU might strengthen those *national* associative systems which retain or enhance a capacity for elementary wage co-ordination (Crouch, 1999; Hall and Franzese, 1998). For national trade unions it is very bad news indeed if the implications of the single currency regime will be severely deflationary, monetarist and neo-liberal. They therefore have a very strong incentive to demonstrate that it is after all possible to assert some basic moderating influence on the labour market through neo-corporatist mechanisms. The situation confronting employers is less clear cut. They will share unions' aversion to perpetual deflationary policies, but may prefer an attempt to achieve completely unregulated labour markets to a revival of corporatism and its concomitant need for dialogue with organized labour. However, if the past record of neo-corporatism has been reasonably successful and uncostly, and if unions are relatively strongly entrenched, they may prefer this path to one of complete deregulation that could be reached only after prolonged conflict. If unions in such a context make the running in re-establishing corporatist arrangements, employers may not be opposed. Governments too have good reasons to avoid deflation and may balk at the social conflict likely to be engendered by a major deregulation struggle. They may be suspicious of neo-corporatist devices as rivals to parliamentary rule, but an attempt at using them might appear as the lesser of several evils. Such actions could provide a functional equivalent of devaluation without many of the latter's negative effects. Therefore, in the foreseeable future we do not look to possibilities of Europe-wide neo-corporatism but at a new lease of life and a new rationale for national responses precisely because of the European development.

A fundamental condition of any form of co-ordination is that it must not merely interfere with or try to prevent the working out of demand and supply pressures; this is especially true of government-imposed incomes policies which have often been temporary alternatives to voluntary co-operation among well organized social partners. Often incomes policies have simply dammed up pay claims until the policy is removed, creating an inflationary pressure that may well be more intense than the problem the policy was originally trying to resolve.[4] To pursue the analogy of damming up, the stream of market forces will insist on flowing. On the other hand it does make sense to talk of diverting a stream. Markets must flow; but they might be able to flow through more than one potential channel; and some potential channels might give outcome mixes that are preferable, both to other available "artificial" ones and to the so-called "natural" one that would dominate were we to do nothing at all. Co-ordination institutions must therefore be mechanisms for diverting the channel; they must correspond to, rather than simply attempt to impede, some kind of market force.

There is of course the danger that such mechanisms incorporate a deflationary bias, as national workforces in different industries try to under-cut each other by accepting lower rates of pay. But a deflationary bias would be less harmful than an inflationary one in the early years of the Union, since it might help the European Central Bank to learn something of the restraint capacities of the wage-bargaining systems, enabling it in turn to pursue more expansive overall policies.

Notes

1   By institutionalists I mean all those contributions to political economy which stress the dependence of markets on specific social contexts and the limitations of the market in shaping rational action, particularly above the level of the individual.

2   Russia and its former satellites also underwent a radical deregulation, and indeed have also seen extreme moves to inequality.

3   An alternative solution occurs when workers are able easily to find new employment in successful firms if they are in a weak one which folds. If this is to happen without major geographical disruption to workers' lives and if they and new employers are to be put into rapid and efficient contact with each other, something of the industrial district model is required (as in parts of Italy and California). These arrangements can dispense with formal associations of employers and unions, but do depend on extensive networks of at least informal interaction.

4   At the same time, of course, firms' attempts to solve labour shortages by increasing wages may also be inflationary and futile if there are no clear mechanisms linking wages with the provision of training for the occupations in which there are shortages.

References

Atkinson, A B (1996), "Income Distribution in Europe and the United States", *Oxford Review of Economic Policy*, 12 (1): 15–28.

Bertelsmann Stiftung und Hans-Böckler-Stiftung (eds.) (1998), *Mitbestimmung und neue Unternehmenskulturen – Bilanz und Perspektiven*. Gütersloh: Bertelsmann Stiftung.

Coen, D (1996), "The Large Firm as a Political Actor in the European Union", PhD thesis, Florence: European University Institute.

Crouch, C (1993), *Industrial Relations and European State Traditions*. Oxford: Clarendon Press.

Crouch, C (1998), "Labour Market Regulations, Social Policy and Job Creation", in Gual, J, ed. *Job Creation: The Role of Labour Market Institutions*. London: Elgar.

Crouch, C (1999), "National wage determination and European Monetary Union", in Crouch, ed., *After the Euro: The Institutional and Democratic Deficits of European Monetary Union*. Oxford: Oxford University Press.

Crouch, C, D Finegold and M Sako (1999), *Are Skills the Answer? ThePolitical Economy of Skill Creation in Advanced Industrial Countries*. Oxford: Oxford University Press.

Due, J, J S Madsen, C S Jensen and L K Petersen (1994), *The Survival of the Danish Model*. Copenhagen: DJØF.

Du Gay, P (1998), in Wilthagen, T (ed.), q.v.

ERT (1996), *Benchmarking for Policy-Makers: The Way to Competitiveness, Growth and Job Creation*. Brussels: ERT.

European Commission (1996), *Enhancing European Competitiveness: Fourth Report*. Luxembourg: Office for Official Publications of the EC.

Giddens, A (1998), *The Third Way : The Renewal of Social Democracy*. Cambridge: Polity Press.

Hall, P A and R J Jr Franzese (1998), "Mixed Signals: Central Bank Independence, co-ordinated Wage-Bargaining, and European Monetary Union", *International Organization*, summer.

Katzenstein, P (1985), *Small States and World Markets*. Ithaca: Cornell University Press.

Merrill Lynch (1998), *"EMU and Corporate Governance: Shareholder versus Stakeholder in Post-EMU Europe"*. London: Merrill Lynch.

North, D C (1990), *Institutions, Institutional Change and Economic Performance*. Cambridge: Cambridge University Press.

OECD (1994a), *The OECD Jobs Study: Evidence and Explanations. Part I: Labour Market Trends and Underlying Forces of Change*. Paris: OECD.

OECD (1994b), *The OECD Jobs Study: Evidence and Explanations. Part II: The Adjustment Potential of the Labour Market*. Paris: OECD.

OECD (1996), *The OECD Jobs Study: Technology, Productivity and Job Creation, Volume 2, Analytical Report*. Paris: OECD.

OECD (1997), *Employment Outlook*. Paris: OECD.

Olson, M (1982), *The Rise and Decline of Nations: Economic Growth, Stagflation and Social Rigidities*. New Haven, Conn.: Yale University Press.

Schmitter, P C and J Grote (1997), "The Corporatist Sisyphus: Past, Present and Future", Working Paper SPS 97/4. Florence: European University Institute.

Strange, S (1988), *States and Markets*. London: Pinter.

Traxler, F (1996), "Collective Bargaining and Industrial Change: A Case of Disorganization? A Comparative Analysis of Eighteen OECD Countries", *European Sociological Review*, 12 (3): 271–87.

Traxler, F (1997), "Collective Bargaining in the OECD: Developments, Preconditions and Effects", mimeo. European Sociological Association Conference, Colchester.

Visser, J (1996), "Trends and Variations in European Collective Bargaining", mimeo. Amsterdam: CESAR, University of Amsterdam.

Visser, J and A Hemerijck (1997), *A Dutch "Miracle"*. Amsterdam: Amsterdam University Press.

Voelzkow, H (1990), *Mehr Technik in die Region: Neue Ansätze zur regionalen Technikförderung in Nordrhein-Westfalen*. Wiesbaden: DUV.

Wilthagen, T, ed. (1998), *Advancing Theory in Labour Law and Industrial Relations in a Global Context*. Amsterdam: North-Holland.

3 European Macro-Economic Policy

Summary of a presentation by LUDWIG SCHUBERT

1. Massive Underemployment: The EU's Reserves of Labour

According to EU statistics the number of unemployed persons is approximately 18 million. The true extent of underemployment is, however, considerably greater, since the statistics do not include all those who are willing and able to work. The rate of employment, namely the ratio between total employment and working age population, is a better indicator: the rate in the EU is only about 60%, whereas in the USA and Japan it is well over 70%. This could mean that in the EU fewer citizens wish to work than in the USA and Japan; yet a more plausible explanation is that more EU citizens would like to work too, but cannot do so because of a shortage of jobs. The divergence in employment rates therefore reveals not only the extent of underemployment but also the vast, untapped potential for employment, income and prosperity in the EU.

How great are the EU's reserves of labour? On the basis of a 67% rate of employment, as existed at the start of the 1960s, its untapped employment potential amounts to almost 22 million persons. Assuming a 72% rate of employment—a valid hypothesis given the sharp rise in the number of working women—the EU-wide potential is roughly 34 million. In addition there is a good deal of involuntary part-time work at present.

These huge reserves of labour not only indicate the extent of underemployment in Europe; they are also a measure of the wastage of labour and the enormous potential for additional income and employment. The integration of 22 or 34 million persons into the world of work could boost the Community's gross domestic product (GDP)—over and above the productivity increase—by an amount equivalent to the current GDP of France or Germany respectively. Such a development would at the same time drastically ease the burden on national budgets and social security systems.

53

2. Full Employment Within Ten Years is Possible

If 22 million extra jobs are to be created over a ten-year period, employment must grow by 1.3% per annum. If there are to be 34 million jobs, annual employment growth of 2.0% is required. Such employment growth can only be realised if GDP growth is higher than the rise in productivity.

In the EU of 15, the trend rate of productivity growth has been stable at 2% per annum since the mid 1970s. If this trend persists over the next ten years, annual GDP growth rates of 3.3% or 4.0% will be needed to fully utilise the above-mentioned labour reserves of 22 or 34 million persons respectively.

About half of the productivity increase over the past 20 years can be attributed to neutral, technical and organisational progress, and the other half to the substitution of labour by capital.[1] If the substitution of labour by capital could be eliminated completely, full employment could be achieved within ten years even at growth rates of 2.3 or 3.0% per annum. Such a reversal of the macro-economic substitution of labour by capital would, however, presuppose a severe downward opening of the wage scale, as happened in the USA in the 1970s and 1980s (a 30% fall in real wages in the lowest quintile). The problem of joblessness would be transformed into a "working poor problem": this would be incompatible with the European social model. Instead, growth in the Community can be made more employment intense, for example, by reducing non-wage labour costs at the lower end of the wage scale or through more flexible collective agreements (see section 5).

Two conditions must be fulfilled in order to make possible the required real GDP growth:

(1) The existing workforce must meet the skill requirements of the economy.

(2) The economy must generate sufficient production capacity and physical jobs over and above the rise in productivity.

(1) The first condition is probably easier to fulfil than would appear, judging by the widespread complaints from industry. Most newcomers to the world of work (young people and the "hidden reserves") possess an adequate basic education, although this needs to be built on during their working lives. The bottleneck has not to do with qualifications, but with the fact that too many people are competing for too few jobs.

The majority of the unemployed (about 11% of the labour force in 1996, 10% in 1998) is still in the turnover of the labour market. Their problem is not "employability", but the fact that there are not enough jobs for all.[2] This applies on the one hand to the relatively low level of cyclical unemployment, which affected some 2% of the labour force in 1996: in this case, labour is available, and the physical jobs exist, but a lack of macro-economic demand prevents them from being taken up.

However, it also applies, in part, to "non-cyclical unemployment"— i. e. to the 9% or so of the labour force for whom there are no physical jobs. Almost half of these (4% of the labour force) still had jobs less than a year ago. They could be permanently employed, with a minimum of retraining, if sufficient physical jobs were created.

Only for the 5% or so of the labour force who constitute the long-term unemployed is there lack of both: physical jobs and the necessary qualifications. But that does not mean they should be "written off": if the economy makes enough jobs available, many of them can be reintegrated into the labour market by means of retraining and other measures.

Thus the employability of the labour force cannot be a major obstacle to strong, lasting economic growth. It should only become a problem once unemployment falls below 3% or so, that is, once it has shrunk by 8 percentage points as compared to today's level.

The widespread claim that "only two percent of the labour force are affected by cyclical unemployment; the rest is structural unemployment which cannot be eliminated through growth" is therefore inaccurate. It overlooks the difference between a cyclical upturn. which utilises spare capacity, and a medium-term growth process, which creates new production capacity and new physical jobs.

This argument does not conflict with the promotion of initial and continuing vocational training. On the contrary, the latter is indispensable to enhancing the skills not only of unemployed people, the "hidden reserves", but also those in work, who are expected to be much more adaptable nowadays. Clearly, initial and continuing vocational training in itself does not create new jobs, although it does improve the vocational prospects of individuals and boost overall economic productivity. Its full benefit, however, can only be realised if the economy makes sufficient jobs available through the growth process.

(2) The second condition, namely the generation of new production capacity over and above productivity growth in the overall economy, and hence the creation of new jobs, is therefore the crucial condition for utilising the Community's huge potential workforce to the full.

This can only be achieved through a medium-term growth process supported by job-creating and capacity-increasing investment. Given the current relatively stable capital output ratio, with an investment rate of around 19% of GDP, the European economy can only grow by about $2^1/4\%$ per annum in the long term without bottlenecks in capacity causing inflationary tension. Thus, a rise in the rate of investment is crucial in order for the EU to embark permanently on the road to higher growth and higher rates of employment.

The prerequisites for this kind of a growth process sustained by investment are more favourable than ever before in the past 30 years:
– Inflation is as low as during the most stable years of the post-war period.
– Returns on investment are as high as at the time of full employment in the 1960s and are still rising;
– The monetary conditions, including exchange rates and long-term interest rates, are extremely favourable to a healthy development of demand.

Under the present structural circumstances (the capital output ratio, productivity trend and extent to which labour is being substituted by capital), this growth process might take the following form:[3] GDP growth of between 3 and 3.5% per annum gradually leads to spare capacity being completely utilised. At the same time, investment growth of 6–7% per annum causes sufficient new capacity to be generated to boost employment and allow private consumption to grow by between 2.5 and 3% per annum. Exports and imports grow by 6–7% per annum in the medium term. In this way, within five years the growth potential—i. e. annual growth in production capacity—could be raised from $2^1/4\%$ now to 3.5% or so because of the increasing rate of investment. Growth could then continue to rise at 3.5% per annum without inflationary tension.

With economic growth of 3.5% and productivity growth of 2%, employment can increase by $1^1/2\%$ per year, thereby generating approximately 25 million jobs in ten years. That would push up the employment rate from around 60% at present to about 70%. Although even higher rates of employment could be envisaged (see section 1), this would still be well on the way to full employment.

If growth can be made more employment-intense through structural and labour-market policy measures, the same employment effect can also be achieved with a lower economic growth rate of some 3% (see section 5).

It is therefore possible and realistic to utilise fully the Community's huge labour potential within the scope of a ten-year growth process with an average of 3–3.5% annual growth, and hence to return to full employment. What is more, the prerequisites for such a process are better than they have been for many years. Now that there are indications of a cyclical upturn, there is an opportunity to convert this into a lasting, non-inflationary growth process as outlined above, and even—something that cannot be explored in detail here—one that is environmentally sustainable.

3. Obstacles to Growth and Employment in the Past

Until the time of the first oil price crisis in 1973–74, there was practically full employment in the European Community. In the 1960s and 1970s, and even until the start of the 1980s, the average unemployment rate in Europe lay below that of the USA. The long-term rise in productivity in the EC (1974–96: 2% p.a.) is comparable with that in Japan (1986–96: 1.9% p.a.) and far higher than in the USA (1974–96: 0.7% p.a.). This applies likewise to the long-term trend in technical and organisational progress (1974–96: EC 1.1% p.a.; Japan 1.1% p.a., and USA 0.6% p.a.).[4]

Europe's economy was not, however, able to achieve sufficient economic growth exceeding the productivity trend to absorb the potential increase in the labour force (1974–96: 0.6% p.a.). If we regard the productivity growth stimulated by technical progress, trade liberalisation and the Internal Market as the basis for Europe's prosperity and competitiveness, the root-cause of its unemployment problem is inadequate GDP growth over and above the rise in productivity.

Why did such a growth not materialise? Looking at developments since 1986, once the effects of the two oil price crises had been overcome, it becomes clear that in the period 1986 90 the Community achieved a remarkable growth rate of 3.3% per annum, which was accompanied by annual employment growth of 1.3% and a significant decline in the unemployment rate (in 1990 the unemployment rate for West Germany was 4.8%; for the EC 7.7%). A total of 9.3 million jobs were created. Over the 1991–96 period, however, the EC achieved a growth rate of only 1.6% per annum. Employment therefore fell by a total of 4.7 million, while the unemployment rate had risen to 10.9% by 1996.

This unsatisfactory trend in employment during the first half of the 1990s is often attributed unjustifiably to globalisation and the introduction of new technologies. In reality it derived primarily from three macro-economic obstacles to growth:

(1) An overheating of the economy (from 1988 onwards), advanced by a lax budgetary policy, fuelled inflation (from 1989 on) and this was reflected in correspondingly higher rises in nominal wages (from 1990 on).

This trend was further exacerbated by the significant increase in the government deficit in the wake of German unification. The inflationary trend caused the Bundesbank to adopt a very tight monetary policy, which had a knock-on effect in all the EU countries. Consequently, rising interest rates and the currency crisis of 1992 led to the stabilising recession of 1992–93. This stability conflict between budgetary, wage and monetary policies was a major macro-economic obstacle to growth.

(2) A rapid adaptation of wage trends, sharp rises in productivity and increased competitiveness contributed in 1993–94 to a healthy upswing, which was led by exports and investment, coupled with a gradual improvement in private consumption and employment levels. This upswing was, however, stifled by the currency upheaval of spring 1995 (which was mainly attributable to the absence of credible economic and more particularly budgetary policies in a number of Member States) and by a rise in long-term interest rates. Such currency upheavals are another major macro-economic obstacle to growth; they have occurred repeatedly in the Community and especially in Germany since the early 1970s.

(3) The fact that healthy upswings have been cut short again and again by stability conflicts and currency upheavals has led to a decline in the investment rate in the Community. This has meant only weak growth in production potential (now around $2^{1}/_{4}$% p.a.), which in itself constitutes an obstacle to growth.

Without these three obstacles to growth, the growth experienced from 1986 to 1990 could have continued, and the Community would by now have been very close to the objective of full employment.

4. The Prerequisites for Full Employment Are Better Now than for a Long Time

As already illustrated, the prerequisites for a return to full employment are more favourable now than they have been for three decades. A lasting growth process underpinned by investment now appears possible—and on such a scale that there are likely to be approximately 17% more jobs ten years from now. The political challenge consists in not jeopardising these favourable prerequisites, and in keeping the macro-economic obstacles to growth under control and not allowing them to resurface.

The completion of Economic and Monetary Union (EMU) could play a crucial role in preventing a revival of these obstacles to growth:

(1) Monetary union rules out monetary turbulence between the participating countries. The more countries belong to EMU, the more favourable the effect on the Internal Market. But even extra-Community trade (which only accounts for some 10% of Community GDP) would stand to gain, since the Euro would probably be strong enough to stabilise the international monetary system too.

(2) The obstacle to growth arising from potential stability conflicts can also be far more readily avoided thanks to the Monetary Union. The provisions contained in Articles 104 to 104c of the Treaty,[5] in particular the ban on the financing of government deficits by printing money in Art. 104, greatly reduce the risk of a conflict between budgetary policy and monetary policy. The implementation of the Stability and Growth Pact with a view to balancing the budget under normal economic circumstances goes in the same direction, in that the reduction of deficits and the burden of debt gives budgetary policy greater scope to take pressure off monetary policy in the course of the economic cycle. Overall, in this way interest rates can settle on a lower level.

The impossibility of exchange rate changes within the Monetary Union, coupled with the credibility of the European Central Bank's stability policy, places greater responsibility on the Social Partners. Under EMU, nominal wages should on average progress in a manner that is compatible with the objective of price stability. Taking productivity gains into consideration, increases in real wages should take into account the need to strengthen both the return on job-creating investment and the purchasing power of wage-earners.

Indeed, the more the stability task of monetary policy is facilitated by a sound budgetary policy and by appropriate wage trends, the more favourable to growth and employment will be the monetary conditions, including the Euro exchange-rate and long-term interest rates.

This means that, in accordance with Art. 105(1) of the EC Treaty, the European Central Bank will pursue in a forceful and credible manner its primary objective, to maintain price stability, but also that, "without prejudice to the objective of price stability", it "shall support the general economic policies in the Community with a view to contributing to the achievement of the objectives of the Community as laid down in Article 2" of the Treaty (including the objectives of growth and employment).

(3) In this way, Monetary Union creates a more stable and less conflictual environment for growth and employment. This, in turn, is the

crucial precondition for overcoming the third obstacle to growth, namely inadequate growth in production capacity. Only if, through strong capacity-increasing investment, the growth in production capacity lies well above the rise in productivity, enough jobs can be created to integrate the Community's huge labour reserves gradually into the production process. The existing high profitability fosters such patterns of investment.

This approach, which promotes both growth and stability, is already the basis of the Community's "Broad Economic Policy Guidelines" and is the subject of EU-wide consensus.[6] Nevertheless, within the EMU stability framework, the promotion of growth and employment should be given far greater prominence, as called for in the "Growth and Employment" resolution adopted at the Amsterdam European Council.

It is important not to jeopardise the favourable prerequisites for growth and employment, and not to permit the emergence of fresh obstacles to growth. The responsibility for this lies with the Ministers for Economic, Financial, and Social Affairs, the Social Partners, and the European Central Bank. A long-term pact for growth and employment would facilitate co-ordination among these players on macro-economic and structural policy, and hence favour the realisation of the full-employment objective.

5. Support for the Growth Process Through Structural, Labour-market and Fiscal Policies

Technical progress and globalisation lead to a permanent structural change in the growth process. The pressure to boost productivity and cut jobs is severe. In sectors with high productivity gains, fierce international and intra-Community competition leads to falling relative prices. Competitiveness is thereby strengthened, and increased productivity, for the most part, is passed on to the rest of the economy through the price mechanism. This market-led transfer of purchasing power allows for rising relative prices in sectors with low productivity gains and less competitive pressure, thus making many jobs in such sectors worthwhile.

This is an age-old process, for which there is clear statistical evidence, and which requires that the price mechanism operates effectively. To a large extent this condition has been met by the opening-up of markets. Nevertheless, in order for the process to create sufficient jobs, there are two further prerequisites:

(1) Sectoral structural change must be socially acceptable.

(2) The growth rate in the economy at large must be sufficiently high for the balance between sectoral job creation and sectoral job losses to be positive and large enough to bring about a fall in unemployment.

These two prerequisites are interrelated. The stronger the overall economic growth, the less painful the process of sectoral structural change, and the more readily its social effects can be cushioned.

Only if efforts to increase competitiveness and productivity are coupled with correspondingly high growth and rising employment levels can the potential prosperity gains from technical progress, the internal market and the international division of labour actually be achieved. Sharply increased productivity accompanied by inadequate growth reduces employment, overburdens social security budgets, and pushes up non-wage labour costs, which, in turn, have a detrimental effect on competitiveness. The policy mix to promote growth and employment, which is feasible under monetary union, offers a way out of this vicious circle.

Structural policies must take account of this overall context. As far as the markets of goods and services are concerned, it is vital to ensure that the price mechanism and competition continue to operate efficiently. But only in a context of adequate growth will the measures still needed to promote competitiveness in the fields of technology, innovation and the information society really bear fruit, as will the Trans-European networks, the Internal Market and the liberalisation of world trade: since they all strengthen productivity, their positive effects on overall employment levels depend on the growth rate exceeding clearly the trend of productivity.

This applies similarly to important aspects of labour-market policy. The promotion of vocational training, retraining, the integration of young people and the long-term unemployed and, more generally, the upgrading of human capital—their positive effects will not be felt in full until the economy has made a sufficient number of jobs available. In the light of technical progress and structural change, continuing vocational training for the entire labour force—and not only for the unemployed—is an important labour-market policy objective: this allows for mobility, occupational advancement and better wages, as well as boosting competitiveness and productivity. Because of these productivity effects, however, here too the impact on overall employment levels depends on the scale of macro-economic growth in excess of increased productivity.

Clearly, labour-market policy also has a social dimension that should not be neglected. The reintegration of problem groups, and in particular young people and the long-term unemployed, into the world of work must be regarded not only in terms of its economic effects but also from the point of view of avoiding social exclusion.

It is necessary, moreover, to devise labour-market policy rules that contribute—in a way that is pragmatic and in keeping with the European social model—to making growth more employment-intense. In this way the goal of full employment can be reached more rapidly, without opening up the floodgates to a USA-style "working poor syndrome" resulting from a severe downward widening of the wage scale. The following approaches are worth considering:

- Flexible arrangements to reorganise and reduce working time, negotiated locally between the parties to collective agreements, and with a neutral impact on costs, including a dissociation of the working hours of humans from those of machines, and, wherever possible, also voluntary part-time work should be encouraged.
- collective agreements between the Social Partners containing greater wage differentiation acccording to skills, regions and—up to a certain point—sectors, together with temporary entry wage rates for the long-term unemployed;
- a budgetary neutral means of easing the burden of taxation and/or non-wage labour costs on the labour factor (especially at the lower end of the wage scale), suitable forms of wage subsidies and negative income taxes in the context of a reform of taxation and social security contribution systems.

The reform of taxation and social security contribution systems should take account of—beside separate objectives, such as fiscal justice and simpliflcation—the objective of full employment through stronger growth. The following principles are of particular importance in this context:

(1) The reduction of government deficits in the process of growth, down to a state of budgetary equilibrium or slight surplus under "normal" economic circumstances, is necessary not only for reasons of stability (to avoid conflicting with monetary policy), but also to encourage the necessary job-creating investment. Since in such circumstances governments no longer absorb private saving, but make a positive contribution to savings in the economy, the increase in the investment rate which is essential to lasting growth can—other things being equal—take place without adversely affecting the balance of payments and without putting pressure on long-term interest rates.[7] Tax and contributions reforms which augment structural government deficits are therefore incompatible with the necessary process of medium-term growth, and hence with the objective of full employment.

(2) The growth process leading to full employment must develop along environmentally sound lines. The progressive introduction of environmental taxes makes it possible to improve the environmental sustainability of growth via the price mechanism. There need be no fear of impairing overall economic competitiveness, as long as the burden of taxes and social security contributions on the labour factor is eased at the same time and in a budgetarily neutral manner.

(3) A budgetary neutral easing of the burden on the labour factor deriving from taxation and social security contributions is most effective in employment terms if it is targeted at the lower end of the wage and income scale. Jobs with a low level of productivity (above all in the service sector) thus become worthwhile, and a successful battle is waged against the underground economy. An across-the-board reduction in the burden of taxation and social security contributions levied on the labour factor is far less effective in employment terms, and would necessitate a considerable amount of compensatory funding to be effective and remain budgetary neutral.

It is worth mentioning that enterprises have already benefited from a substantial easing of the burden of overall wage costs affecting all employees. The moderate trend in real wages as compared with the rise in productivity (in the EU the average annual increase in real wages since 1982 has lagged one percentage point behind the annual productivity growth of 2%) has in fact led to a significant improvement in the profits of enterprises and profitability of investment. Thus the overall increase in social security charges from the early 1970s (1973: 11.8% of GDP) until 1996 (16.1% of GDP) has been shifted back from enterprises to wage-earners. Real unit labour costs in the economy as a whole are currently some 13% below their level at the start of the 1970s.

(4) A reform of taxation and social security systems should also take account of the fact that the budgetary equilibrium sought under "normal" economic circumstances considerably reduces the burden of government indebtedness in the longer term. The room for manoeuvre obtained in this way will give scope for budgetary policy not only to take pressure off monetary policy in stabilising the economic situation, but also to facilitate a reduction in the overall burden of taxation and contributions once the time is ripe.

(5) Gradual attainment of the objective of full employment will considerably ease the burden on social security systems. This does not mean that reforms that are currently under consideration and much needed should be abandoned. But with a return to full employment it is nevertheless possible

to maintain and reform the European social model. This applies in particular to pay-as-you-go pension systems.

As has been demonstrated elsewhere,[8] the ratio of people aged 65 and over to those from 15 to 64 will grow by approximately a third between 1995 and 2020. If the employment rate remains at its present level, pay-as-you-go pension contributions will have to rise likewise by some 33% in order to maintain the current level of pensions in relation to earned income levels. However, if the employment rate can be raised from around 60% at present to 72% over the next ten years and kept at this level or raised even further by the year 2020, the rise in the number of people in work (and hence those paying contributions out of earned income) will more or less offset the rise in the number of pensioners. For the same relative pension level, therefore, only slight increases in contributions would be necessary. The problems of pay-as-you-go pension systems would thereby be minimised for a generation.

Similar considerations apply to sickness, nursing and unemployment insurance. In the case of unemployment insurance, contributions could even be drastically reduced, since the number of beneficiaries would also fall.

These examples show the extent to which the future of the European social model depends on achieving the objective of full employment and a high rate of employment.

Notes

1   Annual Economic Report 1997, European Commission, in: European Economy, 1996, No. 63.
2   Cf. European Economy, 1995, No. 59, Study No. 3.
3   Cf. European Economy, 1993, No. 55; 1995, No. 59, and 1996, No. 62.
4   Cf. Annual Economic Report of the European Commission, 1997, Chapter 2; European Economy, 1996, No. 63.
5   Art. 104: ban on the monetary financing of government deficits; Art. 104a: ban on privileged access of public authorities to the financial markets; Art. 104b: the Community and the public authorities of the Member States are prohibited from assuming liability for the debts of other public authorities; Art 104c: excessive government deficits and debts must be avoided.
6   Cf. "Broad Economic Policy Guidelines of the Member States and the Community", European Economy, 1996, No. 62, and 1997, No. 64.
7   Major economic growth and catching-up processes in the past (e. g. the "economic miracles" in Germany and Japan) have been accompanied by high budget surpluses (compulsory saving).
8   Cf. for example: "Some Economic Implications of Demographic Trends Up To 2020", Study No. 5, European Economy, 1994, No. 56.

4 Is There a Need for a Co-ordinated European Wage and Labour Market Policy?

ULRICH FRITSCHE, GUSTAV A. HORN, WOLFGANG SCHEREMET,
RUDOLF ZWIENER

Introduction

With the introduction of European Economic and Monetary Union (EMU), wage policy is being allocated a decisive role in the EU member states. It is questionable whether the benefits derived from European monetary union in terms of lower transaction costs and lower nominal interest rates will outweigh the additional risks, due to the fact that the ability of the extended currency area to absorb shocks will be weakened. The European single market and with it the free movement of labour and capital have already intensified trade within Europe, triggered off migration and generated higher foreign direct investment and will continue to do so. But with the loss of sovereignty over an independent monetary policy, there will no longer be differences in inflation rates of tradable goods in the individual countries. Fiscal policy will be constrained by the EMU convergence criteria and currency depreciation will no longer be an instrument to compensate for excessive wage and price developments.

Since the mid-1980s, in the process of European unification, the mere anticipation of these restrictions has led to the fact that nominal wage increases in the European countries have become more closely aligned. As a result, price increases in Europe have inched closer together, and the deviation in inflation rates has weakened noticeably (cf. Tables 4.1 and 4.2). In the course of this nominal convergence process, two groups of countries have emerged. One group—consisting of Germany, Austria, the Nether-lands, and Belgium—showed quite a similar development of inflation and unemployment indicators, as well as more or less constant exchange rates. The overwhelming majority of countries examined, differed considerably from this first group. In order to make a conceptual distinction between the

Table 4.1   Rates of Inflation* in Europe, 1981–98

	1981–90	1991	1992	1993	1994	1995	1996	1997	1998**
Belgium	4,6	3,3	2,3	3,5	2,8	1,7	2,3	1,6	1,3
Denmark	5,8	2,4	2,0	0,6	1,6	2,0	2,1	2,3	2,1
Germany***	2,6	3,8	4,9	4,0	2,8	1,9	1,9	1,9	1,7
Greece	18,3	19,7	15,6	14,2	11,0	8,6	8,5	5,5	4,5
Spain	9,3	6,4	6,4	5,6	4,8	4,7	3,4	2,5	2,2
France	6,2	3,2	2,4	2,2	2,1	1,6	1,9	1,1	1,0
Italy	10,0	6,9	5,6	5,4	4,6	5,8	4,3	2,4	2,1
Netherlands	2,3	3,2	3,1	2,1	2,8	1,5	1,3	2,2	2,3
Austria	3,6	3,0	3,9	3,3	3,3	1,5	2,5	1,8	1,5
Portugal	17,3	12,2	9,1	6,6	5,1	4,2	2,6	2,1	2,2
Finland	6,4	5,6	4,1	4,2	1,4	0,3	1,6	1,4	2,0
Sweden	8,2	10,3	2,2	5,7	3,0	2,7	1,2	2,2	1,5
UK	6,0	7,5	5,0	3,4	2,2	2,6	2,6	2,3	2,3
EU	6,5	5,6	4,7	4,1	3,2	3,0	2,6	2,1	1,9
EU Standard Deviation	n. a.		n. a.	3,2	2,3	2,1	1,8	1,0	0,9

* Deflator of private consumption expenditure; year to year percentage changes
** Forecast
*** 1981–91 West Germany
Source: Eurostat.

two groups in this study, the countries in the first group will be referred to as "hard-currency countries", and those of the second group as "soft-currency countries". These terms will be used, even though they no longer apply, due to the nominal convergence of inflation rates during the 1990s. In view of establishing a common currency, the process of convergence—both in terms of levels and deviations—has continued to progress since the early 1990s. At the start of EMU, the rates of price increases within the individual EU countries—as well as increases in average incomes—hardly differ.

With unemployment rates, a similar alignment as in inflation was not observed (cf. Tables 4.1 and 4.2). In the course of the explosion in oil prices, the level of unemployment as well as the variations of unemployment in European countries increased. While employment rates tended to converge again during the 1980s in those countries whose currencies appreciated, the standard deviation in all countries remained virtually constant and even widened in the 1990s.

Thus, one of the central demands being made in connection with the creation of a single currency in Europe is the transition to greater labour market flexibility. However, the term "labour market flexibility" is interpreted in a variety of ways. Very generally defined, the degree of labour market flexibility measures the speed at which an economy adjusts to an exogenous shock. This can include many areas, such as taxation and social insurance systems, labour law, and the institutional organisation of the wage determination process and its ability to adjust to cyclical and structural changes. The flexibility of wage policy in a common currency area is of particular significance in view of the adjustment to real or nominal shocks.

The underlying theory is provided by the imperfect competition model,[1] which states that on the labour market, unions bargain with firms over nominal wage increases while on the product market, firms have sufficient market power to set the price as a mark-up over marginal cost. In principle, unions have an incentive to demand higher wages while firms aim at higher prices. Assuming money supply is given, there is a rate of unemployment that equilibrates the desired mark-up over wages of prices by unions (the real wage) with the desired mark-up of prices over wages by firms (the unit profit). According to such a price formation, the price level is a mark-up (A) on unit labour costs (ULC), according to

(1) $\qquad P = ULC\,(1+A)$

with

(2) $\qquad ULC = W \cdot N / Y_r = W / Q$

Table 4.2   Rates of Unemployment* in Europe, 1981–98

	1981–90	1991	1992	1993	1994	1995	1996	1997	1998**
Belgium	9,7	6,6	7,3	8,9	10,0	9,9	9,8	9,5	8,5
Denmark	7,4	8,4	9,2	10,1	8,2	7,2	6,9	6,1	5,4
Germany***	6,0	5,6	6,6	7,9	8,4	8,2	8,8	9,7	9,8
Greece	6,4	7,0	7,9	8,6	8,9	9,2	9,6	9,5	9,2
Spain	18,5	16,4	18,5	22,8	24,1	22,9	22,1	20,9	19,7
France	9,2	9,5	10,4	11,7	12,3	11,7	12,4	12,5	11,9
Italy	8,8	8,8	9,0	10,3	11,4	11,9	12,0	12,1	12,0
Netherlands	8,5	5,8	5,6	6,6	7,1	6,9	6,3	5,3	4,4
Austria	3,4	3,4	3,4	4,0	3,8	3,9	4,4	4,4	4,2
Portugal	7,0	4,0	4,2	5,7	7,0	7,3	7,3	6,4	6,2
Finland	5,2	7,2	12,4	16,9	17,4	16,3	15,4	14,0	12,3
Sweden	2,7	3,3	5,8	9,5	9,8	9,2	10,0	10,2	9,1
UK	9,8	8,8	10,1	10,4	9,6	8,7	8,2	7,1	6,5
EU	9,0	8,2	9,3	10,7	11,2	10,8	10,9	10,7	10,2

* Eurostat definition; percentage of civilian employment
** Forecast
*** 1981–91 West Germany
Source: Eurostat.

where W is the wage rate per employee, N is the number of employees, Y_r is real GDP, and Q is labour productivity. In logarithmic differentials, the formula is

(3) $$\Delta p = \Delta w - \Delta q + \Delta \alpha$$

Lower case letters denote a logarithmic representation, Δ indicates first differences in time. During the course of an economic cycle, the mark-up will not remain constant, but will, depending on the demand conditions, vary on the goods market; $\Delta \alpha$ is therefore proportional to demand ($\delta \Delta Y_d$). Employment, in turn, develops analogous to Okun's Law, according to $\Delta Y_d = \tau \cdot \Delta N$. With a constant labour supply, this can also be formulated as $\Delta Y_d = \tau \cdot \Delta UR$, where ΔUR is the change in the unemployment rate. Prices then react according to the following equation:

(4) $$\Delta p = \Delta w - \Delta q - \gamma \cdot \Delta UR, \qquad \text{with } \gamma = \delta \cdot \tau.$$

Δq is the target growth rate of real wages that keeps the unemployment rate constant. Hence, it reflects the productivity trend, which is determined by capital accumulation and technical progress. In the long run the equilibrium unemployment rate will be constant, so that $\Delta UR = 0$. Rearranging equation (4) with $\Delta UR = 0$ yields

(5) $$\Delta w = \Delta p + \Delta q.$$

A wage policy recommendation can be deduced from equations (4) and (5). In order to keep unemployment constant, so that the actual unemployment rate and the "natural" unemployment rate do not deviate from each other, nominal wages must rise in line with growth in productivity and the inflation rate. This rule of productivity-oriented wage formation is applicable when the ex-post inflation rate and growth in productivity correspond to ex-ante anticipated values. In the absence of stochastic disturbances, actual productivity growth corresponds to long run trend productivity and the inflation corresponds exactly to the rate tolerated by the central bank. If there is a strict productivity orientation of wage policy, an immediate reaction would be necessary in the event of changes in the general economic conditions.

Economic policy in Europe is faced not only with the challenge of creating more employment in Europe as a whole, but also with the challenge of how to simultaneously reduce the regional disparities that have developed primarily as a result of this kind of convergence process. The key to achieving both is a productivity-oriented wage policy in each country. Such a policy has already been the basis for wage development in some EMU countries, especially the Netherlands, Austria and West Germany. These are also countries whose inflation and unemployment indicators—compared to other participants in EMU show better economic performance Such proposals stand in contrast to the economic strategies often recommended. These strategies are based on improving competitive conditions on labour markets in order to revive employment by lowering real wages.[2] Such approaches do not, however, adequately take into account the interdependence of the entire economic system and the interaction of the economic actions of individual market players on the actions of other market players, as will be shown in the next chapter.

Simulations of the Future Development of the European Labour Market

According to neo-classical ideas, additional competition in the wake of monetary union could contribute considerably to lowering unemployment in Europe. Wage rises that are far below productivity increases would stimulate the substitution of labour for capital, thus increasing the employment intensity of growth. A precondition for the success of this strategy is an economic policy in the EMU geared towards abolishing, or at least weakening, all obstacles to competition, e. g. labour market regulations and highly-centralised wage settings.

Simulations were carried out on the basis of the Oxford Economic Forecasting (OEF) model, a multi-country model that encompasses the main economic links between economies, trade flows, interest rates, and exchange rates.[3] In this particular analysis, the modelling of the labour market is of decisive significance.

The production element of the model by which employment is determined uses both real wages and GDP growth rates as determinants. The long-term results of the model are not based on an econometric, i. e., databased, estimated equation; rather, equilibrium derived from neoclassically shaped theoretical considerations is assumed. As a result, substitution effects explain a large part of the employment trends.[4] This is consistent with the framework of a neo-classical production model. Other (Keynesian) views of the labour market consider the significance of spillover effects from goods to labour markets to be much greater, implying a close correlation between growth and employment within the framework of that approach. In addition, even theoretically, substitution effects are only possible when, for example, increases in real wages lead to a boost in investment, which in turn increases the capital intensity of production while employment is reduced. This link is only contained indirectly in the OEF model, however, since the investment function is based mainly on growth and profits, but not on the relative factor costs, as would normally be necessary in this class of model. In that respect, not even the neo-classical view is illustrated completely. Nevertheless, a series of simulations was carried out, taking stock of the neo-classical recommendations for increasing employment and illustrating their implications. The identified employment effects should, however, in view of their deviation from GDP growth rates, be considered extreme cases.

The second main aspect for the development of the labour market within the scope of the simulations is the nature of wage formation. This also shows the point of convergence attained thus far among the potential EMU participants. Therefore, the specification of the wage function plays a major role in employment trends within the scope of this model. To ascertain the convergence effects and to maintain theoretical consistency, the wage functions used for the simulations below are modifications of the original version of the OEF model.

Monetary policy will primarily take its direction from price stability. For this reason, a reaction function was incorporated into the model aiming principally at constant short-term "real interest rates" (i. e., the short-term interest rate minus the rate of inflation). Trends in German price levels are used as the inflation rate, which actually serves as an indicator for European price trends. Under this assumption, the ECB reacts to each acceleration of rising prices with a similar increase in short-term interest rates.

Apart from the above modifications, the model was not changed. Thus, labour supply is, to a certain extent, positively dependent on real wage levels in keeping with the neo-classical view. Under these circumstances, with increasing real wages, unemployment rises not only for substitution reasons, but, in addition, also because the labour supply also rises. The long-term homogeneity between wage and price trends contained in the original version of the model is also maintained. Each nominal wage increase is then shifted on to prices over the longer term and real wages remain unchanged.

In the following, we present the effects of reductions in nominal wages, in real wages and a reform of the social security insurance system, based on the OEF model. For each case three simulations were calculated: (a) a reduction/reform in Germany (a "large" country); (b) a reduction/reform in the Netherlands (a "small" country); (c) a reduction/reform in all EMU countries.

Reductions in Nominal Wages

Low nominal wages reduce costs for enterprises and thus enable them to lower prices without losing out on profits. However, if the inflation rate decreases too, lower nominal wages do not necessarily also lead to lower real wages. Only if prices are sticky, can the real wage decrease be achieved.

The results of the simulations can be seen from the figures and tables (cf. Figure 4.1 and Table 4.3) in this paper.

Reductions in Nominal Wages in Germany

All in all, the results turn out to be of a mixed nature. On the one hand, growth in Germany is stronger. The main reason for this strength is improved competitiveness in comparison both to EMU countries and other countries. For the other EMU countries, this means a negative shock for their exports and increased imports from Germany. Thus growth is dampened by this strategy. These growth effects are accompanied by a delayed curbing of price movements, which principally has two impacts. First, private consumption will decline in Germany if real incomes shrink. At the same time—it is assumed—monetary policy would be relaxed in view of the lower rates of price increase and nominal interest rates would be lowered by the ECB because of the high weight Germany has in European inflation. This improves investment conditions and induces a positive shock for European growth. Hence all EMU countries except Germany face opposing shocks. As the results show—only Italy, on average, would enjoy a positive net effect (cf. Table 4.3). In all other countries the loss of competitiveness relative to Germany prevails and their growth is lowered.

From a European perspective, it is apparent that despite the relaxed monetary policy related to a strategy of this kind, especially when it is carried out in a large country, the other EMU countries would suffer from a strategy of German wage reductions. Therefore it is not sustainable as a European strategy.

Table 4.3   Reduction of Nominal Wages in Germany

Average deviations from the basis simulation in the simulation period (in %)

	Germany	France	Italy	Nether-lands
Gross Domestic Product, real	1,9	0,0	0,5	−1,0
Private consumption, real	0,0	0,7	2,2	0,6
Gross investment, real	1,5	1,0	0,0	0,9
Exports, real	3,8	−0,9	−1,4	−1,3
Consumer prices	−6,4	0,7	2,3	0,0
Gross wages	−8,5	0,5	2,4	−0,5
Exchange rate national curr./US-Dollar[a]	1,6	1,6	1,7	1,6
Employment	2,0	0,1	0,6	−0,2
memo items				
unemployment rate (%)	−1,8	−0,1	−0,5	0,2
deficit rate (%)[b]	0,8	0,3	0,8	−0,5
short-term interest rate (%)	−1,4	−1,4	−1,4	−1,4
long-term interest rate (%)	−0,7	−0,7	−0,7	−0,7

	Spain	Great Britain	Sweden
Gross Domestic Product, real	0,5	0,0	−0,7
Employment	0,5	0,0	−0,3
Exchange rate national curr./US-Dollar[a]	0,0	−3,2	0,1
memo items			
short-term interest rate (%)	−1,4	0,6	1,9
long-term interest rate (%)	−0,7	−0,5	0,3

[a] (−): appreciation, (+): depreciation.
[b] (−): increase in deficit.

Source: Simulation with the OEF model.

Reductions in Nominal Wages in the Netherlands

The results are somewhat different if nominal wages are reduced only in the Netherlands. The result for the Netherlands itself is a clearly positive effect, for the same reason as Germany benefited from its lower nominal wages. However the effects on other EMU countries are different. The main reason why their growth and employment would remain at the reference level is the fact that no relaxation of a monetary policy can be expected. Dutch prices have little influence on the European price trend; therefore the ECB will have no reason to relax its policy stance. The small influence of the Dutch economy on the European level is reflected in the fact that the increase in Dutch competitiveness does not have any great significance throughout Europe either. Hence the Dutch do not lose much of their export business. The results show that in the end a small country like the Netherlands can enter such a strategy without fear of repercussions from stronger economies.

Reductions in Nominal Wages in all EMU Countries

A reduction in nominal wages in all participating countries would lead to a European- wide expansion in production and employment. The main reasons are improved competitiveness of the EMU countries compared to non-EMU countries and the significant relaxation of monetary policy, since inflation would then be markedly subdued.

However, there are numerous risks involved in this strategy: According to the simulations, private consumption decreases in almost all countries at the beginning. There is no feedback with the investment function used in this model so that investment stays on course. Monetary policy is a further risk factor related to this strategy. It is by no means clear that the monetary policy would be as perfectly accommodating as assumed in this model. On the contrary, it is much more likely that it will react cautiously, due to uncertainty about future developments. Assuming this is true, there is a real danger of deflationary processes, if monetary policy becomes "asymmetric" by showing an inflation fear bias.

Reductions in Real Wages

If one follows the neo-classical approach, reductions in nominal wages do not appear to bring about sustained stimulation of employment. Only a

Deviations from basis simulation

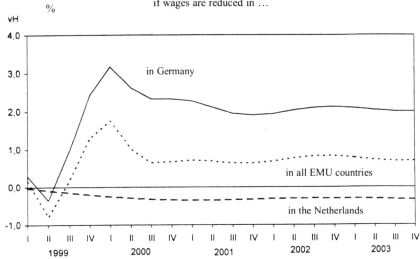

Growth effects for Germany
if wages are reduced in ...

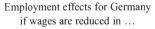

Employment effects for Germany
if wages are reduced in ...

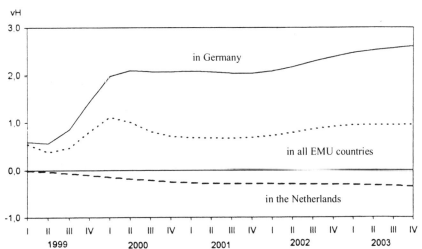

Figure 4.1   Effects in Germany of Reductions in Nominal Wages

Source: Simulation with the OEF model.

DIW 98

significant reduction in real wages will bring equilibrium back on the labour market. This line of thinking, reflected in the labour demand function of the OEF—model, is based on the assumption that there will be ample opportunities to substitute labour for capital.

There are some interesting features connected to this type of simulation (cf. Figure 4.2 and Table 4.4). The first one is: The only way to simulate a real wage decrease with the model used is to keep the prices fixed on the baseline level, while nominal wages are lowered. Beyond doubt, in the long run it is highly questionable whether prices are really independent of unit labour costs. However to illustrate the effects of lower real wages, this kind of imposition is unavoidable. This shows the low realistic content of the following simulation: It is extremely hypothetical. The positive employment showing up in this simulation can be explained solely by the effect of the substitution of labour for capital. Because real wages are lower, firms substitute labour for capital with an elasticity of one. A countervailing effect is the lower growth path, which results from this strategy. Lower real wages mean lower real incomes of the employed, since it takes some time until the positive employment effects materialise. Thus, in particular, private consumption will face a marked adverse shock that will lower growth significantly. In turn, this also lowers employment. Hence the overall effect of lower real wages on employment will be much smaller than the substitution effect. The result is not surprising if one considers that the strategies outlined here are a combination of a positive supply shock with a negative demand shock. Whether the consequences for growth and employment are positive or negative in the final analysis remains uncertain a priori. However, given the empirical relationship as measured by the model, in the end, a positive effect prevails.

One conclusion is obvious. Irrespective of whether the magnitudes of the substitution effects assumed in the neo-classical model are realistic or not, the positive employment effects achieved through a reduction in real wages in the neo-classical approach can also be achieved through restraint on nominal wages in conjunction with an expansive monetary policy. So instead of entering a highly improbable real wage reduction strategy, a strategy of nominal wage restraint and a more expansive monetary policy should be pursued.

Table 4.4   Reduction of Real Wages in Germany

Average deviations from the basis simulation in the simulation period (in %)

	Germany	France	Italy	Nether-lands
Gross Domestic Product, real	− 2,3	−0,4	−0,4	−0,7
Private consumption, real	− 6,3	0,0	0,2	0,1
Gross investment, real	− 0,8	0,0	0,1	−0,1
Exports, real	0,5	−1,5	−1,2	−1,5
Consumer prices	− 0,3	−0,6	−1,1	−1,8
Gross wages	−10,0	−0,5	−1,1	−2,1
Exchange rate national curr./US-Dollar[a)]	− 1,7	−1,7	−1,6	−1,7
Employment	5,1	−0,1	−0,3	−0,3
memo items				
unemployment rate (%)	− 5,2	0,1	0,2	0,2
deficit rate (%)[b)]	0,5	−0,2	−0,1	−0,7
short-term interest rate (%)	− 0,1	−0,1	−0,1	−0,1
long-term interest rate (%)	− 0,1	−0,1	−0,1	−0,1

	Spain	Great Britain	Sweden
Gross Domestic Product, real	− 0,5	−0,2	−0,2
Employment	− 0,3	0,0	−0,2
Exchange rate national curr./US-Dollar[a)]	0,0	−0,5	0,0
memo items			
short-term interest rate (%)	− 0,1	−0,5	−0,8
long-term interest rate (%)	− 0,1	−0,1	−0,4

[a)] (−): appreciation, (+): depreciation.
[b)] (−): increase in deficit.

Source: Simulation with the OEF model.

Deviations from basis simulation

Growth effects for Germany
if wages are reduced in ...

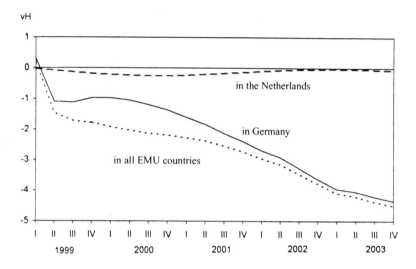

Employment effects for Germany
if wages are reduced in ...

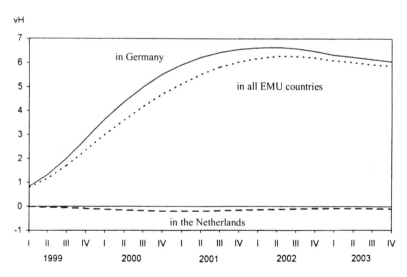

Figure 4.2   Effects in Germany of Reductions in Real Wages

Source: Simulations with the OEF model.

DIW 98

Reforming the Social Insurance System

Given a framework of more or less flexible (adjustable) exchange rates, disparities in the levels of taxes on wages in various countries would be ironed out by means of exchange-rate adjustments, at least in the medium term.

This is unproblematic if the social standards of the participating countries are different at the beginning of a monetary union. After the commencement of monetary union, however, if one country lowers its social standards or chooses another type of financing, there could be repercussions for the other participating countries (cf. Figure 4.3).

There are fears that some European countries in monetary union could raise their growth and employment prospects by lowering social standards or increasing tax financing of social spending at the expense of their neighbours. Such fears are more or less confirmed by these econometric simulation studies, although the negative effects for the neighbouring countries were held in close check. Following the introduction of European

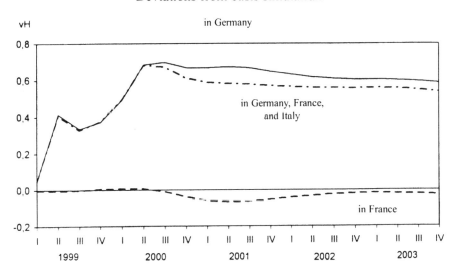

Figure 4.3   Growth Effects for Germany of a Reduction of 3 Percentage Points in Social Insurance Contribution Rates Alongside Increased Indirect Taxes

Source: Simulations with the OEF model.

Economic and Monetary Union, it could become more difficult, for reasons of competition, to raise social security contribution rates in one of the member states even if this would seem sensible, for, say, demographic reasons. If one wishes to raise contribution rates without affecting competitiveness under the conditions of monetary union, a corresponding negative correction of standard wages is necessary—a precondition that cannot be implemented without interfering with wage autonomy. A possible way out might be either to forego raising revenue—and thus cut social insurance spending, or to increase the proportion of revenue financed by taxes. The cut in spending, which is demanded by many, has, at a time of rising unemployment and a growing number of pensioners, certain distribution implications, implying at the very least a relative loss of income for unemployed and retired people.

No "threat" to the big EMU countries would come from changes in expenditure on social insurance or income. It is only the smaller countries that might face difficulties if big countries such as Germany were to make a substantial shift to this strategy. The smaller countries would probably follow suit in order to avoid a decline in their competitive position. Employment gains could probably indeed be achieved in Europe through greater financing of social welfare expenditure by tax revenue. On the basis of the reduction in the contribution rate simulated here (3 percentage points with no inflow bias), the unemployment rate in Europe could be reduced overall by no more than 0.5%.

The Institutional Concept Underlying a European Wage Policy

The institutional concept underlying a European wage policy should thus be expressed a way that allows a successful productivity orientation to be implemented. In this connection it is decisive that the parties involved in the wage formation process are in a position to both take up the signals issued by the central bank and to achieve a productivity orientation. Indeed, they have several strategies and examples at their disposal. In some countries, wage policy in the past has been aligned very closely to inflation targets and economic productivity. In Austria and, to a lesser extent, in Germany, central bank signals are aimed at the wage negotiation partners, who, because of their centralist orientation, take their direction from general economic lines. Wage determination was most closely linked to productivity in Germany, Austria, and the Netherlands and thus fulfilled most of the conditions necessary for positive economic development. In Austria, in particular, where unions and employer confederations are actually represented on that country's central bank council (the *"Zentralbankrat"*) because of their representation on the Labour Council (the *"Arbeiterkammer"*), it has been possible to do away with any impediments to price stability immediately in negotiation with the parties concerned. This is due to the fact that unions and management are able to react to the mere threat of the sanction of higher interest rates, rather than being forced to return to a stability path by means of increased unemployment and a fall in profits following the onset of a recession. The wage policy practised by these countries could be a model for a European wage policy. It would be feasible to strive for a similar institutional shaping of wage policy on a Europe-wide scale—but within national boundaries.

The conditions are most easily fulfilled if the other countries take their orientation from the wage policy of Germany, the one large economy included in the countries mentioned above. In this context, "orientation" does not mean that wage development or, indeed, wage levels should be the same as in Germany, for wage levels must be related to the productivity levels of the country and industrial sector concerned. What this does mean is that wage development defines itself with regard to the trends within a particular industrial sector in Germany. It can be higher if productivity in the country concerned rises more strongly or if greater speed is desired for technological change. It must be lower if productivity does not increase as strongly or structural change is considered too fast. One immediate conclusion that can be drawn from this recommendation is that Germany is the country with the least need to act to reform wage formation following the introduction of monetary union.

Theoretically, smaller European countries would have the opportunity to adopt the concept of wage formation in the "anchoring countries." This could, for example, be assured by legal conditions on whose legal basis wage trends in the reference countries are used as a yardstick for wage disputes. Such a course of action represents the compulsory implementation of the productivity rule.

The development of wage policy institutions can also be left to a process of trial and error in the individual countries. In that case, however, there might be a danger of external effects resulting from economic behaviour adverse to stability. If, in a relevant number of EMU countries, this development is incompatible with the ECB's stability targets, economic development will be slowed down in all countries as a result of interest rate hikes. This could only be avoided if wage development in some countries were moderate enough to compensate for the overshooting in the other countries and the central bank did not need to intervene. In such a scenario, far-reaching regional differences, i. e., the exact opposite of convergence, would be the consequence, and thus a demand for transfers to overcome these imbalances would be fairly likely. Only if the demands for transfers are not acted upon, could the result of a trial and error process be an adjustment of wage formation in the various countries and thus ultimately, a similarly strong productivity-related orientation as in the first group of countries. The result would then be the same as in the initially suggested strategies, only at a much higher cost in terms of loss of growth and employment. If the demand for transfers were acted upon, regional imbalances would remain, and those countries with a stability-oriented concept of wage formation would be permanently burdened with transfer payments.

Conclusion

An orientation along the lines of German wage formation would give German wage policy a special responsibility for all of Europe—similar to the way that German monetary policy was a model in the past. This suggestion stands in stark contrast to the widely held criticism that the German system of wage formation is the main reason for the country's high unemployment rate.

But there are two dangers: First there is the much-debated and obvious danger that German wage policy will in future allow wage increases that lie above rises in productivity and the tolerable inflation rate. However, past experience has shown that, with Germany's institutional wage policy orientation, this has rarely been the case—at least not as often as under alternative institutional arrangements.

The second and more current danger is that Germany could fall below the stability requirements. Thus there has often been a call for German wages to be lowered, despite the fact that through improved competitiveness significant progress in productivity has achieved more exports and higher growth on world markets. From the European viewpoint, such a scramble to lower wages is not a sustainable strategy, since it is based on beggar-my-neighbour effects in which German exports would rise but mainly at the expense of its European trading partners. European growth would experience only a marginal boost, and a process of convergence would not get off the ground. And if monetary policy does not react with expansive momentum at that point, the result would be deflation.

Those who, following neo-classical considerations, suspect that overly high real wages are the root cause of European unemployment dispute such a view. In their eyes, a European scramble to decrease real wages is the only strategy with which underemployment can be overcome. They do not trust the scope for growth of monetary expansion, which is the result of low inflation rates, but, rather, they believe in substitution processes in favour of labour and at the expense of capital. However, the econometric simulations make the errant nature of such a course evident. Even if one were to agree with the neo-classical ideas of a production process with its well-defined substitution opportunities, the result is still sobering: A general decrease in real wages in Europe might well increase employment—but Europe would become a poorer place. Decreases in real wages imply a fall in consumption, since real incomes must fall with decreasing labour productivity. Such decreases also imply a fall in investment, because utilising capital compared with labour becomes too costly and therefore this capital must be disinvested. The losses in growth that are linked with the expansion in employment under neo-classical considerations uncover the regressive character of these ideas. The reason is that such considerations ultimately assume that the wheel of productivity can be turned back at will to achieve present-day incomes with the employment of the past. This is a mistaken assumption, for with the employment of the past, it is only possible to earn the corresponding incomes of the past.

The limitations of supply-side oriented economics become evident when an attempt is made to undercut wage increases that are in line with monetary stability. This is a current scenario in Germany, where wages have been pushed below increases in productivity. The rules for stability orientation must once again take centre-stage, and this implies productivity-oriented wage formation instead of lowering wages at the expense of other European countries.

These considerations on a wage policy for the whole of Europe contain an essential message for economic development: Economic progress may be linked inextricably with competition—but not with every type of competition. Higher growth in Europe and the opportunity for the less prosperous countries to catch up is only possible if competition contains an entrepreneurial element. This means that competition must focus on the more efficient linking of production factors or on the development of new products in the private sector to create competitive advantages for companies. In the public sector, improvements in infrastructure or human capital, the creation of more efficient educational or taxation systems, or new types of development schemes, could help to establish the competitive advantages of particular regions. This type of competition encourages growth through economic creativity and is set against the type of competition that aims to achieve employment by cutting wages, social benefits or taxes. Such an approach might seem promising from the point of view of an individual country or company or from a general economic viewpoint. However, the competitive advantages resulting from such an approach are not based on the creation of something new, but exclusively on the "devaluation" of something that already exists. From an economic viewpoint, this does not open up any additional economic opportunities, but is, at best, a zero-sum game in which the loser is the one who lags behind in the race to cut costs.

Notes

1   Cf. Blanchard (1986), Layard, Nickell, and Jackman (1991), Lindbeck (1993), Franz (1996^b).
2   Cf. Berthold and Fehn (1996), Soltwedel (1997), Sachverständigenrat (1995, 1996, 1997).
3   Cf. OEF (1996).
4   The employment equation shows an error-correction specification in which the real wage level finds its way into the error correction term in the same way as GDP does. The short-term development is determined primarily by GDP growth rates and to a much lesser extent by changes in real wages.

References

Berthold, N and R Fehn, (1996), "The Positive Economics of Unemployment and Labor Market Inflexibility", *Kyklos* 49.
Blanchard, O J (1986), "The Wage Price Spiral", *Quarterly Journal of Economics*, 101: pp. 543–65.
Franz, W (1996), "Theoretische Ansätze zur Erklärung der Arbeitslosigkeit: Wo stehen wir 1995?", in Gahlen, Hesse, and Ramser, eds. (1996). *Arbeitslosigkeit und Möglichkeiten ihrer Überwindung.* Tübingen: J. C. B. Mohr.
Layard, R, St Nickell, R Jackman (1991), *"Unemployment: Macroeconomic Performance and the Labour Market"*, Oxford.
Lindbeck, A (1993), *Unemployment and Macroeconomics.* Cambridge, MA: MIT Press.
Oxford Economic Forecasting (1996), *"World Economic Prospects"*, Summer, Oxford.
Sachverständigenrat (1995, 1996, 1997), *Jahresgutachten*, sev. issues.
Soltwedel, R (1997), "Dezentrale Lohnfindung und gesamtwirtschaftliche Anpassungsfähigkeit", in Bundesvereinigung der deutschen Arbeitgeberverbände, 7. Cologne: Volkswirtschaftliches Kolloquium.

5 Societal Support for Social Dialogue. Europe's Trade Unions and Employers' Associations

JELLE VISSER

"Structure is a function of purpose" —
George Woodcock, General Secretary
Trades Union Congress, 1959–1969

Introduction

One of the interesting phenomena of recent years is the resurgence of concertation or social dialogue in many European political economies. In a number of countries—notably Ireland, Italy, Portugal, Spain, Finland and Greece—this has taken the form of social pacts. In other countries, like Austria, Norway and the Netherlands, concertation has been reinvigorated as the standard operating procedure accompanying national wage bargaining and social policymaking. In Belgium (in 1993 and again in 1995–96) and in Germany (1995–96) attempts to negotiate a national pact for employment failed, but new proposals are on the agenda (for an overview, see Fajertag and Pochet, 1997; Pochet, 1998; *Gewerkschaftliche Monatshefte*, October 1998). Generally speaking, the possibility of a national employment pact does not appear realistic in France or Britain and sits uneasy with current decentralisation trends in Denmark and Sweden, two countries with a tradition of nation-wide policy co-ordination in wage, employment and social policy. It has been suggested that the corporatist Sisyphus, declared prematurely dead in the 1980s, is again toiling his way up the mountain (Schmitter and Grote, 1997).

The resurgence of concertation within the boundaries of national states has led to an increased interest in the possibilities and conditions of social pacts at the level of the European Union. Early (1996) Commission President Santer called for a confidence pact on employment; on several occasions he repeated his plea for a *"social pact veritable"* without, however, receiving much response (see Greenwood, in this volume). As part of the Maastricht Agreement on Social Policy (1991), which, since the Amsterdam treaty (1997) has been incorporated in the EC Treaty, the main European trade unions and employers' organisations are involved in consultations and negotiations about social policy legislation in the European Union. Two agreements have been reached, one on parental leave and one on part-time employment; on other issues—most conspicuously on the European works councils and the procedures for information and consultation in national enterprises—Europe's social partners have failed to negotiate an agreement. The interpretation of this "self-regulatory" path is surrounded with questions: Will it change the shape of interest representation at the European level and produce a kind of "Euro-corporatism" (Falkner, 1996; Obradovic, 1995)? Is the European Commission being "hijacked" by unrepresentative organisations, resulting in a decline of power for European citizens and the European Parliament in a vital policy area (Betten, 1998)? Are the European labour market parties—the *European Trade Union Confederation* (ETUC) on the workers' side; the *Union of Industrial and Employers' Confederations of Europe* (UNICE) for private sector employees and the *Centre Européen des Entreprises à Participation Publique* (CEEP) for nationalised industries and services, well enough equipped for the task?

These questions gain political significance with Economic and Monetary Union. The start of EMU coincides with high unemployment and political pressure for a co-ordinated approach towards economic policy. The new German government wants to project its "alliance for jobs" approach, still under construction at home, onto the European scene and did receive some commitment in this direction during the Vienna summit of December 1998. With so many governments led or dominated by social democratic parties, the *European Trade Union Confederation* (ETUC) appears determined not to waste the opportunity. Having given almost unqualified support to monetary integration in spite of severe misgivings about the deflationary consequences of the EMU qualification criteria (Foden, 1998), Europe's principal union movement now wants to put all emphasis on growth and employment. In November 1998 the ETUC leadership proposed the establishment of a tripartite social-economic council in which a small group of members from each line of industry will meet with finance ministers and engage in a dialogue over a more balanced economic and monetary policy with Europe's new central bank. This demand fell on deaf ears during the Vienna summit, but other attempts at concerted action, including the social partners, remain on the agenda.

What is Social Dialogue and What Support Does It Need?

Extending the definition of *Konzertierte Aktion* of Lehmbruch (1984), I define concertation or social dialogue as a process in which actors inform each other of their intentions and capacities, elaborate on information provided to them by experts, and clarify and explain their assumptions and expectations (Visser, 1998a). Concertation is not to be confused with bargaining; it provides a setting for more efficient bargaining by helping to separate negotiations on "the state of the world" from negotiations on the division of costs and benefits. Negotiators of welfare state reform, labour market regulation or wage setting practices must, first, identify a course of action which is superior to the status quo, and, second, reach agreement over the distribution of costs and benefits of the action they choose. Concertation can help to solve the first problem, spelling out "win win" solutions before engaging in hard bargaining on distribution aspects (Scharpf, 1997). In a decision-making style based on bargaining, each side tries to maximise its own "fair share". In a problem-solving style, negotiators tend to develop a "joint utility function".

Schmitter (1983) argued that organised interest groups, like unions and employers' associations, if engaged in enduring social dialogue, are likely to become "better informed about each other's intentions" and "more respectful of each other's capabilities". This, in turn, may "help them to trust each other's commitments". Trust is essential for a long-term perspective, making it possible for interest groups to accept concessions in the short run because they know that the other side will not exploit the situation and abuse their temporary weaknesses. Trust, a long-term perspective, and the possibility to discuss various policies (issue-linking), help to institutionalise a reform process in many small steps (Visser, 1998b) and avoid veto-positions (Elmeskov, 1998).[1]

A sustained and effective practice of concertation or social dialogue depends on two fundamental conditions: *societal support* and *institutional integration* (Visser and Hemerijck, 1997). Institutional integration underscores the relative importance of enabling public policies. It corresponds with the notion of "shared public space" (Crouch, 1986) and can be viewed as the combined indicator of the capacity and willingness of the public authorities to share regulatory authority with organisations of civil society that they do not administratively control. The institutionalisation of concertation requires state actors not merely to create and maintain a framework for political exchange, but also to develop a certain minimal steering capacity to guide societal bargaining in the direction of the "public good".[2] This particular idea about the role of the state corresponds with the notion of a "shadow of hierarchy" in strategic games (Scharpf, 1993). The ultimate availability of hierarchical intervention and state ratification of social pacts and agreements reached between private interests can help to curb distributive conflict and limit opportunism among bargainers. The state's authority to approve, reward and ratify implies the power to disapprove, punish and nullify, and hence the possibility to insist on *bonafide* processes of representation and negotiation.

Societal support involves the ability and willingness on the part of organised interests to engage in a practice of concertation. Concertation is the most stable if the participating interest groups are sufficiently comprehensive and united. But interest groups must also have the *will* to compromise, be prepared to seek common solutions and have the capacity to make binding decisions on behalf of their members. The key argument is that concertation depends on, and develops, the strategic capacity of "encompassing" societal interests (Olson, 1982).

Operationalisation at the level of peak associations includes four organisational criteria: a) *representation,* or the proportion of potential members who are actual members; b) *cohesion,* or the extent to which members are united in a single peak association; c) *concentration*, or the extent to which members of the peak association(s) are divided over a small number of affiliates; and d) *centralisation*, or the authority of the leadership of the peak association to take and implement decisions that prove binding on their affiliates or members (Lange, Wallerstein and Golden, 1995; Visser, 1984; 1990, for trade unions; Traxler, 1992, and van Waarden, 1995 for employers' associations).

In this chapter I shall limit myself to a descriptive overview of the state of employers' associations and trade unions in the mid-1990s with a view to their participation in social concertation at the national and European level. I shall discuss the organisational capacities in the 1990s under the four headings distinguished above: representation, cohesion, concentration, and centralisation.

Representation

Trade Unions

In 1995 almost 41 of the 128 million employed workers in the European Economic Area were members of a trade union.[3] Overall, the union density rate—the proportion of employed workers belonging to trade union—is 32%, nearly ten percentage points lower than in 1980 (see Table 5.1). Like the early 1980s, the early 1990s witnessed a decline in membership and a contraction of the employed labour force.

Table 5.1   Employed Union Members and Union Density in Europe

year	employed union members		wage and salary earners		union density	
	(1)	(2)	(3)	(4)	(5)	(6)
1980	47,506	–	113,667	–	41.8	–
1985	43,160	– 9.1%	112,048	–1.4%	38.5	– 7.8%
1990 (a)	42,084	– 2.5%	122,934	+9.7%	34.2	–11.1%
1990 (b)	45,550	–	130,312	–	35.0	–
1995	40,928	–10.1%	127,765	–2.0%	32.0	– 8.4%

Source: Visser, *Trade Union Membership Statistics Revisited*, Amsterdam: Cesar, 1998
(a) without former GDR, (b) with GDR

A comparison with the United States and Japan, the two rival global blocs, shows that the European economy is far more unionised. In 1995 union density in Japan stood at 24%, against 31% in 1980; for the US the figures are 14% in 1995 and 23% in 1980.

The variation in membership and density across Europe is very large, though not much larger than between the 50 states of the US. In 1995 union density varied from 87.6% in Sweden to 10.0% in France, a ratio of almost 9 to 1 (see Table 5.2).[4] Compared to 1980 the disparity between the most and least unionised states has increased, mainly because the low-unionised countries have further fallen behind (the 1980 ratios were 4.1 for Europe and 5.5 for the US). In Europe the low-unionised countries tend to be located in the South: France, Spain, Portugal and Greece, together with Switzerland and the Netherlands. Germany and the United Kingdom are around the

European average; Italy,[5] Austria, Ireland, Belgium and the Scandinavian countries are above average. Eight countries—except Italy, all smaller economies—still have a density rate of 40% or more.

Table 5.2   Union Membership, Employment and Union Density in 1995

		all members	employed members	retired and un-employed members	density rate	1990-95 +/–
		(1)	(2)	(3)	(4)	(5)
North						
Sweden	(b)	3,889	3,101	20.3%	87,6	+3.6
Finland		2,118	1,377	35.0%	78,4	+6.4
Denmark		2,170	1,836	15.4%	78,3	+5.2
Norway	(b)	1,256	1,068	15.0%	57,7	+1.7
West						
Ireland		531	483	9.9%	49.1	–5.6
Britain		8089	7,280	10.0%	32.1	–5.8
Centre						
Belgium	(c)	2,480	1,585	36.1%	49.7	–1.5
Netherlands		1,890	1,540	18.5%	25.7	+0.3
Austria		1,583	1,345	15.0%	41.7	–4.6
Germany		11,341	9,300	18.0%	29.1	–7.0
Switzerland		845	724	14.3%	22.1	–1.3
South						
France	(c)	2,267	1,942	14.3%	10.0	–1.0
(a) Spain		1,850	1,606	13.3%	18.6	+5.4
Portugal	(d)	1,000	900	10.0%	28.4	–2.0
Italy	(b)	11,442	6,341	44.6%	44.8	n. a. (e)
Greece	(d)	650	500	23.1%	24.3	–9.8
Total		53,401	40,928	100.0%	32.0	–3.0
unweighted average		–	–		*42.4*	*–1.2*

Notes: (a) 1994; (b) without self-employed members; (c) corrected for inflated self-reported figures; (d) estimates; (e) due to a change of Italian labour force statistics, the comparison with 1990 is distorted.

Source: Visser, *Trade Union Membership Statistics Revisited*, Amsterdam: Cesar, 1998

Union density rates not only vary across countries but also across industries and social groups. In 1992, 45% of the employed union members in Europe had a job in the public or subsidised sector, against 55% in the private sector. Of the latter around 40% were employed in industry and mining, 13% in private services and 1–2% in agriculture.[6] Public sector workers appeared to be twice as well organised as their colleagues in the private sector, 51% compared to 25%. For men and women the rates were 37% and 30%, for manual and non-manual workers 41% and 29%. The proportion of women in unions has risen to 38%, whereas manual workers make up only half of the total union membership and are a minority in today's labour force.

These variations are replicated within most member states. They are most pronounced in countries with overall low levels of unionisation (Visser, 1989). In a highly unionised country like Denmark, differences in union density across industries or social categories tend to be fairly small (see the survey data presented by Scheuer, 1997b). There is not enough reliable data on union membership by firm size, type of employment contract, or working hours to draw firm conclusions for European unions as a whole. Such data exist, for instance, on the basis of labour force sample surveys in Britain and the Netherlands, invariably point to much lower membership levels for youths in comparison to older age groups (and in comparison to previous generations), for workers in small firms, and for workers employed under non-standard contracts or on a part-time basis (Cully and Woodland, 1996; Klandermans and Visser, 1995). All these variations suggest that present trends in labour market structure are making it harder for unions to attract and retain members (Waddington and Whitston, 1997).

In addition to almost 41 million employed members, European unions organise approximately 13.5 million members without a job, the vast majority of them retired from the labour market (see Table 5.2). In many countries—foremost in Italy (in 1996 five million or nearly half of all trade union members were retired workers, CESOS 1996)—trade unions are the largest interest group for retired workers and old age pensioners. Between two and three million of the 18 million unemployed in the European Union have remained in their trade unions. In Sweden, Denmark, Finland and Belgium, where unions are involved in the provision or administration of unemployment insurance, unemployed workers tend to retain their link with the union. Elsewhere they tend to lapse from membership in the case of (longer spells of) unemployment. The claim made by unions that they represent unemployed and retired workers is occasionally challenged.

Movements of unemployed workers, outside the main unions, made their appearance in 1997 in France and Germany and in 1996 and 1997 were involved in the re-negotiation and ratification of a new social pact by the Irish Congress of Trade Unions and the Irish government.

To sum up: On average, one out of three European wage and salary earners in employment—one out of four in the private sector—joins a trade union. Indirectly, however, union representation affects a much greater proportion of workers. Around 70% of European workers employed in the private sector are covered by collective agreements (see Table 5.3). The true outlier in this regard is Great Britain, where since the decline of collective bargaining in the 1980s less than half of all workers have access to collective representation (Brown, 1993). Other countries with comparatively low coverage rates are Switzerland (Fluder and Hotz-Hart, 1997) and, rather surprisingly, Denmark (see Scheuer, 1997a). But in general the major dividing line is between Europe on the one hand and the US or Japan on the other. In the US bargaining coverage extends hardly beyond union membership, in Japan it is even more limited than union membership (Traxler, 1994). We further observe that cross-national variation in bargaining coverage is more limited than variation in union density and that there is hardly a correlation between the two. A high level of union density tends to be associated with a high coverage rate, but the reverse is not true (Traxler, 1994). A high coverage rate, however, does seem to be associated, in both cases, with a high level of employer organisations (see Table 5.3, and below).

Ten out of sixteen countries allow the possibility to "extend" collective agreements between unions and employers to non-organised firms by way of public law. Where this occurs, firms have an incentive to join employers' associations. For unions, extension exerts an influence in two ways (Flanagan, Hartog and Theeuwes, 1993, p. 424): By eliminating the competition from a lower-wage non-union sector, legal extension reduces the incentives for employer resistance to unions (Blanchflower and Freeman, 1990). It also reduces the incentives for consumers to shift purchases to the lower wage non-union sector and therefore increases union bargaining power. On the other hand, by providing for free what unions charge for, legal extension encourages "free riders" among the potential union membership.

Table 5.3   Union and Employers Organisations and Bargaining Coverage in the Market Sector, mid-1990s

countries	% workers joining trade unions	% workers in firms joining the main employers' associations	% workers covered by collective agreements	extension of agreements through public law	Centralisation Index
	(1)	(2)	(3)	(4)	(5)
Sweden	77	60	72	absent	248
Finland	65	58	67	limited	604
Denmark	68	48	52	absent	274
Norway	45	54	62	negligible	678
Belgium	40	80	82	significant	314
Austria	37	96	97	significant	785
Germany	25	76	80	limited	314
Switzerland	18	37	50	limited	199
Netherlands	19	80	79	limited	433
Ireland	37	44	..	negligible	542
Great Britain	21	57	40	absent	100
Italy	32	40	..	absent	347
France	< 7	71	75	significant	124
Spain	<15	70	67	limited	260
Portugal	<20	..	..	limited	128
Greece	<15	..	..	significant	..
average (a)	<26	64	68	n. a	n. a.
average (b)	<36	62	69	n. a	357

Notes: (a) weighted average; (b) unweighted average; column 1 and 2: averages calculated without Portugal and Greece; column 3: averages calculated without Portugal, Greece, Italy and Ireland, column 5: without Greece.
Source: column (1)—(2): appendix A and B; column (3): Sweden (1990), Norway (1992), Great Britain (1990) and Spain (1990): Traxler 1994, table 5.2; Finland (1995): calculated from Lilja 1997: 174; Denmark (1995); Scheuer 1997, table 5.7; Germany (mid-1990s): Jacobi et al 1997: 190; Netherlands (1995): Visser and van der Meer 1998; Switzerland (1994): Fluder and Hotz-Hart 1997: 276; figures for Austria, Belgium, France and Spain refer to mid-1990s and are calculated from Traxler 1994, chart 5.1, assuming a 100 per cent coverage rate for public sector workers (if entitled to collective bargaining); column (4): Traxler 1994, chart 5.2; column 5: see explanation in text (centralisation).

Employers' Associations

It is much harder to establish the membership level in employers' associations than in trade unions and comparable data across time and countries is not easy to come by. Comparing the density rates of trade unions and employers' associations, it should be taken into account that unions organise individuals and employers' associations organise corporate actors. In order to solve the common denominator problem it is customary to calculate employer density in terms of the workers employed by these corporate actors, i. e. firms. Secondly, it is at this point also reasonable to exclude the public sector, since the public sector is not usually in the domain of most employers' associations. In many countries, the finance or home ministry, or some other government department fulfils the co-ordinating role for the purpose of collective bargaining or wage setting in the public sector. For reasons of comparability, Table 5.3 presents data on the proportion of private sector workers organised in trade unions (column 2) and employed in firms that join an employers' association (column 3). These organisation rates, of unions and employers, can best be compared with the bargaining coverage rates in the private sector, again excluding the public sector (column 4).

We observe that in eleven of the fourteen countries for which we have information, employers' associations outnumber trade unions in terms of membership coverage (indirect in the case of employers' associations).[7] Only in Sweden, Finland and Denmark do employers' associations cover fewer workers than trade unions do. Overall, 60% of all private sector workers are employed in firms that join an employers' association, which is double the rate of workers joining unions.

The figures in Table 5.3 may overstate the propensity of employers to organise collectively. The relevant "member" of an employers' association is of course the firm, or possibly the manager, not the worker. In Appendix 5B I have collected the available information regarding the number of firms organised by the main employers' and business associations in Europe. If we neglect the (employment) size of these members, it turns out that these associations organise only a small minority of all firms; in fact, employer density would in most countries be lower than union density. If we exclude firms smaller than, say, one hundred employees (in many countries the relevant borderline between small and large firms may be fifty workers or even less), the employer density rates would be much higher, but the same would happen if we were to exclude workers employed in small firms from the unions' domain.

Cohesion and Concentration

Table 5.4 summarises some major characteristics regarding the cohesion and concentration of the interest organisations of capital and labour in Western Europe. In the first column we list the number of main peak associations and observe at once that unity of organisation is extremely rare. On average, there are three peak associations representing labour and three representing business interests. Among capitalists, the major cleavages are between large and small firms, between industry and services, and between public and private sector employers. Among workers the most important cleavages are political, mixed (with the older religious divisions, as in Belgium, the Netherlands, Switzerland, and—hardly relevant—in France, Germany and Denmark) or pure (as in France, Italy, Spain and Portugal), functional between groups with different education and status (as in the four Scandinavian countries, in Germany, Switzerland and, less important, in France and the Netherlands), or between public and private employees (Greece, Germany). Tensions between these different peak associations can be considerable in the case of political and ideological divisions (France and Portugal in the case of unions, less so in Italy and Spain, still less in Belgium, the Netherlands and Switzerland).

UNICE, Europe's main employers' federation, represents 70% of the organised employers (weighted by employment size). With the exception of Austria, UNICE's affiliates are in a majority position in each of the sixteen countries (information about Greece and Portugal is incomplete, see Table 5B in Appendix).[8] ETUC, Europe's main union federation, represents 91% of all unionised workers. In all but one country its affiliates represent the overlarge majority of unionised workers; the only country where the ETUC's affiliates are only just a majority is France.[9]

In the second column I have calculated the associational monopolies, or the proportion of members organised by the largest peak association, for all employers' and union confederations. On average, the largest union confederation attracts three out of five organised union members; the largest employers' federations attracts three out of four employers (if weighted by the number of employees), probably less than half if just the number of firms rather than their employment size, is taken into account.[10] Across countries there is considerable variation. Leaving aside the exceptional position of the Austrian federations, based on complete monopoly, the main business associations in Sweden, Denmark, Germany, the Netherlands, Ireland, Britain, and Spain attain high scores. Whether this implies a high degree of

Table 5.4   Cohesion and Concentration of the Organisations of Capital and Labour

	peak associations (1)		confederal monopoly (2)		number of affiliates (3)	
	Capital	Labour	Capital	Labour	Capital	Labour
EU	4	3	.70	.91	21 (a)	37 (b)
S	4	3	.81	.56	38	20
FIN	4	3	.65	.52	35	25
DK	4	3	.78	.69	30	23
N	3	3	.61	.57	28	28
B	3	3	.75	.52	35	25
A	2	1	1.0	1.0	–	14
D	4	4	.80	.82	46	15
CH	3	4	.67	.45	30	17
NL	2	3 (c)	.80	.63	150	15
IRL	2	1	.85	.94	53	52
GB	2	1	.80	.84	200	74
I	3	4	.50	.46	110	18
F	3	6	.65	.27	84	19
GR	3	2	..	.78	..	53
E	2	4	.90	.39	..	12
P	3	2	..	.72	..	142

Notes: (a) only affiliates in 16 countries in Table 5.4, total number of UNICE affiliates in 1995 was 32; (b) only affiliates in 16 countries in Table 5.4, excluding transnational industry federations; total number of ETUC affiliates in 1995 was 79, of which 62 were national peak associations, 1 regional peak association, and 14 European industry federations; (c) the fourth peak association (AVC) dissolved and was partly integrated in the Federation of Dutch Trade Unions (FNV).

number of peak associations: *capital*: number of employers' and trade confederations, including the small-firm sector, regional peak associations and semi-public sector, excluding agriculture and the public sector; *labour*: all peak associations, excluding very specialised associations of managerial staff.

associational monopoly: percentage of total membership represented by largest peak association; *capital*: share calculated on the assumption of 100% organisation rate of public sector; *labour*: share of total membership including non-affiliated unions, estimated in the case of Germany, Italy, Spain, Portugal, France, and Ireland (see DUES database).

number of affiliates: number of direct members of largest confederation; *capital*:sectoral employers and/or trade associations, or federations; *labour:* national unions or federations.

cohesiveness depends on the nature of the internal divisions and the external competition from challenging organisations. An estimate of the internal divisions or degree of fragmentation can be made on the basis of the number of affiliates—larger in the case of capital than in the case of labour by a considerable margin (Table 5.4, column 3). The smallest numbers of affiliates and possibly the most cohesive organisations are found in Scandinavia.

On the workers' side, there is the group of Austria, Germany, Ireland, Britain, and Greece, with one dominant federation; an intermediate group of the Scandinavian countries, Belgium, the Netherlands and Portugal, with a majority federation, and a third group of Switzerland, Italy, France and Spain, where all federations are in a minority position. Relations between these federations can of course vary greatly, from severe rivalry (France, Portugal) to pragmatic co-operation (Italy, Spain, the Netherlands) and cartel-like types of co-operation (Scandinavian countries) (Visser, 1990).

The organisational landscape of unions is changing rapidly. In all countries the trend is towards concentration. In all confederations for which we have time series data, the concentration ratio, based on the four largest unions, increased between 1985 and 1995 (Visser, 1990, Table 25; and Appendix 5A). This increase is entirely due to amalgamations and the taking over of small unions by large unions. Smaller size and financial revenue, combined with increased demand for protection and services, has caused a spate of mergers and cost-reduction programmes in trade unions throughout Western Europe. In the second half of the 1990s merger activity tends to lead to the formation of conglomerate (multi-sectoral) unions even in countries like Germany or the Netherlands, with an established tradition of sectoral or industrial unionism. These changes are driven by economics, not or not nearly as much by politics, or deliberate views of class unity, industrial governance or collective bargaining (Streeck and Visser, 1998). As a rule, unions tend to suffer from the same inverse fluctuation of revenue and client needs as do most social security systems. Decentralisation of collective bargaining, increased diversity of needs and conditions of members, increased instability of employment, the availability of alternative providers of advice and insurance, and not least a more self-assured membership increase the costs of union services while requiring a higher quality.

There are similar attempts at organisational restructuring among employers' associations. The traditional functional division of tasks between employers' and trade associations at the level of peak federations has been abandoned in various countries (Ireland, Netherlands, Finland, Norway,

Denmark) in recent times. Within these organisations various attempts are being made at restructuring (through bargaining cartels, straightforward mergers, joint ventures, business spin-offs or other arrangements), the relationship with the (national) peak federations is being redefined together with the application of cost-cutting programmes, similar to what had occurred in many peak federations of trade unions across Europe in the 1980s and 1990s. The average number of affiliates is still much higher in the national federations of employers than on the union side, indicating greater heterogeneity, less capacity of control and more problems of internal discipline.

It is striking that the international or European dimension is absent in the current restructuring process. Union mergers make halt before national borders and thus testify to the national embeddedness of the European union movement. The increase in idiosyncratic structures, which result from current restructuring processes, will make it increasingly difficult to match sectoral unions to national systems and build genuine European-based sectoral organisations capable of aggregating and representing interests.

Centralisation

As a rule, authority within unions or employers' associations is closely tied to where and at what level collective bargaining is conducted (Clegg, 1976; Sisson, 1987).[11] In addition to the level of bargaining, decisions about strikes and lock-outs, and the enforceability of higher-level agreements and peace clauses, backed by the court system, are relevant for the measurement of centralisation (Iversen, 1996; Visser, 1990; Traxler, 1996).

For workers, collective bargaining has a protective function (ensuring adequate pay and working conditions), a voice function (allowing the expression of grievances and aspirations), and a distributive function (providing a share in economic progress and the fruits of training, technology and productivity). For employers the most important function of collective bargaining is probably the aspect of conflict regulation. Management control is more effective when legitimised through joint rules. A "peace rule" may ensure continuous production while the agreement is in force. Finally, collective bargaining relieves the state (and the politicians) from the complex task of intervening in an area with high conflict potential and a high risk of implementation failures. Under single-employer bargaining each employer negotiates independently; under multi-employer bargaining employers combine in employers' associations that have received a mandate to conduct negotiations and reach binding decisions on their behalf. In Western Europe—unlike Japan and the United States—multi-employer bargaining has since the 1930s recession become the dominant type of wage setting. The major exception in Western Europe is Britain, where multi-employer bargaining has disappeared in nearly all sectors. In most countries—Scandinavia, Germany, Austria, Switzerland, the Netherlands, Belgium, Italy (since 1993)—sectoral bargaining is dominant, in Spain, Portugal and France more intermittently so. In Norway, Finland, Ireland, and Portugal central agreements incorporate wage guidelines. In Austria the peak associations are able to influence the timing of negotiations; in the Netherlands targets are set through co-ordination within and between the peak associations.

Multi-employer bargaining may be advantageous for employees to the extent that it generalises the three aforementioned (protective, voice, and distributive) functions across sectors, occupations and firms. Moreover, multi-employer bargaining tends to make the trade unions into a political force and may become an instrument for pursuing egalitarian (wage solidarity) goals, as has been the case in Denmark and the Netherlands. Employers, too, may find multi-employer bargaining to their advantage. First, multi-employer bargaining has a "cartelising" effect by taking wages out of competition. In recessions it may help employers to avoid "cut-throat" competition; under conditions of tight labour markets it may protect them against "whipsawing" tactics of the unions (Commons, 1909). This aspect matters most for employers in labour-intensive industries. Second, multi-employer bargaining takes place far away from the workplace and may help to keep distributional conflicts out of the workplace. Sisson (1987) has shown that in many continental European countries the desire to insulate the influence of unions from workplace management has been a major motive for employers to create or go along with centralised bargaining. Third, multi-employer bargaining may constitute savings on bargaining or transaction costs, especially in homogenous industries and in the case of small and medium-sized firms. Finally, multi-employer bargaining may be used by governments as a means of macroeconomic government aimed at keeping inflation low (Traxler, 1996) or providing collective goods such as industrial training standards, apprenticeship jobs, industrial order, etc. (Soskice, 1990).

There are strong intra-class differences in the balance of advantages and disadvantages of multi-employer bargaining as well (Svensen, 1989;

Iversen, 1996). Multi-employer bargaining does restrict the freedom of individual companies and local unions to do as they like, and they may have deep ideological reasons to prefer autonomy ("self-government"), even at the expense of economic rewards. Air traffic controllers or medical doctors generally prefer single-employer as well as single-occupation bargaining as their best strategy to realise their demands. Unskilled workers do generally better through industry-wide or even economy-wide bargaining (Iversen, 1996). From the point of view of workers, multi-employer bargaining has advantages as well as disadvantages. The voice function is probably more intense when bargaining is conducted "on site", because workers will have more control over their representatives. It seems easier to monitor what management does and new issues and developments are more swiftly recognised. Decentralisation of collective bargaining can be observed in nearly all countries and is mainly driven by employers in the exposed sector of the economy who seek more room to manoeuvre in response to international competition and technological change. It also feeds on growing worker diversity (Locke et al., 1995). Single-level bargaining is exceptional; in nearly all countries unions and employers meet and negotiate at two or more levels. In the case of multi-level bargaining it is crucial that "the different levels are integrated so as to prevent them from mutual blocking their respective purpose" (Traxler, 1994, p. 174). The authority of central organisations over employers and national trade union centres over local bargaining and the strength of the mutual obligations enshrined in higher-level agreements (in particular the peace clause and procedures for conflict resolution) are critical conditions for the efficiency and effectiveness of such multi-level solutions. Internal co-ordination, contract compliance and conflict resolution mechanisms are critically important.

Following the methodology of Iversen (1996) and my earlier work (Visser, 1984, 1990), I have calculated a centralisation index for the mid-1990s. This index gives a proper weight to co-ordination and centralisation and allows both to happen at the level of peak associations and major unions. The weights are based on the role and power of the peak associations and major unions in wage bargaining (is there a central agreement?; is the agreement enforceable?; do peak associations monopolise strike and wage decisions?; what is the principal level of lower-level wage bargaining (industry or enterprise, or both; is lower level bargaining bound by rules controlled at higher level, and is control effective?) In addition, I have taken into account whether all peak associations are working together (as in Italy or the Netherlands) or only one (Portugal, Norway, Ireland) or two (Spain) associations enter into central negotiations with employers and governments. In each case we can use the associational monopoly as measurement. For the establishment of the co-ordinating capacities at the level of sectors, I have used the C4 ratio, or share of the four largest unions of the leading confederation (leading in the sense of leading the negotiations) in total membership (equal to the C4 ratio as given in appendix 5A times the associational monopoly of the relevant peak association). This yields the outcomes shown in Table 5.3, column 5, showing Austria as the most centralised country and Britain as the least centralised country, in terms of how unions influence wage bargaining. Interesting are the low values—very different from the past—for both Denmark and Sweden—and the comparatively high values for Ireland and Italy. The most striking feature, perhaps, is the wide diversity across Europe. Unfortunately it is impossible show similar statistics for employers' associations. A calculation for the ETUC or the European Industry Federation is not meaningful, given the absence of wage bargaining or co-ordination at that level. In any case, values would be extremely low until the moment that these organisations could influence strike decisions or set enforceable wage guidelines.

There are currently 21 European-level union organisations, and about three times as many European employers or mixed associations (not counting the 500 or more trade associations). The organisational architecture of the European system of interest representation is very complex. It differs between unions and employers and is incomparable to any national system. Where UNICE has chosen an open architecture, with networks and direct membership relations of national and multinational companies added onto the primary membership relations with the national peak federations, ETUC has, since its 1991 reform, accepted dual membership of national intersectoral and European sectoral unions and no direct membership (of for instance European works councils). The involvement in central negotiations on social policy issues, under the Social Policy Agreement and now the Amsterdam Treaty, has increased the pressure on the leadership of ETUC to revise internal procedures, improve standards of accountability and design a bargaining mandate with its members. The division of responsibilities and tasks between the peak associations and sector organisations has proven to be a major stumbling block (see Dølvik, 1997). UNICE's bargaining mandate has to be conquered on a case by case basis, and can be clocked by any significant affiliate.

In the national arena, the formation of conglomerate interest associations tends to erode the powers and functions of the national peak federations, both among employers and unions. It is quite possible that in the years to come, conglomerate unions, like multinational firms, will make their presence in Europe in a more direct way, bypassing the national peak federations. This will create a more complex environment for the European confederations, not unlike what has happened in the case of business with the entry of major firms in the European arena (Coen, 1997; Green-Cowles, 1994). One might speculate that it is only a matter of time, once the potential for taking over smaller unions has dried up and the national market for union-mergers has cleared, before large conglomerate unions will try to carry out international mergers. The likelihood of such a development increases, when collective bargaining becomes more devolved from the national (sectoral) to the company level and the main task of national and European-level unions and employers' associations becomes providing information, bargaining skills and services to members in national and European works councils or similar bodies. Indeed, the first immediate effect of European works councils, established and negotiated under the relevant European directive of 1994, is likely to be a closer, direct link between European unions and the development of a professional market for services and information-exchange for these councils and their members.

Appendix

Table 5A   Major Union Confederations, as of 1995

	confederation (1)	member of ETUC (2)	tendency (3)	domain (4)	affiliates (5)	members (6)	confederal monopoly (7)	largest affiliate (8)	C4 ratio (9)
all*	ETUC	–	–	all	49	49,303,400 (–)	.92	18.2	50.3
EU	*ETUC*	–	–	*all*	*34*	*46,556,500 (–)*	*.91*	*19.3*	*53.3*
S	LO–S	yes	socialist	manual	20	2,169,280 (c)	.56	30.0	66.7
	TCO	yes	–	non-manual	20	1,302,147 (c)	.33	26.1	67.2
	SACO	yes	–	professional	23	407,321 (c)	.10	16.8	48.9
FIN	SAK	yes	socialist	manual	25	1,111,350 (b)	.52	20.3	53.3
	STTK	yes	–	non-manual	27	635,446 (b)	.30	17.3	54.7
	Akava	yes	–	professional	32	329,530 (b)	.16	31.4	64.0
DK	LO–DK	yes	socialist	manual +	23	1,495,850 (c)	.69	23.8	67.6
	FTF	yes	–	non-manual	130	340,991 (c)	.16	17.6	57.7
	AC	yes	–	professional	22	141,170 (c)	.06	27.2	59.6
N	LO–N	yes	socialist	all	28	811,423 (c)	.57	28.8	60.8
	AC	yes	–	professional	18	237,445 (c)	.17	21.5	66.3
	YS	no	–	occupational	36	223.524 (c)	.16	23.3	63.2
B	AVB/CSC	yes	Christian	all	25	1,581,516 (b)	.52	16.3	57.4

Table 5A (continued)   Major Union Confederations, as of 1995

	confederation	member of ETUC	tendency	domain	affiliates	members	confederal monopoly	largest affiliate	C4 ratio
	(1)	(2)	(3)	(4)	(5)	(6)	(7)	(8)	(9)
	FGTB/ABVV	yes	socialist	all	11	1,176,701 (b)	.38	25.5	84.6
	LGSLB/ACLV	no	liberal	all	1	216,035 (b)	.07	ca. 50.0	100.0
A	ÖGB	yes	(all)	all	14	1,583,356 (b)	1.0	20.7	60.8
D	DGB	yes	—	all	13	8,972,672 (c)	.82	30.7	65.2
	DAG	yes	—	non-manual	0	501,009 (c)	.04	n. a.	n. a.
	DBB	no	—	state	—	1,101,598 (c)	.09	..	..
	CGB	no	Christian	all	—	303,106 (c)	.02	..	..
CH	SGB	yes	socialist	manual	17	411,072 (c)	.47	29.0	77.3
	VSA	yes	—	non-manual	10	124,042 (c)	.15	52.3	89.7
	CNG	yes	Christian	manual +	11	94,928 (c)	.11	34.0	..
	LFSA	no	liberal	all	0	..	..	100.0	..
NL	FNV	yes	(socialist)	all	15	1,197,218 (c)	.63	40.4	86.4
	CNV	yes	Christian	all	11	350,151 (c)	.18	24.4	72.6
	MHP	yes	liberal	staff	3	160.625 (c)	.08	52.0	100.0
IRL	ICTU	yes	(all)	all	52	690,140 (d)	.94	38.1	55.4
GB	TUC	yes	Labour	all	74	6,800,000 (e)	.84	20.8	52.2

Table 5A (continued)   Major Union Confederations, as of 1995

	confederation	member of ETUC	tendency	domain	affiliates	members	confederal monopoly	largest affiliate	C4 ratio
	(1)	(2)	(3)	(4)	(5)	(6)	(7)	(8)	(9)
F	CFDT	yes	–	all	19	701,180 (b)	.27	11.6 (f)	37.0
	CGT	no	communist	all	34	647,000 (b)	.26	10.3	39.9
	FO	yes	socialist	all	27	400,000 (b)	.17	..	..
	UNSA	no	–	public	7	300,000 (a)	.13	21.4	..
	CFTC	yes	Christian	all	..	130,000 (b)	.06	..	..
	CGC-CFE	no	–	staff	..	130,000 (b)	.06	..	..
	Groupe10	no	–	public	18	70,000 (a)	.03	..	..
I	CGIL	yes	left	all	18	5,211,588 (b)	.46	15.6 (f)	57.9
	CISL	yes	(Christian)	all	23	3,837.104 (b)	.34	11.2 (f)	37.9
	UIL	yes	left–centre	all	24	1,593,515 (b)	.14	13.1 (f)	39.9
	CISAL	no	–	all	53	..	..	..	
	CONFSAL	no	–	all	..	..	..	..	
GR	GSEE	yes	–	private	53	360,000 (a)	.78	..	..
	ADEDY	yes	–	public	..	100,000 (a)	.22	..	..
E	UGT	yes	socialist	all	12	700,026 (a)	.39	19.7	56.3
	CC.OO	yes	(communist)	all	14	656,268 (a)	.38	18.9	47.7
	CSI-CSIF	no	–	all	21	150,935 (a)	.08	13.1	45.1

Table 5A (continued)   Major Union Confederations, as of 1995

	confedera-tion	member of ETUC	tendency	domain	affiliates	members	confederal monopoly	largest affiliate	C4 ratio
	(1)	(2)	(3)	(4)	(5)	(6)	(7)	(8)	(9)
E	ELA–STV	yes	–	regional	7	88,714 (a)	.05	32.4	80.2
	USO	no	Christian	all	17	78,533 (a)	.04	16.1	46.5
P	CGTP–IN	yes	(communist)	all	142	650,000 (a)	.72	6.9	20.0
	UGP	yes	socialist	all	63	200,000 (a)	.22	25.0	50.5
CY	SEK	yes	Greek	regional	..	55,232 (a)	..	..	..
	Türk–SEN	yes	Turkish	regional	..	5,000 (a)	..	..	..
ICE	ASI	yes	socialist	all	..	55,301 (a)	..	..	..
	BSRP	yes	–	public	..	16,437 (a)	..	..	..
LUX	CGT–L	yes	socialist	all	..	47,866 (a)	..	..	..
	LCGB	yes	Christian	all	..	26,000 (a)	..	..	..
MA	GWU	yes	socialist	all	..	26,808 (a)	..	..	..
	CMTU	yes	Christian	all	..	30,409 (a)	..	..	..
SM	CDLS	yes	socialist	all	..	2,585 (a)	..	..	..
	CSdL	yes	Christian	all	..	2,650 (a)	..	..	..
TU	DISK	yes	left	all	..	100,000 (a)	..	..	..
	Türk–IS	yes	nationalist	all	..	500,100 (a)	..	..	..

Notes to Table 5A: * without new members in Central and Eastern Europe. After admission in 1995, ETUC has increased the number of affiliates to 79, of which 14 European sector federations, and 65 national confederation, of which 16 in Central and Eastern Europe.; (a) = 1994; (b) = 1995; (c) = 1996; (d) includes 198,380 members in Northern Ireland; (e) includes approx. 70,000 members outside UK (in Republic of Ireland, mostly included in ICTU figure); (f) calculated without the pensioners' unions, representing 52%, 43% and 24% of the total membership of CGIL, CISL and UIL in 1994.

Table 5A (continued)   Major Union Confederations, as of 1995/6

Columns:

(1) **Confederation:** Major peak association of trade unions, including the public sector (organisations representing less than 5% of all union members have been ignored).

(2) **Membership of ETUC** (*European Trade Union Confederation*, Europe's principal peak federation of trade unions).

(3) **Tendency:** political, ideological or religious orientation (between brackets: weak or fading).

(4) **Domain:** part of working population which the association purports to represent; manual (only blue–collar workers); manual + (including lower–graded clerical and technical staff); non–manual (only white–collar workers); professional (only employees with higher education); occupational (workers and employees with craft–based training); staff (only managerial and supervisory staff); state (only public sector); all (no groups excluded).

(5) **Affiliates:** number of member organisations (national unions or federations only, local unions are not counted).

(6) **Membership:** total number of members of affiliates (including those who are direct member of the confederation, and including retired, unemployed and self–employed workers, students, conscripted soldiers etc.

(7) **Confederal monopoly:** membership of the confederation as a ratio of total union membership in the country (see Table 2, column 1).

(8) **Largest affiliate:** membership share of largest affiliate in the confederation

(9) **C4 ratio:** membership share of four largest affiliates in confederation.

Sources: Visser 1990, 1991, 1992, 1994, 1998 with information added from country chapters in Ferner and Hyman 1992, 1997; Hartog and Theeuwes (1993), CEC (1993); Pichot 1995, ETUI (1995), Van Ruysseveldt and Visser (1996), EIRR, issues 1990–98; DUES database.

Table 5B　Major Employers' Confederations, as of 1995

	confedera-tion (1)	member UNICE (2)	domain (3)	type (4)	affiliates sector (5)	affiliates region	members firms (6)	members employees	density private sector (7)	density total economy (8)
EU	UNICE	–	private	M	..	0		..	..	..
16	UNICE	–	*private*	M	*21 (a)*	0	..	*59,000,000*	*50*	*60*
S	SAF	yes	industry +	E	38	..	42,000	1,300,000	57	75
	SI (b)	yes	industry	T	..	..	..	..	..	..
FIN	TT	yes	industry	M	35	7	5,863	490,500	38	68
	PT	no	services	M	..	..	6,071	250,500	20	..
DK	DA	yes	industry +	M	30	..	30,000	550,000	48	72
	DI (c)	yes	industry	T	59	..	4,300	300,000	..	.
N	NHO	yes	industry	M	28	..	12,000	400,000	33	70
	NSH	no	services	E	..	..	..	250,000	21	..
B	VBO/FEB	yes	all	T	35	3	50,000	1,600,000	80	85
A	BWK (d)	no	all	M	(136)	(9)	320,000	2,600,000	96	100
	VÖI	yes	industry	T	0	9	2,000	420,000	..	..
D	BDA	yes	all	E	46	15	..	20,000,000	76	81
	BDI	yes	industry	T	350	35.	..	..	..	..
CH	SAV	yes	all	E	30	42	..	1,000,000	37	45
	SHIV(e)	yes	industry	T	..	..	..	..	..	..

Table 5B (continued)   Major Employers' Confederations, as of 1995

	confedera-tion	member UNICE	domain	type	affiliates		members		density private sector	density total economy
					sector	region	firms	employees		
	(1)	(2)	(3)	(4)	(5)		(6)		(7)	(8)
NL	VNO–NCW	yes	all	M	150	5	80,000	4,000,000	80	82
IRL	IBEC	yes	all	M	53	..	3,700	300,000	44	55
GB	CBI	yes	all	M	200	(13)	..	10,000,000	57	65
F	CNPF (f)	yes	all	M	84	100	800,000	10,000,000	71	80
I	Confindu-stria	yes	industry	M	110	107	130,000	4,000,000	40	52
GR	SEB	yes	industry	M	..	..	3,000	..	..	..
	EESE	no	services	M	..	..	..	..	..	..
E	CEOE	yes	all	M	..	..	..	5,000,000	70	79
P	CIP	yes	industry	M	..	..	38,000	..	..	..
	AIP	yes	services	M	..	..	..	..	..	..

Notes to Table 5B:
(a)   members are national peak associations (UNICE has no sectoral affiliates); (b) member of SAF; (c) member of DA; (d) BWK is a 'chamber' rather than association, based on compulsory membership; (e) member of SAV; (f) reformed in 1998 (new name: *Mouvement des Entreprises Français*).

Columns:

(1) **Confederation:** Central general employers' (and trade) associations in the private sector of the economy, without agriculture, retail trade, small and medium sized business, and the public or subsidised sector. See for full names appendix A.

(2) **Membership of UNICE** (*Union of Industrial and Employers' Confederations of Europe*, Europe's main central organisation of employers).

(3) **Domain:** part of the economy which the association claims to represent; industry, industry+ (=including parts of trade and private transport, but not financial and business services), services (=commercial and financial services), or all (=private sector).

(4) **Type:** complexity of tasks; E = employers' association only; T = trade association; M = mixed, i.e., employers' and trade association.

(5) **Affiliates:** number of member organisations, divided on the basis of sectors (branches of the economy), and/or regions. Between brackets: subdivisions rather than independent member organisations.

(6) **Members:** number of firms organised directly and/or through affiliates, and total employment in these firms.

(7) **Density private sector:** employment in member firms as a proportion of total employment in the private sector

(8) **Density total economy:** weighted sum of density of all employers' association in the private sector (including minor organisations in banking and other services (in Sweden, Finland, Denmark, Norway, and in Italy)) and public sector employment. (It is assumed that employers' density in the public sector is 100%; on the other hand, agricultural organizations are ignored).

Sources: Van Waarden 1995a and 1995b with information added from country chapters in Ferner and Hyman 1992, 1997; Hartog and Theeuwes (1993), CEC (1993); Pichot 1995, ETUI (1995), Van Ruysseveldt and Visser (1996), EIRR, issues 1990–98; MPIfG database.

Notes

1 "A crucial common feature facilitating the reform processes (...) may have been the notion that individual reforms were part of a wider programme or strategy. Hence, specific reforms that affected particular groups met with less resistance because they were seen as part of an overall strategy affecting much wider groups and thereby possessing an element of fairness (...)" (J. Elmeskov, "The Unemployment Problem in Europe: Lessons from Implementing the OECD Jobs Strategy", Florence: European University Institute, Robert Schuman Centre, working paper 98/24, p. 29).

2 For instance, the objectives of the European Community and the member states, as stated in art. 117 ECT (or art. 136 Consolidated Version), are: "the promotion of employment, improved living and working conditions, so as to make possible their harmonisation while the improvement is being maintained, proper social protection, dialogue between management and labour, the development of human resources with a view to lasting high employment, and the combating of exclusion."

3 Unless stated otherwise, the statistics in this chapter consider sixteen countries, i. e. the fifteen member states of the European Union, minus Luxembourg, plus Norway and Switzerland.

4 In the US the highest rate is found in New York, 27.7%, the lowest in South Carolina, 3.3%, a ratio of 8 to 1 (calculated from Hirsch and Macpherson 1996).

5 The Italian density rates, as shown in Table 2, is calculated on the basis of an estimate of the membership of the unions organised outside the three main confederations (without these unions, density would be around 38 per cent). For a recent overview of the non-affiliated unions: Carrieri 1997, Carrieri and Tatrelli 1997.

6 The figures in this section are averages based on a sample of ten countries, i.e. Austria, Belgium, Denmark, (West-)Germany, France, Italy, the Netherlands, Norway, Sweden, and Great Britain. Data for the other countries were not available or incomplete.

7 Comparable data for Portugal and Greece is lacking.

8 The *Wirtschaftskammer Österreich*, Austrian's main business and employers' association, is based on obligatory membership and for this reason excluded from membership in UNICE.

9 The *Confédération Genérale du Travail* (CGT) in France is the only major confederation of trade unions that is not member of the ETUC, but will probably join before the next congress. It has withdrawn from membership in the Communist World Federation, other ex-Communist federations (including those from Eastern Europe) have been accepted, and the largest French union confederation (CFDT) favours admission.

10 The associational monopolies calculated for capital and labour are not directly comparable. In the case of business and employers' federations we have only considered the private (and semi-public) sector; since non-affiliated unionism is especially widespread in the public sector, the membership share of the main confederations would be higher than those shown in Table 4 if calculated for the private sector only.

11 "Union constitutions vary almost indefinitely, but in most instances the distribution of power within unions can be read off the structure of collective bargaining" (Clegg 1976: 4).

References

Betten, L (1998), "The Role of the Social Partners in the Community's Social Policy Law-Making: Participatory Democracy or Furthering the Interest of Small Elites", in C Engels and M Weiss, eds., *Labour law and Industrial Relations at the Turn of the Century. Liber Amicorum in Honour of Roger Blanpain*, The Hague/London/Boston: Kluwer, 239–60.

Blanchflower, D and R Freeman (1990), "Going Different Ways: Unionism in the US and other advanced OECD countries", London: London School of Economics, Centre for Economic performance, Discussion paper no. 5.

Brown, W (1993), "The Contraction of Collective Bargaining in Britain", *British Journal of Industrial Relations*, 31 (2): 189–200.

Carrieri, M (1997), "I sindacati non confederali", in CESOS, *Le relazioni sindacali in Italia. Rapporto 1994/95*, Roma: Centro di Studi Economici Sociali e Sindacali, 1997: 305–6.

Carrieri, M and L Tatarelli (1997), *Gli altri sindacati. Viaggio nelle organizzazioni autonome e di base*. Rome: Ediesse.

CEC (1993), "Communication on the Application of the Maastricht Agreement on Social Policy", Brussels: Commission of the European Communities, COM 93 600 final.

CESOS (1996), *Le relazioni sindacali in Italia. Rapporto 1993/94*. Roma: Centro di Studi Economici Sociali e Sindacali.

Clegg, H A (1976), *Trade Unionism under Collective Bargaining. A theory based on comparisons of six countries*. Oxford: Blackwell.

Coen, D (1997), "The Evolution of the Large Firm as a 'Political Actor' in the European Union", *Journal of European Public Policy*, 4 (1): 91–108

Commons, J R (1909), "American Shoemakers, 1648–1895. A sketch of Industrial Revolution", *Quarterly Journal of Economics*, 19: 1–32.

Cowles, M G (1994), *The Politics of Big Business in the European Community; Setting the Agenda for a New Europe*, PhD. Thesis. Washington D.C.: The American University.

Crouch, C (1986), "Sharing Public Space: States and Organized Interests in Western Europe", in: J Hall, ed., *States in Societies*. Oxford: Blackwell, 179–80.

Cully, M and S Woodland (1996), "Trade Union Membership and Recognition: An analysis of data from the 1995 Labour Force Survey", *Employment Gazette*, May issue, 215–25.

Dølvik, J-E (1997), *Redrawing the Boundaries of Soliedarity? ETUC, social dialogue and the Europeanization of trade unions in the 1990s*, Ph.D. thesis. Oslo: Arena and Fafo.

Elmeskov, J (1998) "The Unemployment Problem in Europe: Lessons from Implementing the OECD Jobs Strategy", Florence: European University Institute, Robert Schuman Centre, working paper 98/24.

ETUI (1995), *Collective Bargaining in 1993–1994*. Brussels: European Trade Union Institute.

European Industrial Relations Review (n. d.), monthly, various issues.

Fajertag, G and Ph Pochet, eds. (1997), *Social Pacts in Europe*. Brussels: European Trade Union Institute and Observatoire Social Européen.

Falkner, G (1996), "Corporatist Patterns of Decision-Making and Europeanization: No future in the multi-level game", Essex: occasional paper no. 25 in *The European Policy Process* series.

Ferner, A and R Hyman, eds. (1992), *Industrial Relations in the New Europe*. Oxford: Blackwell.

Ferner, A and R Hyman, eds. (1997), *Industrial Relations in the New Europe*, Oxford: Blackwell, second edition.

Flanagan, RJ, J Hartog and J Theeuwes (1993), "Institutions and the Labour Market Contracts and Institutions: Many Questions, Some Answers", in Hartog and Theeuwes, eds., 415–46

Fluder, R, and B Hotz-Hart (1997), *"Switzerland: Still as Smooth as a Clockwork?"*, in Ferner and Hyman, eds., *Industrial Relations in the New Europe*, 262–82.

Foden, D (1998), "Trade Union Proposals Towards EMU", *Transfer*, 4 (1): 88–112.

Gewerkschaftliche Monatshefte, vol. 49, issue 10/1998: "Bündnis(se) für Arbeit in Europa".

Hartog, J and J Theeuwes, eds. (1993), *Labour Market Contracts and Institutions. A cross-national comparison*. Amsterdam: North-Holland.

Hirsch, B and D MacPherson (1996), *Union Membership and Earnings Data Book: Compilations from the Current Population Survey*. Washington DC: The Bureau of National Affairs.

Iversen, T (1996) "Power, Flexibility and the Breakdown of Centralized Wage Bargaining in Denmark and Sweden in Comparative Perspective", *Comparative Politics*, July issue, 399–436.

Jacobi, O, B Keller, and W Müller-Jentsch (1997), "Germany: Facing New Challenges", in Ferner and Hyman, eds., *Industrial Relations in the New Europe*, 190–238.

Klandermans, P G and J Visser (1995), *De vakbeweging na de welvaartsstaat*. Assen: van Gorcum.

Lehmbruch, G (1984) "Concertation and the Structure of Corporatist Networks", in J H Golthorpe, *Order and Conflict in Contemporary Capitalism*, Oxford: Clarendon Press, 60–80.

Lilja, K (1997), "Finland: Continuity and Modest Moves Towards Company-level Corporatism", in Ferner and Hyman, eds., *Industrial Relations in the New Europe*, 171–89.

Locke, R, T Kochan and M Piore (1995), "Reconceptualising comparative Industrial relations: Lessons from international research", *International Labour Review*, 134 (2): 38–161.

Obradovich, D (1995), "Prospects for Corporatist Decision-Making in the European Union: The Social Policy Agreement", *Journal of European Public Policy*, 2: 261–83.

Olson, M (1982) *The Rise and Decline of Nations: Economic growth, stagflation, and social rigidities*, New Haven: Yale University Press.

Pichot, E (1995), *L'Europe des représentants du personnel et de leur attributions economiques*. Brussels: Etude effectue pour la Commission Européenne.

Pochet, Ph (1998), "Les pactes sociaux en Europe dans les années 1990", *Sociologie du Travail*, 40, 2: 173–90.

van Ruysseveldt, J and J Visser, eds. (1996), *Industrial Relations in Europe. Traditions and Ttransitions*. London: Sage.

Scharpf, F W (1993), "Co-ordination in Hierarchies and Networks", in: F W Scharpf, ed., *Games in Hierarchies and Networks: Analytical and Empirical Approaches to the Study of Governance Institutions*. Frankfurt and Boulder Co.: Campus and Westview.

Scharpf, F W (1997) *Games Real Actors Play. Actor-centered institutionalism in policy research*. Boulder Co.: Westview.

Scheuer, S (1997a), "Collective Bargaining Coverage Under Trade Unionism: A Sociological Investigation", *British Journal of Industrial Relations*, 35, 1: 65–86.

Scheuer, S (1997b), "Denmark: A Less Regulated Model", in Ferner and Hyman, eds., *Industrial Relations in the New Europe*, 146–70.

Schmitter, Ph C (1983), "Neo-Corporatism, Consensus, Governability, and Democracy in the Management of Crisis in Contemporary Advanced Industrial-Capitalist Societies", Florence: European University Institute (unpublished paper).

Schmitter, Ph C and J Grote (1997), "The Corporatist Sisyphus: Past, present and future", Florence: European University Institute, EUI Working Papers, SPS 97/4.

Sisson, K (1987), *The Management of Collective Bargaining.* Oxford: Blackwell.

Soskice, D (1990), "Wage Determination: The Changing Role of Institutions in Advanced Industrialised Countries", *Oxford Review of Economic Policy*, 6: 31–61.

Streeck, W and J Visser (1998), "An Evolutionary Dynamic of Trade Union Systems", Cologne: Max Planck Institute for the Study of Societies, MPIfG Discussion Papers, no. 98/4, 1–54.

Svensen, P (1989), *Fair Shares. Unions, Pay, and Politics in Sweden and West Germany.* Ithaca N.Y.: Cornell University Press

Traxler, F (1993), "Business Associations and Labour Unions in Comparison: Theoretical Perspectives and Empirical Findings on Social Class, Collective Action and Associational organizability", *British Journal of Sociology*, 44 (3): 673–91.

Traxler, F (1994), "Collective Bargaining: Levels and Coverage", in OECD, *Employment Outlook 1994*, Paris: Organisation for Economic Co-operation and Development, 167–91.

Traxler, F (1996), "Collective Bargaining in the OECD: Developments, Preconditions, and Effects", *European Journal of Industrial Relations*, 4 (2): 207–26.

Traxler, F (1997), "Austria: Still the Country of Corporatism", in Ferner and Hyman, eds., *Industrial Relations in the New Europe*, 239–61.

Visser, J (1984), "The Position of Central Confederations in the National Union Movement. A ten country comparison", Florence: European University Institute, working paper no. 102.

Visser, J (1989), *European Trade Unions in Figures.* Deventer and Boston: Kluwer.

Visser, J (1990), *In Search of Inclusive Unionism.* Deventer and Boston: Kluwer.

Visser, J (1998a), "Contertation or the Art of Making Social Pacts", in J Delors et. al., *National Social Pacts. Assessment and future prospects*, Paris: Notre Europe, 42–54.

Visser, J (1998b), "Die konzertierte Wirtschaft in den Niederlanden – Lohnt sie?", Keulen: Max Planck Institute for the Studies of Societies, working paper, 14 pp. (internet versie: http:/www.mpi-fg-koeln.mpg.de)

Visser, J (1998c), "Revisiting Union Growth. Recent trends in OECD countries", Centre for the study of European societies and Labour Relations (CESAR), University of Amsterdam, research paper

Visser, J, and A C Hemerijck (1997), *"A Dutch Miracle". Job Growth, Welfare Reform and Corporatism in the Netherlands.* Amsterdam: Amsterdam University Press.

Visser, J and M van der Meer (1998), "Social Partners, Collective Bargaining and the implementation of the Employment Chapter in a Concerted Economy: The case of the Netherlands", Amsterdam: Centre for the study of European Societies and Labour Relations (CESAR), three reports for the European Commission, DG V.

van Waarden, B F (1995a), "The organisational power of employers' associations: Cohesion, comprehensiveness and organisational development", in C J Crouch and F Traxler, eds., *Organised Industrial Relations in Europe: What Future?*, Aldershot: Avebury, 45–97.

van Waarden, B F (1995b), "Employers and Employers' Associations", in J van Ruysseveldt, R Huiskamp and J J van Hoof, *Comparative Industrial & Employment Relations*, London: Sage, 68–108.

Waddington, J and C Whitston (1997), "Why Do People Join Unions in a Period of Membership Decline?", *British Journal of Industrial Relations*, 35: 4, 515–546.

Wallerstein, M, M Golden, and P Lange (1997), "Unions, Employers' Associations, and Wage-Setting Institutions in Northern and Central Europe, 1950–1992", *Industrial and Labour Relations Review*, 50: 3, 379–401.

6 Wage-setting Institutions and European Monetary Union

FRANZ TRAXLER

Introduction

European Monetary Union (EMU) deprives the member states of exchange rates and interest rates as a means to adjust to imbalances in economic performance and compensate for these imbalances. This implies that the labour market will have to bear the main burden of sustaining the competitiveness of a member state. There are two options for labour market adjustment: labour mobility and wage responsiveness. Since cross-border mobility in Europe is very low (Sengenberger, 1993) and this low mobility will probably persist under EMU, due to sociocultural constraints, wage setting will be the key mechanism for economic adjustment. Wage bargaining in the member states will be exposed to competitive pressures all the more as national fiscal policy will be subject to the constraints set by the Maastricht Treaty and the Stability Pact is unsuitable for cushioning adaptive processes. EMU imposes two main imperatives of responsiveness on wage bargaining. On the one hand, total labour costs can increase only to an extent that does not push inflation above the EMU average. On the other hand, wage policy has to respond to both country-specific and sector-specific changes in productivity resulting from inter-industry and intra-industry restructuring, both of which are likely to accelerate within the common currency area.

This paper deals with the *structural* responsiveness of wage-setting to this challenge: that is, the ability of the bargaining institutions to internalise wage externalities in the EMU context. Since wage bargaining takes place exclusively within the member states, the problem of wage responsiveness contains a national as well as a supranational dimension. As regards the national level, the question is whether the bargaining institutions in all EMU member states can meet the requirements for structural (i.e. institution-based, long-term) responsiveness. From the supranational point of view there is the question of whether EMU creates a need for Europe-wide wage co-ordination. One may argue that these two questions are interdependent in that the need for such co-ordination is contingent on the responsiveness of the national bargaining institutions. With regard to the comparative responsiveness of the national bargaining systems, one has to differentiate between three basic, alternative scenarios: (1) all national bargaining systems fail to be responsive; (2) the systems significantly differ in their responsiveness; (3) all systems succeed (Table 6.1).

This analysis will first point to how each of these scenarios relates to the issue of Europe-wide wage co-ordination. The following sections of this paper examine which scenario is most likely. This includes clarification of whether and how distinct bargaining institutions matter in terms of performance and how much the national bargaining systems covered by EMU differ in this respect. The final part of the paper will discuss in more detail the implications of this scenario for the institutional design of wage-setting in Europe.

Wage-setting and EMU: Three Scenarios

When analysing the relationship between the comparative responsiveness of the national bargaining institutions and the requirements for Europe-wide wage co-ordination, one has to take into consideration that governance of money supply by the European Central Bank (ECB) is the only macroeconomic policy instrument that is formally centralised at the European level. It is argued that sound monetary policy is sufficient for attaining price stability, so that deliberate wage policy as an adaptive mechanism becomes pointless. Comparative studies show that an independent central bank significantly reduces inflation (e.g. Alesina and Summers, 1993; Cukierman, 1992). As it is modelled on the German Bundesbank, the ECB meets the institutional prerequisites for independence.

The ECB's role becomes particularly important in the case of scenario one, if the bargaining institutions in all EMU member states fail to internalise the price externalities of their wage policies. The above argument implies that tough monetary policy can work as a functional equivalent to any kind of negotiated wage responsiveness. Yet, this would only hold true if monetary policy could bring about price stability without real economic costs such as unemployment. Such an assumption is controversial. There is empirical evidence from cross-national studies (Hall, 1994; Hall and

Franzese, 1997) that there are interaction effects between central bank independence and wage responsiveness insofar as the unemployment costs of lowering inflation by an independent central bank depend on the ability of a bargaining system to internalise wage externalities by means of co-ordinating wage settlements across the economy. This is because wage settlements encounter a collective-action problem that the presence of an independent central bank cannot automatically solve. Even when a single bargaining unit might be able to synchronise its wage policy with macroeconomic requirements, doing so would not be rational even under tough monetary policies, if the scope of its settlements is too narrow to have a noticeable impact on the economy. Generally, this collective-action problem arises from the fact that imperfect product markets and organised labour markets empower those interest groups that are located in a strong market position to externalise the costs of wage increases, transmitting inflationary pressures from one group to another.

The controversy on the real-cost effects of an independent central bank ultimately comes from differing assumptions on whether this power of interest groups can be contained by market discipline imposed by tight money supply. Real costs become higher in relation to the extent to which such groups can insulate themselves from market pressures. At worst, for EMU this means that dampening inflation merely by a restrictive monetary policy will mean a significant rise in unemployment. At best, real costs will be relatively low when labour markets are slack. Monetary policy might then work as a functional equivalent to wage restraint as long as this condition lasts. If stability-oriented monetary policy is indeed able to flank an effective macroeconomic policy-mix conducive to growth and employment, this arrangement will undermine the preconditions of its own success if wage responsiveness is lacking. The reason is that market discipline imposed on wage-setting will wither away as growth recovers and employment increases. At least in the long run, there is a need for Europe-wide wage co-ordination even when price stability can be maintained by monetary policy with or without real costs in the short run.

In the second scenario there are stark differences in the abilities of bargaining systems to behave responsively. This will result in growing imbalances in economic performance across countries. As monetary policy is a non-wage mechanism of transnational co-ordination in the case of the first scenario, so are compensatory payments from the EU's structural funds in the second scenario. However, to the extent to which differences in responsiveness are really structural (i.e. entrenched in institutional properties), compensation for economic imbalances would certainly overstretch available resources. Additional transfers conflict with the budgetary constraints mentioned above. The aggregate monetary outcome from this scenario is much more uncertain than in the other scenarios. It depends on the economic weight of those countries characterised by structural wage responsiveness, the bargaining policies pursued in the member states and the monetary/inflation target set by the ECB. Monetary policy itself becomes very difficult whenever wage responsiveness significantly varies across countries. From this perspective, differences in the responsiveness of the national bargaining systems require Europe-wide co-ordination even more than with the first scenario.

At first glance, the third scenario does not seems to create any co-ordination problem of European scale. If all systems are able to synchronise their wage policy with economic requirements, everything looks perfect. Closer consideration reveals that there is a risk of overdrawing responsiveness so that such a synchronisation may result in a deflationary race for the lowest labour costs. For some time, smaller countries (e.g. the Netherlands) of the "hard-currency bloc" (which one might consider the "virtual" predecessor of EMU) improved their competitive position through wage restraint that kept the increase in their labour costs consistently below that of Germany, the bloc's core member. They could do so without causing disruptive imbalances because of their small size. However, even the large countries (if able to do so) may embark on competitive wage restraint in response to the special pressures of EMU. In fact, Germany has recently countered with a rise in unit labour costs that is below the average of the hard currency bloc (Flassbeck, 1997). While productivity-oriented wage policy offers a means to respond to EMU requirements without wage dumping, the problem with this concept is its operationalisation. Productivity growth of a country's economy varies within and across sectors and may change at these levels in the course of economic restructuring. Such a variation can also induce competitive wage settlements unless a transnational consensus on what productivity rate should be adopted as a guideline can be achieved. This scenario also underscores the point that Europe-wide wage responsiveness is more than simply the sum of national wage responsiveness: In fact Europe-wide wage responsiveness presupposes a transnational (i.e. cross-border) approach to wage co-ordination.

The upshot is that any of the alternative basic scenarios creates a need for such co-ordination (Table 6.1).

Table 6.1   The Comparative Responsiveness of National Bargaining Systems to EMU Requirements: Three Basic Scenarios

Scenarios of comparative responsiveness	Risk in the case of absent transnational co-ordination
1 None of the systems is responsive	Inflationary wage settlements
2 The systems differ in responsiveness	Growing inequality in performance combined with either inflationary or deflationary tendencies
3 All systems are responsive	Competitive wage dumping

The Bargaining System and Economic Performance

The performance effects of the institutional properties of bargaining have attracted considerable attention from crossnational empirical research. Although studies differ in their theoretical premises, most of them nevertheless suggest that bargaining that is co-ordinated across the economy has beneficial employment and inflation effects. However, relevant literature disagrees on how other, less co-ordinated bargaining systems perform. The corporatist school and the hump-shape hypothesis are the most prominent in this debate. While the former has found a monotonic and positive relationship between the degree of bargaining co-ordination and performance (e.g. Cameron, 1984), the latter has reported that extremes (i.e. both the most co-ordinated and the least co-ordinated systems) work best, whereas intermediate degrees of co-ordination do worst (e.g. Calmfors and Drifill, 1988). After all these studies which came up with significant (albeit more or less differing) performance effects of the bargaining institutions, an OECD study published more recently (1997) concludes that there is little evidence that any particular bargaining system is either better or worse on performance criteria than others.

This broad range of differing and even contradicting findings ensues from several shortcomings that permeate the debate. The most apparent weakness is that these studies directly relate the bargaining institutions to macro-economic performance indicators such as employment and inflation, but never deal with the impact of institutions on labour costs, even when they come up with significant effects on macro-economic indicators. This is strange because the causal link between the bargaining institution and macro-economic performance is labour costs (Therborn, 1987). Moreover, control over labour costs—or put more precisely—over an increase in unit labour costs is the essence of wage responsiveness in the EMU context.

Re-analysis of the most influential studies (including that by Calmfors and Driffill) does not yield any significant effect on measures of labour costs (Traxler and Kittel, 1997). These findings do not mean that bargaining institutions do not matter. Rather, they indicate conceptual shortcomings in the way in which the impact of the institutions on performance is empirically tested. One shortcoming is that most studies tend to equate co-ordination with centralisation of bargaining, which in turn is considered a one-dimensional concept. Such conceptualisation misses the complexity of bargaining. Centralisation, in its strict sense, merely points to the level at which agreements on wages and working conditions are concluded (Soskice, 1990). Co-ordination refers to whether and how bargaining on behalf of distinct employee and employer groups takes place in a synchronised way. The critical point is that co-ordination does not necessarily coincide with centralisation in reality. In several OECD countries (such as Japan, Germany and Austria) wage bargaining is co-ordinated across the economy, without collective agreements being concluded at the central (i.e. cross-sectoral level). In these countries bargaining co-ordination rests on the pattern-setting role of one particular sector (i.e. generally the metal industry) which defines the going rate for overall wage increases. Put in another way, the equation of centralisation with co-ordination neglects non-hierarchical forms of economy-wide bargaining co-ordination. Another dimension which conventional measurement concepts ignore concerns the question of whether co-ordination rests on either voluntary co-operation between the two sides of industry or on state intervention. Finally, empirical studies rarely differentiate between the horizontal and vertical problem of bargaining co-ordination (Moene et al., 1993). Horizontal co-ordination refers to whether bargaining on behalf of workers in different types of jobs is synchronised. The vertical problem of co-ordination involves compliance of the rank-and-file with agreements concluded by their representatives.

This multi-dimensionality of bargaining has essential implications for scaling. If there are qualitatively differing dimensions of bargaining, constructing an ordinal scale of bargaining co-ordination along the centralisation axis—as conventional concepts do—is not valid. For instance, there is no reason to believe that economy-wide co-ordination when based on central agreements generally delivers more beneficial performance effects than co-ordination based on pattern bargaining does. As regards the role of the state, ordinal rankings according to the mere degree of centralisation/co-ordination imply that the distinction between voluntary and state-guided co-ordination does not matter. Such an assumption is—to say the least—debatable. It is also misleading to measure the degree of horizontal and vertical co-ordination on one and the same scale. This is because horizontal co-ordination and vertical co-ordination each represent a distinct collective-action problem. As a result, horizontal co-ordination across the economy when agreed upon by the bargaining parties may fail, due to defection by the rank-and-file. This happened to several "social pacts" struck centrally in countries like Britain, Italy and Spain.

Following this line of reasoning, the author of this paper and Bernhard Kittel conducted a comparative study of the performance effects of wage bargaining, which included 18 OECD countries from 1970 to 1990 (Traxler and Kittel, 1997). As far as horizontal co-ordination is concerned, the study empirically identified six main patterns, when differentiating between hierarchical and non-hierarchical forms of co-ordination on the one hand and between different forms of state involvement on the other. These patterns are: (i) uncoordinated (i.e. "decentralised") bargaining; (ii) pattern bargaining; (iii) state-imposed co-ordination (i.e. authoritative wage control); (iv) intra-associational co-ordination by the peak associations (i.e. the central-level associations of employers and employees internally synchronise bargaining of their respective affiliates); (v) inter-associational co-ordination (i.e. central agreements concluded by the peak associations of employers and employees); and (vi) state-sponsored co-ordination (i.e. tripartite, central agreements in which the government joins the peak associations as a third party). The degree of vertical co-ordination was measured as bargaining governability, the latter referring to whether labour law contains opportunist behaviour of the rank-and-file. The argument is that labour law most effectively contains opportunism when establishing: (i) the legal enforceability of collective agreements; and (ii) a peace obligation as long as a collective agreement is in force. Bargaining governability was operationalised as a composite index derived from whether the two provisions mentioned above form part of a country's legal framework of bargaining. Low governability lacks either legal enforceability or the peace obligation.

Figure 6.1 The Relation between Centralisation of Wage Bargaining and Economic Performance

Performance*

		pattern setting	voluntary, centra-lised (i.e. peak-level) co-ordination** with high bargaining governability
high			
medium	unco-ordinated bargaining		state-imposed co-ordination
low			voluntary, centra-lised (i.e. peak-level) co-ordination** with low bargai-ning governabili-ty
	low	medium	high

Degree of Bargaining Centralisation

*	measured as wage responsiveness in terms of the increase in unit labour costs from 1970 to 1990 for 18 OECD countries.
**	inter-associational co-ordination, intra-associational co-ordination, state-sponsored co-ordination.

Source: Traxler and Kittel (1997).

Regression analysis, which uses these measures of horizontal and vertical co-ordination for country classification, yields indeed a significant impact on economic performance, including labour costs for the countries and time period mentioned above. Since this impact points to the same direction with regard to all performance indicators, this report can concentrate on the increase in unit labour costs as the criterion most important to EMU requirements. Related findings are summarised in Figure 6.1, which refers to three institutional properties of wage bargaining: centralisation, governability and co-ordination. Most importantly, economy-wide co-ordination proves to be effective only if the problem of vertical co-ordination can be overcome. This can be achieved in three ways. The first way is through voluntary co-ordination, which takes place within a rather decentralised framework so that the problems of vertical co-ordination emerge only on a relatively limited scale. The second way is compliance of the rank-and-file to be enforced by the state. In comparison to voluntary pattern bargaining, the results of this form of co-ordination are less beneficial. Third the performance of voluntary, central-level forms of co-ordination (i.e. inter-associational, intra-associational and state-sponsored co-ordination) comes close to the performance of pattern bargaining when they are combined with a high degree of bargaining governability. However, voluntary, central-level forms of co-ordination definitely perform worst if bargaining governability is lacking. This contingency is due to the enormous problems of vertical co-ordination resulting from centralised bargaining. Voluntary systems can cope with these problems only if they rely on a supportive (legally-backed) framework that makes bargaining governable. If the problem of vertical co-ordination cannot be solved, unco-ordinated bargaining is the (second) best choice. The fact that the performance of unco-ordinated (i.e. decentralised) bargaining is inferior to that of governable economy-wide co-ordination may seem surprising from a neoliberal point of view. It can be explained by the imperfect product-market competition that does indeed enable employers and employees to share rents from their company's dominant market position, thus externalising the costs of wage increases (OECD, 1994). As with pattern bargaining and state-imposed co-ordination, the performance of unco-ordinated bargaining is not especially contingent on the degree of bargaining governability.[1] This is because state-imposed co-ordination solves the co-ordination problem by force and this problem becomes diminished in the comparatively decentralised context of pattern bargaining so that governability is less important. By definition, any kind of co-ordination problem disappears when bargaining is unco-ordinated. Overall, findings confirm that there is a significant impact of bargaining institutions on performance, which results from a rather complex interplay of horizontal and vertical co-ordination problems.

Recent studies have stressed the importance of an economy's sectoral composition for bargaining outcomes, contending that strong public-sector unions dampen performance (e.g. Garrett and Way, 1995; Franzese, 1997). This adverse effect is attributed even to economy-wide concertation when the public sector dominates the exposed sector. The general argument is that the public sector, being sheltered from market competition, can easily externalise pay hikes. However, the empirical evidence from these studies is questionable, since they all somehow refer to the size of public employment as an indicator of strong public-sector unions. This raises a problem of reliability, as there are no good data series on employment by sector (particularly the public sector) available. Furthermore, there is a problem of validity, since neither the mere share of the public sector in total employment nor the share of public-sector unionism in total union membership simply translates into relative strength vis-à-vis public employers and other unions. A re-analysis, using the membership share of the three largest public-sector unions under the umbrella of the largest union confederation did not confirm the above-mentioned argument (Kittel, 1997). Similarly, a crossnational analysis of the performance effects of the wage-setting institutions in the public sector (including their impact on real wages) did not detect a systematic relationship, but suggests that such effects are highly contingent on circumstances (Traxler, 1998). This holds true even for the Scandinavian countries, which indeed show evidence that public-sector expansion has a negative effect on both economy-wide bargaining co-ordination and performance. Without the contingent element of a very tough solidaristic wage policy inherent to co-ordination in these countries, redistributive conflicts between distinct sectoral employee groups would have been less acute and destructive.

The Comparative Responsiveness of National Bargaining Systems to EMU

From the above findings, one can deduce a prediction on the comparative responsiveness of the national bargaining systems to the requirements of the EMU. This can be done by relating the bargaining practices of the EMU members to the categories of bargaining patterns from Figure 6.1. Table 6.2 presents this classification (except for Luxembourg) for the 1980s.[2] For interpretation, it is worth mentioning that several countries have more or less frequently moved from one category to another. Hence, Table 2 shows only the most important (i.e. most durable) pattern. For the same reason, the performance of the individual countries in terms of control over unit labour costs cannot directly be derived from Table 6.2. Needless to say, changes in the national bargaining patterns also took place during the 1990s. It is, however, important to note that all these changes concerned only the horizontal dimension of wage co-ordination. None of the countries listed in

Table 6.2 records a substantive change in bargaining governability. As a consequence, none of these changes affected the divide in terms of governability between countries.[3] Given the fact that this divide constitutes contrasting capacity to control unit labour costs in the case of voluntary peak-level co-ordination of wages, it is evident that scenario three (implying significant differences in the structural wage responsiveness of the EMU members) will be most likely.

Table 6.2   The Structural Responsiveness of the Bargaining Systems of EMU Member States

Bargaining patterns ranked by responsiveness*	Most durable patterns per member states** (1980–90)
1 pattern bargaining voluntary peak-level co-ordination*** (with high governability)	A, D FIN, NL
2 unco-ordinated bargaining state-imposed co-ordination	F
3 voluntary peak-level co-ordination*** (with low governability)	B, E, I, IRL, P

*	Responsiveness (in terms of control over unit labour costs) decreases with score 1–3.
**	Most durable pattern derived from annual observations on the countries' bargaining practices.
***	Inter-associational co-ordination, intra-associational co-ordination, state-sponsored co-ordination.

A = Austria, B = Belgium, D = Germany, E = Spain, F = France, FIN = Finland, I = Italy, IRL = Ireland, NL = Netherlands, P = Portugal.

Significant variations in wage responsiveness across EMU members will place adaptive pressures on those countries that perform particularly poorly, since they combine voluntary peak-level wage co-ordination with low governability. It is primarily the state that is cast in the role of the agent of adjustment because any bargaining unit that is able to externalise the cost of its wage policy will find little reason to revise its behaviour to meet performance requirements. In principle, the state has three options when a lack of structural responsiveness requires institutional change. The first option is to increase bargaining governability, allowing the country to shift from group 3 to group 1. However, given the stickiness of governability, this would require introducing a far-reaching legal reform of industrial relations (e.g. the introduction of a legal peace obligation for the validity of a collective agreement). Such reforms would be a very conflict-provoking issue, since they would fundamentally re-define the scope for action of the bargaining parties. Analogous implementation problems emerge in connection with the second option, that is, dismantling collective bargaining institutions in order to arrive at unco-ordinated bargaining. As Table 6.2 reveals, all EMU members have developed a strong tradition of horizontal wage co-ordination which would conflict with such a neoliberal project. In fact, Britain is the only EU member state in which bargaining has been unco-ordinated for a longer time period. As the British experience also shows, such neoliberal politics of industrial relations improve performance in comparison with co-ordination efforts burdened with low governability only over the medium term. In this respect, state-imposed co-ordination as the third option is more attractive, since it promises to establish wage restraint in the short run. Furthermore, this option creates fewer implementation problems since bargaining units can lay the blame for income losses on the state.

For all these reasons, state-imposed wage moderation is the most probable adjustment strategy in countries suffering from a lack of structural responsiveness, provided that they are able to adopt an effective adjustment strategy at all. The example of Belgium is instructive in this context. Since the problems of a lack in responsiveness have accelerated under the pressure to curb labour costs, which is one result of the country's accession to the hard-currency bloc, the government has exercised tough wage control since 1993. Depending on whether, in poorly performing countries, the state manages to implement a shift to more wage responsiveness, the comparative responsiveness of the EMU members will either reproduce scenario two or move to scenario three. This brings us to the issue of cross-border co-ordination, an issue that becomes important in either of these cases.

EMU and Cross-border Bargaining Co-ordination

There is a functional and a genetic aspect of the prospects for transnational bargaining co-ordination. From a functional point of view, the question is what type of cross-border wage co-ordination may amount to a working

European regime of economic and social policy under EMU. The genetic aspect concerns the chance of the emergence of such co-ordination. In functional respects the argument as summarised in Table 6.1 is that there is a general need for transnational co-ordination regardless of what scenario, in terms of the comparative responsiveness of the national bargaining systems, will come into effect. If transnational co-ordination is absent, any possible scenario is likely to entail economically and socially suboptimal results for the EMU area as a whole. In the short run, the problem of growing inequality among the member states will prevail since the structural responsiveness of the national bargaining systems differ significantly. Longer-term developments depend on how poorly-performing systems react and how their reactions interact with monetary policy. If adjustment is delayed, manifesting itself in inflationary tendencies in the common currency area, the ECB will presumably tighten monetary policy. If adjustment is fast and tends to overcompensate (e.g. in the wake of massive state intervention in wage policy), this may trigger competitive wage dumping. Hence, any kind of longer-term development that fails to establish cross-border co-ordination runs the risk of getting trapped into deflationary policies.

Even if there is a need for transnational bargaining co-ordination, this does not automatically create the preconditions for its fulfilment. Hence, it is necessary to differentiate between the functional requirements for such co-ordination and the prospects for its emergence. The established institutions of the European Social Dialogue do not seem to be well prepared for assuming this co-ordinating task, as the following short review demonstrates.

The Social Policy Protocol in the Treaty of Maastricht formally excludes pay policy from the range of issues negotiable within this framework. Aside from this, the practice of negotiations that has developed so far does not provide a suitable basis for wage co-ordination. Dealings according to the Social Protocol are macro-centred in that all negotiations and agreements concluded so far refer to cross-sectoral issues. European wage co-ordination cannot rest on such centralised macro-agreements, since the problems of both intraclass and interclass unification of interests would magnify at this level to an extent which is beyond any manageable scale. In comparison to this, the sectoral Social Dialogue, which raises fewer problems of interest unification, is underdeveloped (Keller and Sörries, 1997). Also of importance, UNICE has been willing to negotiate only under pressure by the European Commission. Most sectoral Euro-associations of business even hesitate to take on the task of an employer organisation at all and see themselves as trade associations. Overall, the Social Dialogue, neither at the cross-sectoral nor at the sectoral level, provides a basis for regular and enduring bargaining, which a negotiated approach to transnational wage co-ordination would require.

Using the European works councils as another possible institutionalised starting point for European bargaining also raises a formal problem, since only information rights are attributed to them. While the European works council may have a role in crossnational adjustments of the wage structure, its co-ordinating activities are confined to the company level, and thus fail to meet the macro-economic requirement for synchronisation of wage determination with monetary goals.

The Euro-associations of business and labour which have to assume the key role in a European system of bargaining co-ordination face manifold problems of attaining corresponding co-ordinating abilities. Euro-associations are poorly resourced—at least in comparison to many of their national affiliates which are also rather reluctant to transfer competencies to the supranational level. Furthermore, the incoherence in the structure of national affiliates and the diversity of the national systems of labour market regulation make supranational interest aggregation extremely difficult. Organisational incoherence is a particularly serious problem for the employers at Community level. There is rivalry over representational domains, namely between UNICE and UEAPME over participation in the framework according to the Social Protocol. In addition, there is the problem of how sectoral interests should be inserted into the cross-sectoral structures. The sectoral Euro-associations of business are not incorporated into UNICE. This situation contrasts with national associational systems, which are characterised by the affiliation of most sectoral associations with the general peak associations.

Finally, any decision taken at Community level needs implementation by the national actors in the member states. As outlined above, the capacity for vertical co-ordination is precisely the precondition for structural responsiveness that several national bargaining systems are lacking. Even when the European representatives of business and labour manage to embark on wage concertation, low governability of some national bargaining systems poses a serious problem in implementing cross-border co-ordination.

All this leads to a sceptical assessment of the prospects for cross-border wage co-ordination. In fact, one has to rule out any possibility of its emergence, when applying conventional wisdom of the institutional requirements for socio-economic governance: Accordingly, only a coherent system of Euro-corporatism, consisting of encompassing associations and centralised bargaining would assure the capacity for pan-European co-ordination. However, as argued above, this wisdom suffers from several analytical shortcomings and also lacks empirical evidence. The following lessons from effective patterns of national wage co-ordination are particularly relevant for the co-ordination of wage settlements in the EMU context.

Economy-wide wage *co-ordination* does not mean *centralisation* of bargaining. This argument is important for two reasons. In structural respects, a centralised approach to European wage co-ordination would certainly overstretch the limited capacities of the European institutions. In substantive respects, the combination of macroeconomic co-ordination and decentralised bargaining is the only way to make two EMU requirements for wage policy compatible: These two requirements are control over aggregate wage increases in line with employment and stability goals and a wage structure that responds in a flexible way to inter-industry and intra-industry restructuring. The example of Austria is instructive in this regard, since it is among the OECD countries with the most effective co-ordination of wages and at the same time records one of the highest degrees of wage dispersion.

Voluntary wage co-ordination across the economy does not necessarily rest on bipartite *negotiations*, as the case of intra-associational co-ordination by the national peak organisations documents. Again, this is essential to the European situation, due to the employers' reluctance to enter bipartite negotiations.

Economy-wide co-ordination does not presuppose encompassing involvement of all groups and sectors of the economy. There is hardly a working national system of bargaining co-ordination which has been able to incorporate all groups. By contrast, it is often a rather small core group that actively contributes to the realisation of economy-wide co-ordination. This becomes apparent when examining the size of the pattern-setting group in those countries characterised by lasting pattern bargaining. In Austria and Germany, the share of the pattern-setting metal industry in the total number of employees was no more than 8.3% (in 1996) and 16.3% (in 1990) respectively. Although it may be true that pattern bargaining is backed by certain supportive conditions in these two countries, the point is that arriving at economy-wide co-ordination is rather independent of group size. Accounts on collective action theory that abandon the assumption of independence of individual action have stressed that a relatively small "critical mass" may suffice to overcome the collective-action problem (Granovetter, 1983; Oliver and Marwell, 1988; Oliver et al., 1985). Under certain circumstances (such as high heterogeneity of interests and resources, and the fact that co-operation costs are rather insensitive to group size), the prospects for collective action even increase with group size because larger groups are more likely to find a critical mass for co-operation, particularly if there is a core subgroup with members socially tied to one another. It follows from this that the large size of the EU is not a structural impediment to economy-wide wage co-ordination. The metal industry, which is highly unionised in most EMU countries, may form the critical mass for Europe-wide co-ordination.[4]

Overall, cross-border wage co-ordination is possible only on the basis of non-hierarchical, network-style structures, most probably launched by a combination of intra-associational co-ordination and pattern bargaining at Community level. At least in an early stage, this co-ordination may be informal and implicit, resulting from "tacit" intra-associational arrangements rather than from negotiations between the Euro-associations of business and labour. Such Europeanisation of wage policy constitutes a complex multi-level framework that requires elaborate articulation of these levels. This means that the distinct levels must deliberately be geared to one another and form part of a coherent system of division of labour (Crouch, 1993). Since it is very difficult to arrive at agreements on substantive issues (even within the union movement) at the European level, it is reasonable to concentrate Europe-wide co-ordination on procedural issues. This implies devolution of bargaining over substantive issues to lower-level actors in the member states, whereas higher, European levels confine themselves to defining the guidelines for bargaining. As mentioned above, these guidelines may include the precedence of the exposed sector as the pattern setter. Another guideline has to link wage increases to productivity growth in an unequivocal, operational way. Such a guideline would be flexible enough to respond to variations of performance across Europe in that it enables the national bargaining units to fix different wage rates in accordance with differences in productivity growth. Accordingly, the basic principle of a European system of articulation would be that the importance of both *procedural* issues and *co-ordination* in comparison to *substantive* issues and *bargaining* increases with the level of interest aggregation.

While a network-style co-ordination of that kind has not come into existence so far, there have nevertheless been some tendencies from both "below" and "above" in this direction. Tendencies from below originate in the member states all of which have tried to moderate comparative labour costs in the context of the coming EMU. In many cases this has led to tripartite "social pacts" (Regini, 1998) which most strikingly indicate the revival of corporatism in the member states, as predicted by Traxler and

Schmitter (1995a,b). This national incomes policy constitutes a *negative* form of cross-border co-ordination in that its raison d'être is to prevent national pay hikes from exceeding those fixed in the respective country's most important trading partners. In practice this means that particularly the smaller countries have aimed to keep their wage increases below those in Germany. So far, this has been facilitated by the fact that in Germany the effect of wage restraint on comparative labour costs has often be nullified by concomitant revaluations of the Deutschmark. EMU will relieve Germany's bargaining parties of this burden so that they will be able to counter competitive wage bargaining much more effectively than in the past. As Table 6.2 shows, a high degree of structural responsiveness characterises the German bargaining system. Therefore, the race for the lowest labour costs under EMU more than ever implies a "beggar-my-neighbour" policy with deflationary, self-defeating consequences for all countries involved. Growing insight into this risk (possibly arising in the course of a trial-and-error process) may pave the way for a *positive* approach to cross-border co-ordination. Similarly, state intervention, which may occur in order to enforce wage responsiveness to EMU in place of a lack of bargaining governability, may push the bargaining parties towards more voluntary and positive forms of cross-border co-ordination. Indeed, initial activities directed to positive co-ordination practices have been launched. Since 1997 attempts at co-ordination of bargaining on behalf of the steel industry in Belgium, the Netherlands and North Rhine-Westphalia have been made by the national unions which—inter alia— agreed on mutual participation in their respective bargaining rounds.

Tendencies from above are located at the Community level. Under the umbrella of the ETUC the European Metalworkers' Federation has developed into the vanguard of cross-border co-ordination. Related measures follow a three-stage procedure consisting of the mutual participation of the national affiliates in their country's wage commission; joint discussion and preparation of minimum standards of wage policy; and an "accountability obligation" when jointly agreed wage rules are not implemented (Hoffmann and Hoffmann, 1997). On the side of employers, the informal European Employers' Network initiated by UNICE in the early 1990s may become a first step towards intraclass co-ordination insofar as the Network's aim is to co-ordinate employers' organisations in order to obviate incoherencies in socialpolicy strategies (Hornung-Draus, 1994).

It is well-known that a chain as a whole is no stronger than its weakest link. None of the above tendencies towards Europe-wide co-ordination has addressed one of its key issues: legally-based governability of bargaining. In no less than six of the ten EMU members bargaining governability is very low (Traxler, 1998). Voluntary peak-level co-ordination in these six countries as an element of the overall process of cross-border co-ordination will thus face considerable implementation problems. There are, nevertheless, two factors which may mitigate these problems. As outlined above, the coverage of economy-wide wage co-ordination is incomplete even in those countries, where it has proved successful. This indicates that such co-ordination patterns can tolerate free-riding to some extent without losing their beneficial effects. Sound monetary policy can help to keep the area of free-riding small. Characteristically, the Austrian Trade Union Federation (ÖGB) strongly supported the adoption of a "hard-currency policy" in the 1970s, since this could be instrumentalised as a means to suppress autonomous shop-floor movements and wage drift (Traxler, 1995). Since 1987, Ireland's tripartite concertation has been more successful than its predecessors because of the explicit commitment of its peak organisations to ERM parity (O'Donnell and O'Reardon, 1997).

The question of whether these factors suffice to compensate for low bargaining governability in several EMU members is empirical. At any rate, their supportive function in relation to wage co-ordination will be weakened to the same extent the labour market recovers.

Conclusions

It is evident from both the feasible options for and the real tendencies towards cross-border wage co-ordination that Europeanisation of wage policy will not formally be integrated into the established institutional framework of the European Social Dialogue. Any kind of a Europe-wide wage concertation will thus add a new dimension to the Social Dialogue not only in substantive but also in institutional respects. For all the reasons outlined above, the institutional setting of European wage policy would be far more informal and even less based on explicit agreements than is the case with the current Social Dialogue. Notwithstanding these differences, the two settings would probably complement and reinforce each other. For instance, participation in Community decisions according to the Social Protocol has strengthened the position of the cross-sectoral Euro-associations, namely UNICE, vis-à-vis their affiliates. This in turn facilitates intraclass/intra-associational wage co-ordination. Conversely, the interactive effects among wage policy, monetary policy and fiscal policy are likely to pull the Euro-associations of business and labour into policy fields other than the labour market, as soon as they manage to acquire co-ordinating capacities for wages.

It remains to be seen whether the Euro-associations can actually deploy co-ordinating capacities to an extent that provides structural responsiveness to EMU requirements. If so, medium-term success in reconciling employment goals with inflation/monetary targets may erode the long-term base of co-ordination. As long as labour markets are slack, "market discipline" imposed by high unemployment, possibly connected with state-imposed wage restraint in some member states, may help to make the rank-and-file comply with co-ordinating efforts. If labour markets become tight again, the effectiveness of these mechanisms will wither away. Given that the lack of shop-floor compliance was the Achilles heel of neo-corporatist incomes policy in many European countries during the 1960s and 1970s, there is hardly an alternative to legal reforms aimed at enhancing bargaining governability in those member states in which governability is still lacking.

Notes

1   Nevertheless, one should not underestimate the importance of governability for pattern bargaining in the European context. Among the OECD countries characterised by this bargaining pattern, both European countries, where it has been most durable (i.e. Austria and Germany), rely on high governability.

2   In France, wage-fixing in the public sector sets the pattern for the private sector (Redor, 1997). Hence, wage co-ordination is state-imposed in the sense that it is not the outcome of negotiations between the bargaining parties of the private sector.

3   It is not mere coincidence that this divide between these two types of bargaining co-ordination, by and large, reflects the divide between the hard-currency bloc and the rest of the EMU countries. With the exception of Belgium, all countries belonging to the bloc can rely on bargaining backed by a high responsiveness. This excludes France, which takes an intermediate position. The series of effective upward revaluations the hard-currency bloc encountered have made a responsive wage policy indispensable, unless the exchange rate is defended by restrictive monetary policy at the cost of high unemployment.

4   Since employment in the metal industry is shrinking, one may doubt that the industry's organisational strength will continue to be strong enough for establishing the critical mass. However, the prevailing trend towards amalgamations throughout Europe's unions gives rise to more encompassing organisations in the manufacturing sector. This rather broadens the basis for forming a critical mass. Furthermore, the Single European Market and privatisation have enlarged the exposed sector to most services, which, due to their market exposure, share the interest in synchronising wage policy with employment goals.

References

Alesina, A and L H Summers (1993), "Central Bank Independence and Macroeconomic Performance: Some Comparative Evidence", *Journal of Money, Credit and Banking*, vol. 25: 151–62.

Calmfors, L and J Driffill (1988), "Bargaining Structure, Corporatism and Macroeconomic Performance", *Economic Policy*, vol. 6: 13–61.

Cameron, D (1984), "Social Democracy, Corporatism, Labor Quiescence and the Representation of Economic Interests in Advanced Capitalist Countries", in J H Goldthorpe, ed., *Order and Conflict in Contemporary Capitalism. Studies in the Political Economy of Western European Nations*, Oxford: Clarendon Press, 143–78.

Crouch, C (1993), *Industrial Relations and European State Traditions*. Oxford: Clarendon Press.

Cukierman, A (1992), *Central Bank Strategy, Credibility, and Independence*. Cambridge: MIT Press.

Flassbeck, H (1997), "Und die Spielregeln für die Lohnpolitik in einer Währungsunion?", *Frankfurter Rundschau*, 31. September 1997.

Franzese, R J (1997), "Monetary Policy and Wage/Price Bargaining: Macro-Institutional Interactions in the Traded, Public and Sheltered Sectors", Ann Arbor: The University of Michigan, Unpublished Paper.

Garrett, G and C Way (1995), "The Sectoral Composition of Trade Unions, Corporatism, and Economic Performance", in B Eichengreen, J Frieden and J von Hagen, eds., *Monetary and Fiscal Policy in an Integrated Europe*, Berlin: Springer, 38–61.

Granovetter, M (1978), "Threshold Models of Collective Behavior." *American Journal of Sociology*, 83: 1420–43.

Hall, P A (1994), "Central Bank Independence and Coordinated Wage Bargaining: Their Interaction in Germany and Europe", *German Politics and Society*, 31: 1–23.

Hall, P A and R J Franzese (1997), "Mixed Signals: Central Bank Independence, Coordinated Wage-Bargaining, and European Monetary Union", Unpublished Paper.

Hoffmann, J and R Hoffmann (1997), "Globalization – Risks and Opportunities for Labor Policy in Europe", DW P97.04.01 (E), ETUI.

Hornung-Draus, R (1994), "Union der Industrie- und Arbeitgeberverbände in Europa UNICE", in W Lecher and H-W Platzer, eds., *Europäische Union-Europäische Arbeitsbeziehungen: Nationale Voraussetzungen und internationaler Rahmen*, Köln: Bund, 230–41.

Keller, B and B Sörries (1997), "The Sectoral Social Dialogue und European Social Policy", Universität Konstanz, Unpublished Paper.

Kittel, B (1997), "The Impact of Trade Unions on Economic Performance: Theoretical Elegance and Empirical Ambiguity", Paper prepared for the 48th Annual Conference of the Political Studies Association of the United Kingdom, Keele University, April 7–9, 1997.

Moene, K O, M Wallerstein and M Hoel (1993), "Bargaining Structure and Economic Performance", in R J Flanagan, K O Moene and M Wallerstein, eds., *Trade Union Behavior, Pay-Bargaining, and Economic Performance*, Oxford: Clarendon Press, 63–131.

O'Donnell, R and C O'Reardon (1997), "Ireland's Experiments in Social Partnership 1987–96", in G Fajertag and P Pochet, eds., *Social Pacts in Europe*, ETUI, Brussels, 79–95.

OECD (1994), *The OECD Jobs Study. Evidence and Explanations. Part II The Adjustment Potential of the Labour Market*. Paris: OECD.

OECD (1997), "Economic Performance and the Structure of Collective Bargaining", in *OECD Employment Outlook*, Paris: OECD, 64–92.

Oliver, P E and G Marwell (1988), "The Paradox of Group Size in Collective Action: A Theory of the Critical Mass. II", *American Sociological Review*, 53: 1–8.

Oliver, P E, G Marwell and R Teixeira (1985), "A Theory of the Critical Mass. I. Interdependence, Group Heterogeneity, and the Production of Collective Action." *American Journal of Sociology*, 91: 522–56.

Regini, M (1998), "Different Trajectories in 1990s Europe: De-Regulation Vs. Concertation", Paper presented at the International Sociological Association XIV World Congress, Montreal, July 26–August 1.

Sengenberger, W (1993), "Labour Mobility and Western European Economic Integration", in IIRA, ed., *Economic and Political Changes in Europe: Implications on Industrial Relations*, Bari: Caccucci Editore, 415–39.

Soskice, D. (1990), "Wage Determination: The Changing Role of Institutions in Advanced Industrialized Countries", *Oxford Review of Economic Policy*, 6: 36–61.

Therborn, G (1987), "Does Corporatism Really Matter? The Economic Crisis and Issues of Political Theory", *Journal of Public Policy*, 7: 259–84.

Traxler, F (1995), "From Demand-side to Supply-side Corporatism? Austria's Labour Relations and Public Policy", in C Crouch and F Traxler eds., *Organized Industrial Relations in Europe: What Future?*, Aldershot: Avebury, 271–86.

Traxler, F (1998), "Der Staat in den Arbeitsbeziehungen. Entwicklungstendenzen und ökonomische Effekte im internationalen Vergleich", *Politische Vierteljahresschrift*, 39: 235–260.

Traxler, F and B Kittel (1997), "The Bargaining Structure, its Context, and Performance", Paper prepared for the Conference on "Economic Internationalization and Democracy", December 14–15, University of Vienna.

Traxler, F and P Schmitter (1995a), "Arbeitsbeziehungen und europäische Integration"; M Mesch, ed., *Sozialpartnerschaft und Arbeitsbeziehungen in Europa*, Wien: Manz, 231–56.

Traxler, F and P Schmitter (1995b), "The Emerging Euro-Polity and Organized Interests", *European Journal of International Relations*, 1: 191–218.

7 Reforming the Channels of Representation for an Eventual Euro-democracy

PHILIPPE C. SCHMITTER

The European Union is not only difficult to label—Jacques Delors liked to refer to it as *"un objet politique non-identifié"*—but it is even more difficult to evaluate. It has all the formal institutions of a democracy, but it does not function as a democracy. Its rulers are not accountable to its citizens acting through the competition and cooperation of their representatives.[1] Should the member states of the EU ever decide to fill its "democracy deficit," they will at a minimum have to reform its existing institutions in three directions: (1) they will have to come up with mutually acceptable decision-rules for its rulers; (2) they will have to specify a unique set of rights and obligations for its citizens; and (3) they will have to provide legitimate and effective channels of representation linking citizens and rulers.

In this essay, I will address only the third dimension—that of representation. First, I will describe the existing situation and evaluate its implications and, then, I will advance some proposals for reform that should make the European Union more democratic. The reader should note, however, no matter how much progress is made in this domain, the EU will not become a performing democracy until its norms of citizenship and decision rules are also reformed.

The Present Situation

As befits a large-scale, multi-layered and diverse polity, the EU already relies heavily on multiple channels of political representation. Member states in the Council of Ministers, national political parties in the European Parliament, selected functional interests in the Economic and Social Committee and, most recently, sub-national territorial units in the Committee of Regions are formally present in its decision-making processes. Informally, a very large number of classes, sectors, professions and causes have organized themselves at the level of Europe and found their way to Bruxelles, Luxembourg or Strasbourg, along with a steadily increasing phalanx of national interest associations and transnational firms. Some of these representatives are explicitly "weighted" according to the size of their respective constituencies; others depend exclusively on the voluntary efforts and relative intensities of their members. Some have the right to participate with "voice and vote" in the making of binding decisions; some are invited by EU authorities to enter the obscure corridors of "comitology" where the projects for eventually binding decisions are drafted; still others resort to less formal ways of exercising their influence.

All this conforms to the generic nature of modern political democracies, each of which has multiple channels of representation and most of which have several layers of authoritative decision-making. One could hypothesize that the more the levels of aggregation and the greater the diversity in interests and identities, the more "representative" the democracy is likely to be. The EU, being the most complex polity ever devised by human agency, is bound to be especially dependent on the functioning of its mechanisms of representation.

Everywhere, the exercise of citizenship, whatever its level, scope or content, has become less and less confined to voting periodically in elections. It also can be expressed by influencing the selection of candidates, joining parties, associations or movements, petitioning or pressuring authorities, participating in the drafting of legislation, engaging in "unconventional" protests, and so forth. Nor is the accountability of authorities only guaranteed through the traditional mechanisms of territorial constituency, partisan competition and legislative process. Much of it can circumvent these mechanisms and focus directly through functional channels and bargaining processes on elected or appointed officials within the administrative-cum-executive apparatus of the state.

The problem with the EU, therefore, lies not in the absence of representation, but in the systematically skewed distribution of the interests and passions that do manage to find their way into its complex and secretive decision-making process. From its origins, the integration process tended to privilege two sets of interests: first and formally, those of the governments of member states (so-called national interests) and, second and informally, those of the business sectors most directly affected by its functional policy domains. This left out many citizens of Europe whose individual and collective well-being was indirectly, gradually and often surreptitiously affected by EU policies: (1) large and diffuse quasi-groups of "policy-takers" within each member state such as wage-earners, unemployed persons, women, consumers, pensioners, youth, etc.; (2) intense and compact movements committed to some specific cause or the provision of some particular public good such as environmental protection, abortion rights, conscientious objection, international solidarity, etc.; (3) inhabitants of sub-national political units—regions, provinces, communes, municipalities —who do not feel adequately represented by their national governments; and (4), most importantly for the future of the integration process, transnational or cross-border coalitions of any of the above three categories. Whatever the formula applied, if the Euro-polity is to democratize its multiple channels of representation, it must provide greater incentives for the collective articulation and the access of these systematically under-represented interests and passions.

Exactly what these incentives should be hinges very much on the type of polity that is emerging at the level of the European Union. If it were merely a *confederatio*, the issue would scarcely arise and attention could be focused exclusively on improving forms of collective action and accountability within the respective national polities. As a purely intergovernmental organization with easy entry and exit and with unanimity as its predominant decision rule, a confederal EU could co-exist comfortably with democratic member states. If it were to become a supra-national *federatio*, most of one's attention would be focused on the formation of a European-level party system sufficiently anchored in citizen perceptions, an electoral mechanism which was uniform, reliable (and acceptable) enough to produce winning candidates and an institutional arrangement which could ensure that decisions binding on the public would be held accountable to properly elected representatives and implemented uniformly and fairly by EU authorities.[2]

But if the (medium-term) problem is to design a more democratic form of representation for either a *consortio* or a *condominio*, then, it may be necessary to use more imagination. The central issue revolves around the "peculiarity" that members of the Euro-polity may have different rights and obligations (in the former mode) and also be constituted by different countries (in the latter mode). Moreover, there would be no clear hierarchy of institutions that would exercise sovereignty and, hence, provide the focus for ultimate accountability—just a complex network of multi-layered bargaining between organizations with overlapping jurisdictions. If this functional and territorial variation were only provisory, i. e. due to explicit temporary *dérogations*), the problem would eventually eliminate itself and those who are full-members might not object to partial-members enjoying "voice and vote" even in matters to which they had not (yet) accepted an equal commitment. Or, if one could be certain that Euro-sovereignty would eventually assert itself, the usual federalist mechanisms of equal status for participants, territorially differentiated powers, checks and balances, and constitutional review should suffice.

However, in the scenario of an indefinite and perhaps permanent diversity within European institutions—and, even more especially, in an eventual *condominio* with its "eccentric" configuration of multiple Europes, each with its own functions and set of members—democratization will have to hinge on inventing more appropriate ways of representing citizen interests and passions.

Some Modest, but Possible Reforms

Now let us examine some reform measures that address both of the above-noted issues. They recognize the "non-state," "eccentric" and "multi-layered" nature of the emerging Euro-polity; and they seek to mitigate (but not eliminate) distortions in the existing channels of representation.

Universal (but limited) and Equal (but proportionate)
Representation in the EP

Let first us assume that, regardless of eventual variation in their commitment with regard to specific functional domains and territorial boundaries, all the countries that join the EU (or any part of it) voluntarily accept to submit themselves to a minimum common denominator of obligations and, hence, to the supranational authority of the Commission and the Court of Justice in these (restricted) matters. This *noyau dur* of obligations would presumably incorporate key aspects of the present *acquis communautaire*, but it should be the subject of explicit negotiations and limits with regard to eventual expansion so that "partial" participants can feel secure from "creeping entanglements" in the future. While it would certainly be a mistake to attempt to produce a *Kompetenzkatalog* based on subsidiarity that would definitively fix the distribution of functional *compétences* and institutional jurisdictions, some kind of distinction between "primary obligations" and "secondary commitments" would be indispensable. If I am not mistaken, something like this was negotiated during the formation of the European Economic Area. Needless to say, in order to accommodate the special situations of the Eastern applicants, it will be necessary to include apposite temporal *dérogations*—even for the primary obligations.[3]

Acceptance of this common denominator would entitle all of the signatory states—perhaps as many at 30 or 35 of them, depending on what happens to the bits-and-pieces from the former Yugoslavia—to representation in the European Parliament. There seems to be general agreement that the size of this body should be limited, in the interests of efficiency, to approximately 700 deputies. Both this cap and common political sense preclude the distribution of seats in the basis of absolute population size. My proposal would be to apply a standard formula, with room for minor modifications to guarantee at least one seat for each country and to round off fractions (it would be difficult to seat 1.75 or 13.38 deputies!). Each country would be entitled to a number of members of European Parliament (MEPs) roughly proportionate to square root of its population. This could be called "proportionate proportional representation" (PPR) and has the virtue of being relatively close to the formula currently in use for votes in the Council and seats in the EP.[4] Admittedly, the eventual adhesion of mini-states such as Andorra, San Marino and Liechtenstein —should they apply—would bias the representation even more against large states, since each would merit at least one seat. Perhaps, some form of rotational representation could be devised for those that do not reach a pre-specified minimum threshold. In any case, each time new members would be admitted, it would be necessary to make a proportionate downward adjustment in the allocation of seats among existing members in order to keep the total within reasonable bounds—something which might have interesting effects on both the nomination and electoral processes. Needless to say, all MEPs, regardless of the size of their constituency and the scope of their commitment to the integration process, would be entitled to participate with equal "voice and vote"—but, as we shall now see, only in the plenary sessions of the European Parliament.

Differential Representation in Functional Committees of the EP

Which is where the role of functionally differentiated representation comes in. The effective legislative activity of the EP would be delegated to standing committees—with at least one assigned to monitor and render accountable the activities of each of the EU's policy domains, e. g. one for Monetary Europe, one for Agricultural Europe, another for Energy Europe, yet another for the "Schengen" Europe of Internal Security or the "Trevi" group on police cooperation, etc. Only those countries which had accepted the full *acquis* in that specific domain would be eligible to participate in the deliberations and make the binding decisions of its corresponding committee. In effect, the EP as a whole would meet only for limited ceremonial occasions, for the approval of major rules changes and for the accession of new members. Most of the actual deliberation and decision- making would take place in a series of "functional sub-parliaments" whose decisions would be automatically given the *imprimatur* of the parliament as a whole.[5]

A rules committee—elected by the EP plenary—would assign draft legislation to the appropriate committee or committees.[6] Some form of appeal procedure would have to be established to allow both members and non-members of the specialized committees to have something to say with regard to resolving the inevitable externalities generated between policy domains and quarrels between competing agencies. For example, if a certain proportion of the MEPs—say, $1/3$ of the total—objected either to excessive "free-riding" by those who were not committed to joint policy-making in a specific domain or to excessive provision of "selective goods" by those who were, the plenary could be empowered to come up with appropriate regulations or compensatory measures. In addition, the fact that all members recognize the general jurisdiction and principles of the ECJ should permit that institution to play a role in mediating inter-functional disputes, as well as the inter-state ones they have more typically had to deal with.

Variable Constituencies and Candidacies

These changes in parliamentary representation and procedure seem (to me) appropriate adjustments to make given the increasing disparities between territorial scope and functional domain that are likely to characterize the emerging Euro-polity, but they would do little to resolve the more fundamentally democratic problem of systematic under- and over-representation of certain interests and passions. To correct for this, it would desirable in the long run to modify the constituencies that the MEPs represent and the conditions under which they are nominated to compete for these positions of representation. Needless to say, this will be no easy matter in the short run since contemporary MEPs—not to mention even better entrenched national politicians—benefit considerably from existing rules that ensure three things: (1) that most Euro-deputies are elected by PR from closed lists representing the country as a whole (except in Great Britain where a first-past-the-post system prevails, and Germany, Belgium, Ireland and Italy where there are multi-member regional lists);[7] (2) that control over nominations to these lists lies exclusively in the hands of national party directorates; (3) that funds to pay for campaigning in Euro-elections are paid directly (and unaccountably) to these same directorates. Under these conditions, sub-national and cross-national constituencies only get represented "by accident".

Ideally, Euro-citizens should be given some direct say in the nomination process, either through local party caucuses or primaries, but this is rarely observed in the national politics of member states and would be even more difficult to implement at the supra-national level where partisan identities and organizational structures are much weaker. With so little possibility for their participation in the nomination process, attention has been focused almost exclusively on expanding the electoral role of Euro-citizens. For example, it has been suggested that they be accorded the opportunity to vote twice in each election; once by simple majority for individual candidates in sub-national constituencies; and again by proportional representation for closed lists established by trans-national political parties.[8] This has the virtue of resembling a well-established (if not always well-understood) procedure followed by one of the EU member states, the Federal Republic of Germany, but it seems unlikely that such a far-reaching change would be accepted unanimously by the others—which, after all, would have to be the case under the existing rules of the Council. If these countries cannot even agree on a much simpler common electoral procedure, how can one expected them to agree on something that would so dramatically empower trans-national parties that barely exist!

I propose something more modest; indeed, so modest that it might initially be implemented by simple majority vote of the EP under its present rules. What if the existing European party formations in the EP were given control over one half of the EU electoral funds allotted for each member state? And what if these funds were distributed in support of national lists in which one half of the candidates would be nominated by these very same, admittedly embryonic and often fragmented, European party secretariats?[9] Would this be enough to bring out latent voter preference for candidates with more trans-national connections and appeals? Would national party oligarchies find it increasingly desirable to place candidates with more Euro-experience higher on their lists? Would politicians, especially if they had the incentive of serving possibly longer terms in the EP, come to attach their professional expectations more securely to that level of aggregation?

If it could be demonstrated on this reduced scale that such candidacies and campaigns are viable, then it might become feasible to consider eventually more consequential reforms such as sub-national or explicitly cross-national constituencies (with either single member districts or smaller PR pools by region), double lists and voting for national and European candidates, strictly uniform procedures for nomination and vote assignment, even additional financial and legal incentives for the formation of supra-national party identities and structures independent of national ones. But this is for the distant future. In the meantime, just increasing the proportion of funds controlled by Euro-parties at each successive Euro-election should provide a badly needed impetus for change—and might even generate some desirable side-effects.

Support for Euro-Associations and Movements

Modifying the channels of EU representation in the ways indicated above, should provide significant incentives for the expression of trans-national and even sub-national *territorial* interests—without suppressing the well-established centrality of national ones.[10] It would, however, do little or nothing to correct the second great source of over- and under-representation in the Euro-polity, i. e. its *functional* bias in favor of business and, to a lesser extent, professional interests.

This is, of course, a bias that is not unique to the EU. In all national liberal democracies, one major problem with the "interest group chorus" is that it sings in an upper-class accent—to use the imagery that E. E. Schattschneider coined in 1960.[11] Wolfgang Streeck and I have argued that the EU is a rather extreme case of weakness in the self-organization of larger scale and more diffuse interests such as workers, women, consumers, patients, the unemployed and pensioners[12]—not to mention the difficulties that passionate causes such as environmental protection, international solidarity, abortion rights and feminism have encountered in articulating themselves at this level.

After reflecting on this issue of systematic distortion in national interest representation, I have advocated a set of reforms that might produce equally or even more beneficial results at the supra-national level.[13] The core of what I propose consists of three, closely interrelated, reforms in the nature of liberal, i. e. voluntary and individual, associability:

(1) the establishment of a semi-public status for interest associations and social movements;

(2) the financing of these associations through compulsory contributions; and

(3) the distribution of these funds by means of citizen vouchers.

In the case of the EU, only associations and movements that were "European" in nature, i. e. had members and some degree of organization in several European countries could acquire the semi-public status. They would have to agree to obey a European set of norms and submit themselves potentially to the jurisdiction of the ECJ (as well as be prepared to operate within the legal norms of whatever member country they might find themselves in). The financing of these representative organizations would come from designated EU funds—much as the present subsidies and contracts do—but receipt of these funds would not preclude their also receiving funds from national governments, private organizations or individual persons. And the voucher system would be run in tandem with the holding of Euro-elections, alongside voting for MEPs and eventual Euro-referenda.

The most obviously analogous reforms at the national level have been the provision of public funding for political parties and the extension of guarantees that accused persons will be provided with adequate legal counsel, paid for by state or local authorities. Vouchers, of course, have been proposed by a wide variety of advocates as a means for introducing competition and accountability into the provision of public service, and some experiments with them have already been carried out and evaluated. To my knowledge, however, this is the first suggestion to use vouchers for the purpose of choosing and funding interest representatives—something which fits nicely with my general objective of making the experience of Euro-democracy different from its national counterpart without, of course, diminishing or damaging the latter.

The system I am proposed here would deliberately avoid the specification by European authorities of any fixed category of representation based on class, status, sector, profession or cause, but would leave the task of determining the organizational boundaries surrounding these entities to the initiative of interest entrepreneurs, the self-determination of social groups, and the subsequent competition for vouchers from individual citizens. The central purpose behind the development of such a semi-public status for Euro-associations and movements is to encourage them both to become better citizens, i. e. to treat each other on the basis of greater equality and mutual respect, and to dedicate greater attention to the interests and passions of the European public as a whole, i. e. to articulate those issues that transcend national boundaries.

This effort would involve nothing less that an attempt to establish a "Charter of Rights and Obligations" for European associations and movements which would, thereby, be recognized as "secondary (organizational) citizens of Europe"—alongside the usual individual variety that we have discussed above. It would be naive to suppose that merely imposing certain forms and rules would *eo ipso* make them into more "fact-regarding, other-regarding and future-regarding"[14] actors. The legislation of most national democracies is strewn with unsuccessful attempts to regulate lobbies and pressure groups. What is distinctive about this approach is the coupling of respect for certain conditions of self-organization and management with quite concrete incentives for support and a competitive process of allocation.

1. *Obligatory Contributions*: No one advocates the creation of a new tax lightly—especially these days in the face of neo-liberal diatribes against fiscal obligations that are supposed to be already too high. But this proposal rests squarely on the need to develop a new method for financing interest intermediation that is independent of the ability and willingness of individual citizens to pay—and that means extracting resources involuntarily from all those who ultimately will benefit. It may be disguised under some innocuous label, for example: "the EU representative contribution", but it would still have to be a coercive levy.[15]

The contribution/tax should be extracted from all persons resident in a given territory, but not from firms or corporations since they would be forced to pay twice and could, therefore, exert more influence over the resultant distribution of revenues (and would, in any case, just pass on the cost to their consumers). Persons who wished could also give voluntarily to various national and European causes, but this would not exempt them from the general "representative contribution". Note that, by tolerating such a freedom, small and compact "privileged groups" would still be more likely to attract and spend disproportionate resources in the European policy process, since their members would continue to have greater incentives to give voluntarily above and beyond their involuntary contribution. Nevertheless, given the large numbers involved across Europe as a whole, a very considerable dispersion of resources across interest categories and passionate causes would be likely.

The most feasible manner for doing this would be to attach the proposed voucher system to the election of Euro-deputies. Even if the amounts involved are quite small, it will not be difficult to generate rather considerable sums. For example, if each Euro-citizen would be required to contribute the equivalent of a modest 10 euros that would raise the tidy sum of 2.81 billion euros in the EU(15) of today. That could fund a lot of associative action and, depending on how citizens "spend" their vouchers, it could go a long way to rectifying existing inequities in organizational resources and systemic under-representation within Euro-institutions. What is important is to retain the low level of individual payments in order not to scare away potential supporters of the reform, but to make the aggregate level of resources provided sufficient to compensate for persistent inequalities between interests. It is also essential to convince the public that such an arrangement would constitute an important extension of democratic rights—analogous to the previous extension of the franchise. This is where the voucher notion comes in.

2. *Choice by Voucher*: What pulls the entire scheme together is the mechanism of vouchers. These specially designated, non-transferable units of account could only be assigned to European-level interest associations with a semi-public status, in proportions chosen by the individual Euro-citizen. Their value would be established by the EP at some uniform level and there would be no way of avoiding paying for them. The only cost involved in spending them would be the individual's time and effort in getting acquainted with alternative recipients, plus the few moments it would take to check off boxes or fill in blanks.

There are many attractive features of vouchers in the domain of specialized representation:

— They would permit a relatively free expression of the multiplicity of each Euro-citizen's preferences—rather than confine them to one party list or a single candidate as do most territorially-based voting systems.

— They allow for an easy resolution of the "intensity problem" that has long plagued democratic theory, since their proportional distribution by individuals across associations should reflect how strongly the citizenry "really" feels about various interests and passions.[16]

— They equalize the amount and sever the decision to contribute from the disparate command over resources that individual citizens unavoidably have in an economic system based on the unequal distribution of private property.

— They offer no rational motive for waste or corruption since they cannot provide a direct or tangible benefit to the donor and can only be spent by certified associations for designated public purposes with the EU.

– In fact, they should provide a very important incentive for reflection on the nature of one's interests, thereby encouraging the opening up of a new public space at the level of Europe as a whole. Since they would be repeated over time, the distribution of these vouchers would present a virtually unique opportunity to evaluate the consequences of one's past choices.
– They would, therefore, become a powerful mechanism for enforcing the accountability of existing Euro-associations and movements since, if the behavior of their leaders differs too remarkably from the preferences of those who spent their vouchers on them, citizens could presumably transfer their vouchers elsewhere.
– They make it relatively easy, not just to switch among existing rival conceptions of one's interest, but also to bring into existence previously latent groups that presently cannot make it over the initial organizational threshold.
– Finally, they offer a means of extending the principle of Euro-citizenship and the competitive core of Euro-democracy[17] that neither makes immediate and strong demands on individuals, nor directly threatens the entrenched position of elites.

Granted that in the initial iterations of the scheme, existing Euro-associations and movements which accepted semi-public status would naturally be at an advantage, although less so than the national ones whose names and symbols are better known and whose members are less likely to defect from the group loyalties they have already acquired. On the one hand, this could be thought of as desirable since it should lead these established Euro-level organizations to support the scheme in the first place. On the other hand, it might initially have the undesirable effect of perpetuating organizations that are no longer representative. Eventually, the logic of competitive appeals for vouchers should have the effect of either reviving moribund groups or displacing them by more authentic rivals.

Semi-Conclusions on Representation

As we have seen, the problem with democratizing the Euro-polity's system of representation is not to create something *ex novo*. Plenty of interests and passions have already found their way to the corridors of Brussels. It is just that they are too skewed in functional terms towards business interests and too confined in territorial terms to groups articulated at the national level.

Ironically, it may prove more difficult to improve this evolving system with its entrenched modes of access than to convince individual Europeans that the emerging Euro-polity can make a positive contribution to extending and guaranteeing their rights as citizens. Nevertheless, the potentiality for mobilizing the interests of other classes, sectors and professions at the supra- and sub-national levels—not to mention for reaching the passions behind so many social movements and environmental causes—exists and, if realized, it could provide a new momentum to the whole integration process. The modest proposals for reform suggested in this essay will definitely not eliminate the favored treatment of national governmental and private business interests (if they did, these proposals would be rejected *sine die*), but they should encourage the opening of new channels of representation and the experimenting with new means for holding authorities accountable. In the absence of a large-scale refounding of the EU, i. e. constitutionalizing, of the entire enterprise, I doubt if one could ask anything more at this stage. And, who knows, once some groups have demonstrated their success in representing "other" responses.[18] Whether this sort of politicization would—on balance—prove to be positive for European integration in the future is a calculated risk, but one which should be taken. Without such an effort at enlarging the sphere of representation and without much further prospect for cultivating functional spill-overs surreptitiously, those who favor such an enterprise could, at best, find themselves defending a stagnant process and, at worse, managing a retreat to the *status quo ante integratio*.

Notes

1   For a more detailed exposition of this generic definition of democracy, see Philippe C. Schmitter and Terry Karl, "What Democracy is … and is not", *Journal of Democracy*, Vol. II, No. 3 (Summer 1991), pp. 75–88.
For an application of this definition to the European Union, see Philippe C. Schmitter, "La démocratie dans l'Europe politique naissante: déficit temporaire ou caractère permanent?" in Mario Telò et Paul Magnette (eds.), *Repenser L'Europe* (Bruxelles: Éditions de l'Université de Bruxelles, 1996), pp. 45–68.

2   My hunch is that, even in an orthodox federation—national or supranational—this may no longer be an adequate view of the process of democratic representation. It ignores the very substantial changes that have already taken place in the nature and role of parties in well-established democracies, and it anachronistically presumes that parties in today's emerging Euro-polity will go through all the developmental stages and perform all the functions of their national predecessors. It seems preferable (to me) to assume that the citizens of contemporary Europe—have quite different organizational skills, are less likely to identify so closely with partisan symbols or ideologies, and are

inclined to defend a much more variegated set of interests. Moreover, the Euro-polity is emerging in an international environment virtually saturated with different models of successful collective action. All this may not preclude a hegemonic role for political parties in the representation of social groups, but it does suggest that they will be facing more competition from interest associations and social movements than their predecessors, and that we should revise our thinking about democratization accordingly.

3   Another way of putting the issue is that, while future European integration will have to give up the presumption of a uniformly expanding *acquis communautaire* for all members in all policy arenas, it should be possible to safeguard a core subset of mutual obligations sufficient to prevent excessive "free-riding" and "predation".

4   Elsewhere, I (with José Torreblanca) have developed the idea of PPR along with a *Colegii* system of decision-making and simulated the results for a series of EUs with up to 35 members: "Old 'Foundations' and New 'Rules' for an Enlarged European Union," Working Paper No. 97/1, Robert Schumann Centre, European University Institute, 1997.

5   According to my understanding, this has long been the practice in the Italian parliament—perhaps, not a model of legislative probity, but a formidable producer of laws. Giuseppe Di Palma, *Surviving without Governing* (Berkeley: University of California Press, 1977).

6   The European Parliament already has a "bureau" composed of its President and 14 vice-presidents, all elected by the plenum.

7   The fact that Euro-deputies are elected according to rather disparate electoral regimes is, no doubt, regrettable from a strictly democratic point of view, but it is not clear whether this has significant consequences for the way in which they "process" the demands of their constituents. For a comprehensive discussion of the different regimes, see Julián Santamaría, Josep María Reniú and Vicente Cobos, "Los debates sobre el procedimiento electoral uniforme y las caraterísticas diferenciales de las elecciones europeas", *Revista de Estudios Políticos*, No. 90 (Oct–Dec. 1995), pp. 11–44.

8   *Flexible Integration. Towards a More Effective and Democratic Europe* (London: CEPR, 1995), pp. 172.

9   The best and most up-to-date treatment I have read on this subject is Frank L. Wilson, "The Elusive European Party System", paper presented to the ECSA Meeting, Charleston, SC, 11–14 May 1995. For an earlier analysis, see Karl-Heinz Reif and Oskar Niedermayer, "The European Parliament and the Political Parties", *Journal of European Integration*, Vol. 10, Nos. 2&3 (1987), pp. 157–172.

10   Actually, the possible impact on sub-national groups would be much more mitigated and indirect—unless, of course, more substantial changes were to be introduced by creating regional or even municipal constituencies and nomination procedures.

11   *The Semi-Sovereign People* (Hinsdale, Ill.: Dryden Press, 1975), originally published in 1960.

12   Wolfgang Streeck and Philippe C. Schmitter, "From National Corporatism to Transnational Pluralism: Organized Interests in the Single European Market", *Politics & Society*, Vol. 19, No. 2 (June 1991), pp. 133–164; also Franz Traxler and Philippe C. Schmitter), "The Emerging Euro-Polity and Organized Interests," *European Journal of International Relations*, Vol. 1, No. 2 (June 1995), pp. 191–218.

13   "Interests, Associations and Intermediation in a Reformed Post-Liberal Democracy", *Politische Vierteljahresschrift*, 35. Jg., Sonderheft 25, "Staat und Verbände", 1994, pp. 160–174.

14   For this "trilogy" of types of regardingness, I am indebted to Claus Offe.

15   The tax would be novel, but the amounts of revenue transferred to interest associations might not be. Since first presenting this idea in Norway several years ago, I have become increasingly aware of the very substantial sums that some continental European governments provide as subsidies to specific organizations—ostensibly because they are accomplishing some public purpose. Norway, Spain and France are three cases in point, even if the amounts involved are rarely publicized.

    At the level of the EU, no one knows for sure how much funding is devoted to the purpose of supporting Euro-associations, although they have been so substantial that the EP has periodically demanded an investigation of them. This subsidization of civil society by bureaucratic means is much less democratic than the one that I propose since the criteria used to determine eligibility are secret and non-competitive; whereas, under a voucher-based scheme, this would all take place publicly and accountably—and would be accompanied by specific binding obligations to behave as "secondary citizens". If the countries (and the European Union) that are presently subsidizing associations by clandestine means would agree to stop these practices, they might be able to switch to a better arrangement at virtually no cost!

16   And not incidently they would generate a fabulous new source of data on preferences for social scientists to analyze—much cheaper and much better in quality than what they have been collecting *via* survey research.

17   Cf. my earlier essay, "Democratic Theory and Neo-Corporatist Practice", *Social Research*, Vol. 50, No. 4 (Winter 1983), pp. 885–928. where the role of competitiveness is evaluated along with such other normative standards for democracy as participation, access, responsiveness and accountability.

18   There are already some signs of this, especially coming from the pressure of environmental movements. The EP has recently rejected several directives coming from the Commission. For a case study of one such "footnote", see David Earnshaw and David Judge, "The European Parliament and the Sweeteners Directive: From Footnote to Inter-Institutional Conflict", *Journal of Common Market Studies*, Vol. 31, No. 1 (March 1993), pp. 103–116.

8 The Role of the Associations in a European Constitution

JUSTIN GREENWOOD

The Role of Associations in the European Union

Whilst the precise number of European level interest groups and fora is disputed, no one doubts the overwhelming predominance (75%?) of producer interests amongst them. This is unsurprising, given the history of the EU as an economic community. Business interests, in particular, have long been cast as central players in institutionalist based accounts of European integration, where the relationship between business interests and European institutions interested in deepening integration, and actions by organised business in shaping the preferences of member states, identified them as dynamic agents of integration. Some of the high points of European integration, such as the drive to create a single European market, have been attributed to actions by (large) business interests such as the European Round Table of Industrialists (Cowles, 1995). The contribution by business interests to market integration in a range of sectors is now widely recognised (see, for instance, the plethora of case studies and analysis presented in Greenwood, Grote and Ronit, 1992; Mazey and Richardson, 1993; van Schendelen, 1993; Pedler and van Schendelen, 1994; Stern, 1994; Greenwood, 1995; Greenwood, 1997; Wallace and Young, 1997; Aspinwall and Greenwood, 1997). This role sometimes extends someway beyond simple "lobbying" or "influence" into more advanced forms of interest intermediation, where private interests have crossed the boundary between public and private and become a routinised part of the machinery of European governance itself. Whilst the impact of interests other than those representing business has been somewhat less dramatic, commentators have noted the steadily increasing efficacy of trade unions (Leisink, van Leemput and Vilrokx, 1996) and of public interests (Harvey, 1995; Wallace and Young, 1997) acting on the European policy arena. Even collective action issues within European associations may be relatively unproblematic because the vast majority of associations are confederal by design, with member organisations already politically active (Greenwood and Aspinwall, 1997). Even where interests (such as firms) may affiliate direct to Euro groups, the pressure placed by European institutions on dialogue with single encompassing associations, the "insurance policy" nature of membership, the need for formal or informal types of information, or the need to use associations as one of a number of public affairs strategies, seems to push the logic in favour of associability to Euro groups. "Weak Euro groups" (Grant, 1990) are no longer the rule (Greenwood, Stancich and Strangward, 1998), and in the late 1990s European level interest representation has reached a level of maturity, with a critical mass of often effective associations existing alongside a diverse range of structures and channels of representation for interests which enable and enhance their participation in the European policy arena.

The Role of Associations in European Industrial Relations

The contribution of private and public interests to European integration in low politics is by now well recognised by most scholars of the integration process, irrespective of the perspective (principally divided between traditions informed by a neo realist, or institutionalist, theoretical base) from which they write. There is less certainty about the contribution of interests to high politics. By definition, high politics are heavily politicised issues which have entered the wider public arena of debate, and to which a multiplicity of players has access. In these settings, interests are just one of a number of players and are unable to command monopolistic access to issues which are so typical of "low" politics settings, where governance often arises from relatively closed policy communities. European industrial relations are very definitely "high" politics, and have increasingly been so since President Delors set out to extend the benefits of project Europe beyond the single market. Associations of private interests are thus one voice among many, and can never be the dominant players in a system of European industrial relations.

A developed basis for European citizenship would require a constitution for Europe, embodying political and social as well as economic values. Whilst the rhetoric of citizenship is there at the highest level,[1] the substance is not. The European Union is *sui genesis,* without state like properties. In a social constitution of a territorial sovereignty, personal security and freedom might be at the top of a pyramid of constitutional rights, closely followed by freedom of association, the right to strike (and the right to lock out) and some protection of collective labour law (Fitzpatrick, 1997). Most of these are excluded from the Treaty, reinforcing the architecture of the EU where economic rights are the top layers of constitutional rights. The EU remains primarily an economic union, a polity which has responded aggressively to the threat and opportunities of globalisation, in which the mass restructuring necessary to boost Europe's competitiveness on the world stage requires only a secondary level of social participation through mechanisms such as the social dialogue. Following the classic definition of social policy as redistributive and market correcting, it is by nature unlikely to be successful in a political project in which business is the main force (Walby, 1997). Whilst there are some directives—such as those concerned with equal treatment, and parental leave—which are not solely based upon the economic criteria of market integration, they are relatively few in number. Whilst representation and collective defence of the interests of workers, including co-determination, is included within the Treaty of Amsterdam, it is only governed by unanimity rules. Whilst the Community Charter of fundamental social rights is there, it is not binding, is riven with subsidiarity, and leaves the most contentious areas of social policy firmly in the hands of member states (Fitzpatrick, 1997).

European social policy has been used by writers to illustrate the potency of intergovernmental forces in the integration process. Writers in this tradition argue that member states remain in control of social policy, and have prevented the EU from developing significant social rights. Even where some level of agreement is possible on economic issues, disagreement between member states on social issues continues to prevent the development of enabling European legislation. The latest example of this concerns the 20 year long deadlock for a European Company Statute to provide a legal basis for pan European companies, which, despite the best efforts of the 1998 Austrian Presidency, continues to be stalled on the issue of the rights to be accorded to workers in such legal entities (European Voice, 1998a). Certainly, a full-blown concept of European citizenship would require member states to relinquish some national values, and there is no sign of this. It is possible that the Social Charter may well be used to protect national rights from intrusion by the EU's higher level economic rights (Fitzpatrick, 1997). Both the Commission and the Court of Justice are now much less likely to advance challenging interpretations of Community law than in previous decades. The Social Dialogue, in its present minimalist usage, may even be a threat to social standards in the highest standard member states (Fitzpatrick, 1997). The ETUC[2] has become socialised with EU values and agenda priorities such that its work does not make it a bastion standard bearer for European social rights; witness its present adherence to the monetarist convergence criteria of EMU. EU macroeconomic policy represents a strange mixture of economic monetarism, with Keynesian social rhetoric a secondary force. Pay bargaining is explicitly excluded from European social policy. These are difficult circumstances for producer associations to play a leading role in the creation of a European social constitution, or indeed in establishing a European system of industrial relations.

The obstacles to European collective bargaining include: the exclusion of pay bargaining; the failure of an effective European labour market to develop; the diversity of member state industrial relations systems; and the continued vitality of national systems, and the investment made in them by employers and unions at the national level (Threlfall, 1997). Yet there are those, most notably within ETUC, who see the social dialogue, in particular, as embryonic collective bargaining, whilst some analysts also share the optimism about the general significance of the process (Falkner, 1997a and b; Obradovic, 1997). Certainly, national unions are no longer opposed to ETUC playing a major role in advancing the collective rights of European workers, and EU collective bargaining is now widely seen within the European trade union movement as a necessity (Rhodes, 1995). Despite this conversion process among labour interests, the social dialogue, whilst providing for an institutionalised role for the social partners in European public policy making, cannot develop into a system of European collective bargaining without the support of employers. At the core of economic restructuring in Europe has been market principles involving deregulation, enabling capital to compete in the global market place through strategies such as exercising more control over labour market costs, and it is difficult to identify how business interests would benefit from unpicking these advantages.

At the time of writing, the social dialogue stands at a crossroads. The most significant part of the social dialogue is undoubtedly the social protocol, first appended as an annex to the Treaty on European Union (TEU), in which UNICE,[3] CEEP,[4] and ETUC (only) are accorded constitutional legislative status in European policy making. Whilst some commentators (Falkner, 1997 a and b; Obradovic, 1997) have attached considerable significance to this specific mechanism as a possible form of nascent corporatism, its future is at best uncertain. Firstly, UEAPME,[5] the intersectoral European association representing small businesses, has issued a series of legal challenges to the entire basis of the social protocol in response to its exclusion from it. Whilst it has now (November 1998) withdrawn these following discussions with UNICE in which the two parties have agreed to try to identify a more significant role for UEAPME than hitherto, the events are illustrative of broader tensions within the Dialogue. UEAPME's actions took the form of referring both of the agreements so far concluded (to the status of European Directives) between UNICE, CEEP and ETUC, on Parental Leave, and Part Time Work, to the Court of First Instance (CFI) for annulment. Whilst the Court of Justice did not uphold the first of these challenges in its ruling on the Parental Leave Directive in June 1998 (T-135/96), the issues remained far from settled. Firstly, the ruling of CFI was made subject to appeal to the European Court of Justice, and informed legal opinion suggested at the time that there were good reasons for UEAPME to be hopeful about the outcome of its appeal. The Commission's basis for recognising only CEEP, ETUC and UNICE has no status in law, and the document in which the recognition is provided, COM 600/93, is only an opinion document (about the degree of representativity of the social partners) with only the status of "soft law". The Commission's ability to make rulings on matters of representativity is not included in the Treaties. Secondly, in the event that UNICE and UEAPME are unable to reach a lasting understanding, UEAPME still has the option of pursuing the challenge to the Part Time Workers Directive in the Court of First Instance. For its part, UNICE remains irritated by UEAPME's actions to date, which it sees as evidence that UEAPME may be unwilling to co-operate as part of a wider business platform in the legislative section of the Social Dialogue (European Industrial Relations Review—EIRR, October 1998). For a long time UNICE simply ignored UEAPME's claims to inclusion, on the grounds that UNICE also represented a significant small business constituency. Whilst a change in leadership to UNICE seems to have removed part of the stumbling block to a rapprochement between the two parties, it remains to be seen whether the two organisations can work together, in that the basis of UEAPME's participation, via the back door of UNICE, does not appear to be the basis for long term stability.

A second reason to question the significance of the social protocol is its record of achievement to date. In six years, only two agreements have been concluded using this mechanism. Even ETUC, the most enthusiastic participant in the social dialogue, concedes that "the list of achievements remains meagre" (Gabaglio, 1998). On four further occasions, UNICE has refused to use the protocol mechanism (European Voice, 1998b). The most recent of these concerned the proposal for an agreement on the negotiation and consultation of workers at the national level. The antecedents to this latter case are numerous, but reflect a central mechanism in the development of European social integration—the confluence of interests of the Commission (in expanding the frontiers of integration) with those of ETUC (in seeking to enhance the interests of its worker constituency). One antecedent to the national consultation measure concerns the European Works Council Directive (the first of the four cases in which UNICE refused to negotiate under the social protocol) aimed at creating formal systems for dialogue with employees over issues likely to significantly affect their interests, in large European companies (with over 1,000 employees, and a base in at least two member states). The proposal for information and consultation at national level sought to extend the principles of this to smaller firms (in one early draft, with as few as 20 employees) based in just one member state. The measure was given particular prominence by the decision by Renault in 1997 to close a profitable plant in Belgium with the loss of significant employment, announced unilaterally with apparently no worker consultation and to take effect at very short notice. The incident quickly became a matter of "high politics", attracting criticism at the highest level from politicians (including the condemnation of President Santer), workers and the general public, and was used by the Commission and ETUC as a symbol of the need for further, and strengthened, legislation to govern the behaviour of firms to regulate the economic and social consequences of their decisions.

The Commission/ETUC intervention was designed to put pressure on UNICE to negotiate an agreement. Whilst UNICE announced its decision in March 1998 to refuse to do so, the pressure regime sought to maintain the issue with the status of high politics. In response to UNICE's refusal, the Commission called what it termed a "crisis mini summit" of the social dialogue, playing high stakes by using the rhetoric of the need to consider the very future of the dialogue. Commission Flynn's spokesperson told *European Voice*

> We are hoping this summit will save the social dialogue. For their own sakes the employers need to show they are committed to the process. (European Voice, 1998b)

The mini summit, in the event, did not resolve the crisis. The new General Secretary of UNICE, Dirk Hudig, came out of the summit and commented that "there is an underlying tension, with one side wanting to draw everything to the European level with collective bargaining at the European level. But that is not the way things are going ... you have to go down to the national level and solve things there" (European Voice, 4–10 June 1998). In effect, UNICE were challenging the Commission to issue legislation on the subject in the belief that it would not attract sufficient support in the Council of Ministers. There followed a game of bluff and counter bluff. The Commission responded to the challenge by drafting a proposal and leaking it to UNICE. UNICE were requested to think again, and given an extension under the rules of the social protocol to do so. This UNICE did, but only to reaffirm (in October 1998) its original decision not to negotiate, arguing that the measure, aimed at national companies, was not properly a matter for European legislation. In fact, the strength of the opposition within UNICE is highlighted by two factors. The first is that the vote was taken by secret ballot, while the second is that six countries—double the number required for a blocking minority under UNICE's rules, and two more than when the issue was first considered by UNICE in March—voted against negotiating. This confirms the long held suspicion that there are many more business associations than simply a laggard minority (most prominently including the UK Confederation of British Industry) who remain opposed to significant social legislation, and that these associations have for some time conveniently used UK opposition to mask their own unease. The "two level game" of apparent support for social legislation as long as an apparently small number of national associations could be relied upon to block it, was therefore exposed. The Commission has now issued a proposal for a Directive in response to UNICE's "non", and whether it will attract sufficient support in the Council of Ministers remains to be seen, but in the meantime at least the lines are somewhat clearer. The Commission wants further social integration, and the employers do not. Other proposals it has placed on the agenda of the social protocol, for agreements on various aspects of working time, may well follow the same pattern.

In 1998, UNICE appointed a new General Secretary and elected a new President. The commitment of General Secretary Hudig to the Anglo-American model of capitalism, where there is little tradition of social dialogue, is well noted, whereas the new President, George Jacobs, is known to take a somewhat more enthusiastic view of the social dialogue. Certainly, the key to the social dialogue remains the perspective of the employers. UNICE surprised many in October 1991 when it drafted, along with CEEP and ETUC, the social protocol annexed to the TEU, following years of refusal to enter into a meaningful dialogue which might develop into collective bargaining. But rather than signalling a change of attitude of

UNICE, it simply reflected political realities at the time. The intergovernmental conference leading up to the TEU signalled certain extensions to QMV in social policy, and in the UK the election of a Labour government committed to being at the heart of social Europe seemed a certainty. UNICE's members simply took the view that an extension of the social agenda was inevitable, and they would be better off placing themselves in a position to be able to exert some influence over it. At least the social protocol represented a way for UNICE to by pass the Parliament, and perhaps to delay the introduction of legislation by at least 9 months. Certainly, this remains the viewpoint of one interested observer. ETUC Secretary General Emilio Gabaglio reflected recently that

> UNICE has never made any secret ... that its acceptance of the agreement on European negotiations owed more to its desire to seek ways to slow down the purported excess of social regulation by the European legislator than to a positive vision of the role of collective negotiations and their necessary extension to the European level. (Gabaglio, 1998)

In the recent case of information and consultation at the national level, UNICE, by using the procedures to the full and in achieving a time extension to them, has been able to at least delay legislation even further. Looking beyond the recent past, the signs are not more hopeful. The present negotiations on the regulation of fixed term contracts seem beset by protracted difficulties between the partners, and the next round, on the organisation of work, has already begun by the employers stating their reluctance to even debate the issues (EIRR, December 1988). The age-old problem of reconciling labour interests in security with employer needs for flexibility and control over labour costs remains a lasting tension for even the most established social dialogue traditions. Whilst ETUC has ceded much to keep the European level social dialogue going, UNICE continues to cede little, and ETUC has signed agreements on worker flexibility that seem to challenge the core concerns of its members.

Whilst there is much low level agreement and examples of collaboration between the partners on relatively uncontentious issues such as training, youth unemployment and opportunities for people with disabilities, and clear evidence (from interviewing the main protagonists) of social learning between them as a result of their interactions, there must be a limit to how long the social partnership can be interpreted as more significant European collective bargaining in the making. The social dialogue as a whole has a considerable history. At the sectoral level, it dates from agreements in agriculture concluded in 1963, with little else of note being achieved until a further agreement, again in the agricultural sector, was reached in 1997. There are certainly some signs of achievements in the sectoral social dialogue, and in anticipation of this the Social Dialogue has recently (May, 1998) been restructured with the creation of "Social Dialogue Committees", although whether this will amount to any more than a change of nomenclature and bureaucratic organisation remains to be seen. Some recent agreements have been concluded (or are nascent) such as those in the transport (most notably, maritime and rail transport), cleaning, clothing/ textile and metalworkers sectors, while the term "virtual collective bargaining" has now been coined to include the range of framework discussions and joint opinions under consideration by sectoral social partners (Marginson and Sisson, 1998). Nonetheless, the actual agreements cited above are only a handful of approximately 30 sectors which have developed dialogue at Community level with joint committees or informal working parties, and the majority of these have produced nothing more substantial than joint opinions or the exchange of divergent opinions. Where employers have participated, they have tended to do so somewhat unenthusiastically, participating largely as a result of the pressure placed upon them by the Commission. In any event, whilst there are (only) seventeen European sectoral trade unions ("industry federations"), these often lack sectoral business counterparts willing to act, or capable of acting, on employment related issues.

At the intersectoral level, the social dialogue dates from the 1970s, moving up a gear in 1985 following a determined push by Jacques Delors. Whilst reforms to the three first level partners (ETUC, 1991; UNICE, 1992; CEEP, 1994) have made them better able to conclude agreements under the social protocol by removing requirements for unanimity, none of these organisations enjoy a general bargaining mandate, but rather must seek the agreement of their members afresh each time in order to enter negotiations, i.e. on an issue by issue basis. Whilst these are not surprising rules of engagement for business and employers associations to enter into any substantive negotiations, both UNICE and CEEP remain on extremely tight reins from their members. For instance, the statutes of CEEP insist that its General Assembly, normally a tier of any organogram reserved principally for rubber stamping policy positions agreed at lower levels in the organisation, and for policy presentation and member relations, to be kept informed throughout negotiations.

Institutional self interest makes the three social partners have a greater stake in the social dialogue than their members. The Social Protocol has to some extent rescued each of them at a key turning point in their history by institutionalising their role in European public affairs. This has been a source of strength for ETUC and CEEP, who might otherwise have been marginal actors in European public affairs. CEEP, for its part, is enjoying something of a renaissance, with significant new membership, and the organisation exudes optimism about the future of the dialogue and warmth for its relationship with the other partners. The future of both CEEP and ETUC has become inextricably linked with the progress of the social dialogue. For UNICE, the social dialogue has undoubtedly strengthened its positions vis other, potentially competing organisations such as the ERT, but at the cost of increasing control over it by its members. Whilst there are signs that a small number of UNICE's members (mainly from those countries with a tradition of social dialogue, such as Belgium and the Netherlands) are not unhappy with business participation in social Europe, the majority have deliberately taken measures in the design of its organisational structure to prevent the organisation and its permanent delegates from "going native" (Ebbinghaus and Visser, 1996; Gorges, 1996). Certainly, the secretariat of UNICE appear to have more interest in, and enthusiasm about, the social dialogue than do its members. Ironically, however, it is ETUC's historic lack of strength that may have prevented employers from investing in strong European employers" organisation. In any event, the sheer diversity of UNICE, whose membership spans organisations with product market interests as well as labour market (either separately or in combination), makes it difficult to reach agreement of any sort, let alone meaningful agreement, on common positions. For employers federations, it is far easier to get agreement to say no to a legislative proposal than it is to find ground for even a qualified "yes".

ETUC has most to gain from the social dialogue, and it has been successful in socialising their members in support of it. Its recent unity is borne of its natural advantage of homogeneity over business in representing labour market interests, rather than the combination task faced by business in representing product market interests. One of its central aims is to develop the social dialogue into a coherent pattern of industrial relations, and the entire nature of ETUC's work has shifted so that the social dialogue has become one of its major priorities (Abbott, 1997). Its enthusiasm to develop the dialogue has led it to adopt positions which may be questionable for a representative of labour interests to adopt, and one which may eventually become a source of tension with its members again. Whilst the hope is that monetary union may lead to convergent collective bargaining through transparency and the need to involve unions in wage restraint deals, there is very limited evidence of European collective bargaining emerging at present,[6] and the convergence criteria for EMU is resolutely monetarist and may be a source of job losses for its members. In macroeconomic policy, ETUC has signed relatively "expensive" joint opinions with UNICE under the social dialogue, such as one where the two parties agreed on a "Renewed Co-operative Growth Strategy for More Employment" where the main strategy was to cut government spending and keep wage settlements low; in return, employers only "gave" exempting capital spend from the curbs, and more investment in training and in research and development (Compston, 1992)—all "concessions" well within the interests of business to have.

ETUC's principle hopes of developing the social dialogue into a system of European level collective bargaining seem to lie in four directions. The first of these is in an enhanced role for the social partners in macro-economic policy, reviewed below. The second is the ever hopeful change for political forces as a result of member state elections, such the recent changes in government in Germany, Italy and in the UK, and whilst these have certainly resulted in changes they will not be sufficient to match the aspirations of ETUC; the UK, for instance, remains opposed to a proposed Directive on Information and Consultation at the national level. The third hope lies with the Commission, and in particular DG V, seen by one commentator as a "union lobbying organisation, old style" (Ross, 1994, p. 507). The entire interest configuration of DGV is the expansion of social integration. Certainly, the key personnel in the section of DGV responsible for the dialogue come from those countries with the most established tradition of social partnership, although the personal interconnections with the trade union movement are not quite as strong as in the Delors days. President Delors is quoted as saying that "I want to make sure that the trade unions are written into Europe's social and economic decision making" (Tongue, 1989, cited in Compston, 1992). Support for the dialogue continues to exist at the highest level; President Santer and Commission Flynn (who both see the social dialogue as strategically important for the development of EU social policy) took the initiative to jointly convene the recent crisis mini summit on the social dialogue. The Commission, as an actor whose interests lie in the further development of European level competencies, continues to be the most proactive force in the development of the social dialogue, to the point of UNICE and other business associations complaining about being "pressurised" by it. ETUC's principal "whip" at the negotiating table is that it will ask the Commission to bring forward legislation if business refuses to reach an accord, and recent examples (information and consultation at the national level; extension of working time in road sector) suggests that the Commission will usually oblige. Certainly, the Commission is a classic political entrepreneur in the social dialogue (Falkner, 1997b), acting as initiator, policy broker, and progress chaser, as well as providing the administrative infrastructure support. Once the Commission strays outside its own initiative areas, however, it is likely to be drawn into institutional conflicts, particularly with the Council, and there is every sign that it is increasingly less willing or able to do this. The Social Dialogue therefore represents a key strategy for the Commission, and DGV in particular, to seek to expand social integration, because the social protocol puts the responsibility firmly on the shoulders of the social partners to present legislative measures to the Council. The Commission is therefore constantly on the look out for ways of involving the social partners in a wider range of its policies, such as the free movement of workers, and the equal treatment of men and women. Parallel to this, it has also sought to develop a "civic dialogue" with the representatives of social (non labour market) interests, such as voluntary organisations and civic campaign groups, although these have also met with limited success.

The fourth hope for the development of the social dialogue lies with its linkages with the Employment agenda for Europe. Since the Essen European Council, this issue has steadily progressed, through its linkages with EU democratic legitimacy and of a "Citizen's Europe", to President Santer's 1996 "Confidence Pact for Employment" (where a role for the social partners was specifically identified), the Essen follow up reports (in which the social partners were given a surveillance role) with annual national employment a dedicated chapter in the Treaty of Amsterdam, the Luxembourg Council of November 1997 with its jobs targets, through to recent Presidencies (the UK, for instance, made employment and labour market policy the top agenda item for their Presidency of the Council during the first half of 1998). Indeed, as Commission Flynn remarked in June 1998, Employment has now become the very top issue on the European policy agenda, with all policies required to contribute to Europe's employment strategy. "Employment" and a "Citizen's Europe" have gone far beyond "cheap talk" into a momentum of their own, and it is possible that these issues may carry the social dialogue along with them in a more significant direction in the future. Certainly, this is the hope of Commissioner Flynn, who recently commented that "employment is at the heart of social policy because it is a Europe at work that will enable us to sustain and develop the core values of the European social model ...". (Scotland Europa, May 1998, p. 49). Employment creation, and changing forms of work organisation, can hardly proceed without some level of involvement by the social partners, and in recognition of this some recent changes to the social dialogue structures have been introduced. These include a political meeting between the macro (CEEP, ETUC, UNICE) social partners and the "Troika" of heads of state and government or with the Council under the Presidency, and a formal recognition of the partners" role in meeting employment targets identified by the Luxembourg summit, but the real significance of these mechanisms in delivering hard results is likely to be somewhat questionable. However, it is undoubtedly the case that the key to growth and employment lies in a conducive macro economic environment, and here there are signs that an enhanced, renewed role for the social partners is being sought in a field which is less likely to draw objections from employers. EMU is seen as the key driver to such an enhanced role.

The Role of Associations in European Union Macro-economic Policy

The macro-economic social dialogue is riddled with as many uncertainties as the employment based "social" dialogue for its participants. Formal social partner input to macroeconomic policy has historically been channelled through the Economic and Social Committee; the Standing Committee on Employment (for dialogue between the Council, Commission, employers and unions, although economic and finance ministers are largely absent from Council representatives); and the Social Dialogue itself, through the Macro-economic Group.[7] All of these structures have advisory powers only. The Macro-economic Group, like the wider social dialogue itself, also has a stop start history, with the most recent Group dating from 1992 after a period of dormancy. Even more than in the case of the employment based dialogue, much of the impetus comes from the Commission, a responsibility shared in this case between DG II and DGV. One senior ETUC official told me that

> The real economic agenda is pushed by the Commission ... we go along with them ... we've helped, but the key players have been the Commission.

Whilst there is little tangible to have come from the macro-economic dialogue to date, there is also an expectation that it might grow into something more significant. After several unsuccessful years of trying, the social partners had their first formal meeting with the Chair of the ECOFIN Council in May 1998, the key macro-economic decision making structure, and (somewhat predictably) is scheduled to be repeated under the Austrian Presidency. Whilst nothing of substance emerged from the May 1998 lunch meeting, the partners are hopeful that there will be further opportunities to develop the dialogue with ECOFIN, and recognise that any meaningful role in macroeconomic policy for them cannot succeed without a structured interface with ECOFIN. Similar hopes are also invested in the European Central Bank, where there have been informal contacts initiated by ETUC, and with the EURO 11 Council, which has already commenced a low-level dialogue with the social partners. There are also specific hopes about the Macroeconomic Group of the Social Dialogue. Whilst business has a wide range of access points to macroeconomic policy making, the social dialogue structures have been almost the main opportunity for ETUC to make input outside of informal contacts. The same ETUC official quoted above told me that

> It is not a major driving force. But we need this body to help us build something ... we're not quite sure where we'll talk ourselves to, but we have to have a forum.

This view was echoed by an official from CEEP, who reflected that "it may be the beginning of a process, but we don't know how it will be developed ..." A Commission official from DGV confirmed something similar, when he told this author that

> We don't see a change over the next two years in the degree of involvement of the social partners in macro-economic affairs. I'm not optimistic in the short term, but in the longer term EMU will be the big driver.

ETUC places particular emphasis upon EMU as its gateway to a role in macro-economic policy making, and has done so by seeking to exploit the Commission's interests in European monetary union. It has argued that, in the run up to EMU, the strict monetarist criteria would require trade union participation to ensure that wage settlements do not threaten the key convergence criteria of inflation. Their view is that, in particular, the need for inflation to be no more than 1.5% above the average of the three lowest inflation member states would ensure that wage rises were co-ordinated with those in the lowest inflation countries. In this version of events, EMU would thus give unions the bargaining power they need because of their ability to block its successful implementation unless their demands were satisfied. A second pressure expected by ETUC would arise with the introduction of the EURO, in that prices, wages and collective bargaining would become transparent across the EURO area, making apparent the need for cross border collective bargaining. Wage bargaining policy would need to be co-ordinated with economic policy, leading for a more important role in EU decision making for ETUC, including with ECOFIN and the European Central Bank. In short, EMU, in the view of ETUC, would necessitate the introduction of some form of European wage bargaining (Compston, 1992). The reality is, however, that this scenario did not arise in the run up to the qualifying date for the convergence criteria for a number of reasons, including high unemployment and trends to casualisation of work, and diversity of union interests as national economies compete for inward investment. Some accounts do indicate changes in some national wage policies and enhanced cross national co-ordination (most notably, in the German satellite countries and in Belgium) as a result of monetary union, but the evidence as a whole is at best patchy or of unclear significance to date (European Industrial Relations Observatory, 1998; EIRR, October 1988; Traxler, this volume; Visser, this volume), and, prior to the commencement of monetary union, still remains in the realm of futurology (Marginson and Sisson, 1998). Equally, monetary union may have been a factor in the enhanced national and cross border co-operation of trade unions, but it has not been an independent variable, and alliances tend to have arisen more from difficulties in the operating environment of trade unions (Visser, this volume). Evidence for changes in the role of social partners in national policy making contexts is even more dubious. Where tripartite relations existed, so these have tended to incorporate the convergence criteria, but Ireland is the only case where new structures of social dialogue have arisen as a result of the convergence criteria. There may even be some limited evidence for dismantling of institutional structures based around the social partners, in response to major economic restructuring (Crouch, this volume; Martin, 1998). In any event too much cross national trade union unity would be required for phased upward wage convergence, particularly in a context where there is already considerable differences within the European trade union movement in language, ideology, political (and even religious) affiliation, regional identity, and sector. The incompatibilities of national industrial relations systems make it unlikely that unions could ever unite behind a common European strategy for collective bargaining. Business interests will continue to rely on national governments to prevent a European system of industrial relations, and in any event it would be difficult to imagine EU level wage claims being successfully imposed on employers at the national level. Once the EURO is introduced and exchange rates are irreversibly locked, wage rises in one country which are much greater than those elsewhere would simply result in a loss of competitiveness and jobs (Compston, 1992).

It is one thing for there to be contact between the social partners, and with outlets such as ECOFIN, the European Central Bank (ECB) and the EURO 11 Council, and quite another for the partners to share with them any sort of role in economic policy making. The ECB is dedicated to the control of inflation above all other economic factors, and it has no remit whatsoever to balance employment needs with this. Like most central banks, it is by design relatively insulated from sectional interest representation. The key potential role for social partnership is clear in the present context of EU macroeconomic policy making. Partnership is intended as a buffer to mass unemployment in the context of monetary union and its monetarist foundations. Yet the infrastructure to do this simply does not exist at the European level. Wage bargaining and control is specifically excluded from the Treaties, whilst prices control supersedes that of employment criteria. There is no sign of wage co-ordination between employers in response to EMU. As Traxler argues in this volume, some limited cross border wage co-ordination is possible in a European environment, and there is certainly evidence of attempts by trade unions to co-ordinate in response to EMU, but there is no possibility of fully fledged collective bargaining at the European level itself.

Once again, much seems to depend on the relationship between the Commission, with its interests in expanding the scope and depth of European integration, and ETUC. However, ETUC's over reliance upon this relationship is a source of weakness. Whilst Community economic guidelines are subject to qualified majority voting rules, the Council still retains unanimity on major economic and monetary policy making issues. The European Council, and ECOFIN in particular, remain largely dominated by a neo liberal outlook; indeed, the entire "project Europe" post 1985 has depended upon preference convergence amongst member states for market solutions as the principle behind economic restructuring. There is a limit to the amount a Commission still largely on the retreat can only be expected to deliver. In the circumstances of prevailing neo liberalism, the predominance of monetarism in European economic policies and the primacy of inflation control, and the high politics nature of employment and macro-economic policy and of the institutions surrounding these, associational roles will always be somewhat limited. Associations will continue to contribute vigorously to the "low politics" of European integration, but only in a somewhat limited sense to such high politics domains as are covered by the scope of the social dialogue. Beyond this, the key obstacles are: enduring national interests and a strong Council; the architecture of unanimity in high politics domains; the primacy of economic interests in a European constitution; the lack of substance of European citizenship, and the significant exclusions of elements of it from the competence of the EU, and of wage bargaining; irresolvable conflicts of interest between the key actors; and limitations in the associational capacities of organisations with such vast functional responsibilities. In the light of these difficulties, the main hope of ETUC and CEEP in the strength of the present "Employment Agenda" may in reality offer little prospect for advancement. Whilst the "optimists" keep predicting something significant just around the corner (and have done so since the relaunch of the dialogue in 1985 and again following the TEU and the social protocol annexe in 1992), there is a limit to the length of time such forecasts can be credible. Social partnership at the EU level is neither embryonic corporatism nor the start of a European wide system of wage bargaining, because the means for these to happen, through associations or otherwise, simply does not exist.

Notes

1   President Santer has called for the EU to give itself a "social identity" amounting to "more than just the social counterpart of the developing market" and calling for a "veritable social pact". See Threlfall (1997).
2   European Trade Union Confederation.
3   Union of Industrial and Employers Confederations of Europe.
4   European Centre of Public Enterprises.
5   European Association of Craft, Small and Medium Sized Enterprises.
6   A recent exception was Belgium, where the government took the decision to put forward a wage increase based on the average of wage increases in immediately surrounding countries.
7   A further structure, tripartite conferences between unions, employers and the Council, ended in 1978.

References

Abbott, K (1997), "The European Trade Union Confederation: Its Organization and Objectives in Transition", *Journal of Common Market Studies*, 35 (3), September, 465–81.

Compston, H (1992), "Trade Union Participation in EC Economic Policy Making", *Strathclyde Papers on Government and Politics*, 90. Glasgow: University of Strathclyde.

Cowles, M G (1995), "The European Round Table of Industrialists: The Strategic Player in European Affairs", in J Greenwood, ed., *European Casebook on Business Alliances*, Hemel Hempstead: Prentice Hall, 225–36.

Ebbinghaus, B and J Visser (1996), "European Labour and Transnational Solidarity: Challenges, Pathways and Barriers", in Klausen, J and L Tilly, eds. (1997), *European Integration in Social and Historical Perspective*, Lanham, MD: Rowman & Littlefield, 195–222.

European Industrial Relations Observatory (1998), EIRO 1997 Annual Review, www.eiro.eurofound.ie/1997/review/index.html.

European Industrial Relations Review (EIRR) (October 1998), *Unions agree common strategy*, EIRR 297: 1, 21–2.

European Industrial Relations Review (EIRR) (December 1998), *The social dialogue—the social partners" view*, EIRR 299: 18–21.

European Voice (1998a), *"Social dialogue in jeopardy"*, 4 (11): 1.

European Voice (1998b), *"Crisis talks fail to reconcile social partners"*, 4 (22): 2.

European Voice (1998c), *"Company statute plan still blocked"*, 4 (42): 4.

Falkner, G (1997a), *"Corporatist Governance and Europeanisation: No Future in the Multi-level Game?"* European Integration online Papers (EIoP), 1 011; http://eiop.or.at/eiop/texte/1997-011a.htm.

Falkner, G (1997b), *"Multi-level plus multi-actor: Co-operative governance in the European Union"*, paper prepared for presentation to the Fifth Biennial International Conference of the European Community Studies Association, Seattle, Washington, May 29–June 1 1997.

Fitzpatrick, B (1997), *"Inverted Pyramids and the EU Social Constitution"*, paper prepared for presentation to the conference on "The UK and the Social Dimension of the European Union", University of Leeds, 7 November 1997.

Gabaglio, E (1998), *An obvious partner in social relations*, UNICE Special Edition, February, Brussels, UNICE, p. 5

Gorges, M (1996), *Euro-Corporatism? Interest Intermediation in the European Community*, Lanham (MD): University Press of America.

Grant, W (1990), *"Organised Interests and the European Community"*, paper prepared for presentation to the 6th International Colloquium of the Feltrinelli Foundation, Corton, May 29–31.

Greenwood, J (1995), *European Casebook on Business Alliances*, Hemel Hempstead: Prentice Hall.

Greenwood, J (1997), *Representing Interests in the European Union*, London: Macmillan.

Greenwood, J and M Aspinwall, eds. (1997), *Collective Action in the European Union: interests and the new politics of associability*. London: Routledge.

Greenwood J, J Grote and K Ronit, eds. (1992), *Organized Interests and the European Community*. London: Sage.

Greenwood J, L Stancich and L Strangward (1998), "The Capacities of Euro Groups in the Integration Process", *Political Studies*, forthcoming.

Harvey, B (1995), *Networking in Europe: A Guide to European Voluntary Organisations*. London: NCVO.

Leisink P, J van Leemput and J Vilrockx, (1996), *The Challenges to Trade Unions in Europe*. Cheltenham: Edward Elgar.

Marginson, P and K Sisson (1998), "European Collective Bargaining: A Virtual Prospect?", *Journal of Common Market Studies*, 36 (4): 505–28.

Martin, A (1998), *"EMU and Wage Bargaining: The Americanization of the European Labour Market"*, paper prepared for presentation at the Eleventh International Conference of Europeanists, Baltimore, February.

Mazey, S and J Richardson, eds. (1993), *Lobbying in the European Community*. Oxford: Oxford University Press.

Obradovic, D (1997), *"Eligibility of Non-State Actors to Participate in European Union Policy Formation"*, paper prepared for presentation to the conference on "Non State Actors and Authority in the Global System", University of Warwick, 31 October–1 November.

Rhodes, M (1994), "Labour Markets and Industrial Relations", in Nugent, N and R O'Donnell, eds., *The European Business Environment*. London: Macmillan.

Ross, G (1994), "Inside the Delors Cabinet", *Journal of Common Market Studies*, 32 (4): 499–523.

Scotland Europa (1998), *Monthly Bulletin to Members*. Brussels: Scotland Europa.

Stern, A (1994), *Lobbying in Europe after Maastricht*. Brussels: Club de Bruxelles.

Threlfall, M (1997), *"Is European Social Integration Necessary? Rationales for EU Social Policy"*, paper prepared for presentation to the conference on "The UK and the Social Dimension of the European Union", University of Leeds, 7 November.

van Schendelen, M P C M, ed. (1993), *National Public and Private EC Lobbying*. Aldershot: Dartmouth.

Walby, S (1997), *"The new Regulatory State: the social powers of the European Union"*, paper prepared for presentation to the conference on "The UK and the Social Dimension of the European Union", University of Leeds, 7 November.

Wallace, H and A Young, eds. (1997), *Participation and Policy Making in the European Union*. Oxford: Clarendon Press.

9 Summary of the Conference

MICHAEL MESCH, CLARISSE PÁSZTORY, THOMAS ZOTTER

Subject Area 1: The European Economic and Welfare Model in the Context of Global Competition

Bernhard Ebbinghaus (Max-Planck-Institute for the Study of Social Sciences, Cologne), Does a European Social Model Exist and Can It Survive?
The question raised here is not merely an academic question, but an issue of political relevance in European integration as well. An integration, which not only profited from but also fostered convergence among its member states.

It is also of importance in the context of increasing international competition. Facing this competition, which also leads to regime competition, the following question must be asked: Is the adaptation towards the US-American model and a downward spiral of labour market and welfare regulation the only option for Europe? Before turning to this issue, one should try to find some characteristics that could be seen as something like the "core European model", despite the diversity of European models.

There are significant national variations among the major components of the European model, which on the one hand provide some obstacles to Europeanisation but on the other hand also contribute to the richness and plurality of Europe, which is needed to develop and implement multiple adaptation strategies for Europe.

European integration did not follow a single model approach, but rather a variable geometry of partially overlapping social institutions and national models that co-exist in the core and periphery of Europe. The various regimes did not develop by themselves, but were constituted by social choice.

In order to identify the characteristics along which the nations set their institutions vis-à-vis the Japanese or the Anglo-American model, one has to look at the particular set of institutions (foremost the production system, industrial relations, employment regimes and welfare state). These institutions heavily depend on each other and therefore somewhat determine the patterns of development.

173

Within Europe four distinct patterns can be identified. Two of them are the most constitutive for the European social model: the Central European Social Partnership model and the Scandinavian corporatist model. The Southern European and the British model showed somewhat different development patterns.

The production sphere of the Scandinavian and the Central European model is characterised by export orientation, a high skilled labour force and a high value-added strategy. In the realm of industrial relations they share relatively encompassing interest organisations and high social security standards. All of these elements are, among others, important for a permanent upgrading.

Important differences between the Scandinavian and the Central European model are a different employment regime and different forms of the welfare state. The Scandinavian universalist welfare state provided a high level of overall and particularly female employment through a large public sector and through part-time work, though at the cost of high taxation.

The continental social insurance states have been less successful in creating sheltered jobs and employing women and high unemployment and early retirement schemes have increased the social costs and thus payroll taxes.

The Southern European model has not succeeded in achieving a balance between state intervention and market principles. Nationalised or recently privatised companies producing mass consumer products and a relatively flexible sector of small and medium enterprises co-exist. Labour markets and industrial relations are still marked by state intervention and often lack self co-ordination.

The British model, particularly since the Thatcher revolution, has followed the Anglo-American free market model and therefore constitutes an outlyer in Europe. Here a low-wage mass production strategy finds institutional support by voluntarist labour relations, a relatively unregulated labour market and low social benefits. The competitiveness problem is tackled by further labour market deregulation, decentralisation of wage bargaining, and lowering of the reservation wage.

The sources of strength of the European model are or at least have been manifold. By and large, the European welfare model allows a more socially acceptable and peaceful adaptation to the economic imperatives and global pressures, thanks to the more developed welfare state and better employment relations. Despite all rigidities, national and European-level consultation strategies provide opportunities and means for co-ordinated adaptation while keeping negative social consequences at a minimum.

In those European economies with established practices of co-ordinated capitalism, the high skill and high value-added long-term strategies have provided a positive growth perspective.

The role of organised interests through institutionalised co-ordination procedures has been important to the support of these models. Their viability rests on the beneficial constraints and institutional incentives that foster the provision of quasi-public goods—wage moderation, social peace, apprenticeship training, professional education, etc.

The European model—if we can speak of one model—has, however, come under considerable pressures. A strategy to ensure the survival of the "core European model" might run along the following lines:

Welfare state reforms, some degree of wage moderation and a reconsideration of wage schemes especially at the lower end are necessary, but not sufficient conditions. Strategies are needed to increase employment, to reintegrate the unemployed into the labour market; here some rigidities of the employment regime should be reconsidered. In order to allow for the more differentiated work profiles and diversified production systems, regulation of collective contracts and employment laws need to be moderated and made more flexible.

Finally, the crises of organised interests—declining membership, crises of legitimacy and the decentralisation pressure—will require a renewal of the system of collective bargaining and interest representation. The efforts to negotiate social pacts between the Social Partners and success stories of some countries have indicated a European route of adaptation.

The necessary reforms have to be undertaken by the collective bargaining parties via co-ordinated forms of more decentralised bargaining, by the state as a regulator of employment conditions, and by more long-term social pacts between the state and the Social Partners. Given Europe's laboratory of diverse national policies it might be more advisable to look for best practices within Europe.

Joachim Lamel (Austrian Federal Economic Chamber, Vienna): To summarise Prof. Ebbinghaus' presentation, one might say that a European model exists if you look at it from the outside. The view from inside gives a somewhat differentiated perspective, but one can still see enough common characteristics of the economic and social models to be able to identify a common European model, especially for the core of Europe.

Having said that, the next question that arises is whether this European model can survive given increased competition in good markets that eventually leads to regime competition. The answer here is a "yes, if ...".

The "ifs" are especially remarkable for two reasons: 1) The decisive elements remain national despite the EU. 2) The core of the European model is industrial relations, a field in which the national level is still prevailing (this might be an obstacle for further European integration).

Many of the conditions critical for the survival of the European model affect the Social Partners directly or indirectly. Consequently, the policies adopted by the Social Partners have a decisive influence on the success of the European model.

Erwin Bendel (Federation of Austrian Industrialists, Vienna): We are not seeing and will not be seeing one European model.

Benchmarking could help us to identify the best features of each single model by looking at the economic performance of each model.

In the **general discussion** the following question is raised: What should the right yardstick for the judgement in a benchmarking process be? In this connection, it should be taken into consideration that in order to identify a best practice, every party should clearly be able to understand what the others do and how these approaches work with existing institutions. There seems to be no one answer at hand (just as an example, one should consider the different labour market strategies adopted by Denmark, Ireland, or the Netherlands).

New institutional economics permits insights into the importance of corporate governance, corporate finance and its relation to the welfare state in the discussion of socio-economic models.

To some extent, whether the Dutch model should continue to be used as a benchmark should be reconsidered, since it is based to a large extent on the creation of part-time jobs.

In talking about social pacts from the point of view of the trade unions, the *"Paktfähigkeit"* of employers associations can come into question, if the only outcome of wage moderation is higher profit rates and stagnant investment.

Colin Crouch (European University Institute, Florence), Adapting the European Model: the Role of Employers' Associations and Trade Unions
There are two very different perspectives on the role of economic interest organisations, leading to directly opposed but equally clear sets of policy

recommendations. According to the logic of neo-liberalism, these associations and institutions should be weakened and marginalised as much as possible.

If unregulated economies are systematically superior to regulated ones, this ought to be true for all times and all sectors. We then have great difficulty explaining why US unemployment was higher than that in some key regulated economies (Germany, Sweden) for most of the post-war period. It is also difficult to explain why according to some very important indicators (productivity improvement, export performance, overall performance in certain manufacturing sectors), several of the continental European economies continue to out-perform the USA.

According to the logic of institutionalist theories, these organisations should be encouraged and enabled to play neo-corporatist governance roles—that is, roles in which they are constrained to share responsibility for developing collective goods for maximising economic gains and in which they have significant negative and political incentives not to use their strength largely for lobbying and rent-seeking.

The matter cannot be resolved by ruling one of the rival perspectives on organisations as somehow in error; there is too much evidence on both sides for that. While they produce contrasting policy prescriptions, they are not mutually incompatible as accounts of how institutions may work.

The policy challenge is to reshape the environment of associations so that they behave in entrepreneurial and developmental ways rather than protectionist and cartelistic ones, if possible trying to give them incentives to do this before global markets place them under severe pressure. This is the nub of the conflict between neo-liberals and neo-institutionalists: The former insist on the viability of only one way of achieving economic success; the latter see a diversity of solutions.

Attempts at establishing the future scope for associational economies need to recognise both the reality and the limitations of the threat posed to them by globalisation. To deal first with the second, the limitations, it is important to bear the following in mind: Large parts of economies remain dominated by non-global firms in sectors that continue to have a future and also where a system of gradual adaptation will work just as well as radical innovation and complete shifts of forms of production. But if associational systems are to recover a role in economic governance, they must achieve the following: to sustain the participation of the global players that do indeed exist and will probably grow in number; to be able to facilitate moves into new production sectors; and to enable company autonomy within an overall framework of effective governance. They also need, in certain cases, a reorientation towards true collective goods. Some of the relevant action lies within the scope of associations themselves; others need stimulation from public actors of various kinds.

Rather than simply decline, these organisations might demonstrate capacity for radical internal change—provided a large enough number of their active members perceive that either an abolition of the structure or allowing it to continue in a worn-out fashion as undesirable.

Innovation comes from social actors themselves working under pressure to find a way out of difficult dilemmas. The appropriate context for the reform of associative systems is for the association actors to be forced to find solutions (rather than being relieved of responsibility), but protectionist and rent-seeking options should be blocked off by government refusal to respond. In the case of EU countries, competition law usually provides a convenient exogenous Leviathan for blocking off this option.

Similarly, domestic rent-seeking has historically been of little use to organised actors in the small open economies. However much the domestic market might be regulated by government on insiders' behalf, the global context remains highly open, and firms must succeed in it. These cases all demonstrate that the behaviour of associative systems will depend on the structure of incentives (to behave either entrepreneurially or defensively) determined by their context, a context which can often be articulated and shaped by public policy or indeed by associations themselves if they are determined to improve their own mode of behaviour. If the problem is that firms are exiting the associational system in order to avoid its obligations, governments have the capacity to make it clear that they will only take note of direct enterprise lobbying only by firms that have reputations as good associational citizens.

We here encounter again a central irony of economic organisation: The more an interest organisation system reflects the free market ideal, the more this system is likely to take the form of a pluralistic rent-seeking system. The greater the neo-corporatist architecture of shared governance, the more likely is it to be pushed into constructive roles.

The need for greater autonomy of firms results primarily from the fact that, in conditions of great uncertainty, a great number of firms must search, in various directions, for success, so that some might find it. This produces a difficult situation for organised labour. Workers' security becomes particularly important at precisely the moment when it becomes very difficult to give it: Not only are firms unwilling in their insecure environment to accept burdens of worker security, but the fact that many firms will fail makes the demand for security an urgent one. This is, however, an argument not for the abolition of collective relations, but for their enhancement and improved sophistication, since the way in which workers' security can be reconciled with firms' needs has to be a matter for constant experiment. Once workers' security and firms' flexibility are both recognised as necessary, rather than being seen in zero-sum competition, it becomes clear that co-operative approaches of various kinds will be in the best position to resolve the dilemma, since workers' security has to be treated as a collective good rather than the responsibility of a single employer.

Cross-sectoral associations are often less likely to be rent-seekers at a time of rapid technological change than single-industry organisations are. The problem with an industry-specific association is that it cannot deal with any need to wind down a sector and find alternative activities and an economy dominated by associations representing the interests of such sectors is unlikely to be able to innovate. The same problems do not apply to general, non-sectoral organisations of the *Kammer* type. These can be particularly useful at local level, where, in the face of a decline of existing industries, their central motivation is to find new activities for their city or area. They are motivated to provide the collective goods and the infrastructural facilities which will attract and be valuable to new kinds of business—especially where local governments and cross-sectoral union organisations are also involved. Again, it is within the capacity of public policy to encourage developments of this kind by involving this kind of association in local economic development strategies.

EMU might strengthen those national associative systems that retain or enhance a capacity for elementary wage co-ordination. National trade unions have a very strong incentive to demonstrate that it is, after all, possible to assert some basic moderating influence on the labour market through neo-corporatist mechanisms. The situation confronting employers is less clear-cut. They will share unions' aversion to perpetual deflationary policies, but may prefer an attempt to achieve completely unregulated labour markets to a revival of corporatism and its concomitant need for dialogue with organised labour. However, if the past record of neo-corporatism has been reasonably successful and uncostly, and if unions are relatively strongly entrenched, they may prefer this path to one of complete deregulation, which could be reached only after prolonged conflict. Governments too have good reasons to avoid deflation and may balk at the social conflict likely to be engendered by a major deregulation struggle. Social pacts could provide a functional equivalent of devaluation without many of the latter's negative effects. Therefore, in the foreseeable future we do not look to possibilities of Europe-wide neo-corporatism but at a new lease on life and a new rationale for national responses of this kind, precisely because of the European development.

Gerhard Huemer (Austrian Federal Economic Chamber, Vienna): The most outstanding feature of the institutional set-up of many European countries is certainly the fact that organised interests play an important role.

The main function of institutions is certainly stabilisation. Having said that, we have to ask ourselves the following questions: Do we see a convergence of systems? There are not many indications of such a process. In the context of EMU, do we need problem-solving mechanisms and institutions on the European level or on the national level? And, if we need institutions on a European level, do these meet the stabilisation requirements resulting from EMU?

The **general discussion** focuses on the effects of globalisation. Evidence found by Traxler suggests that investment decisions of transnational corporations are not influenced significantly by differences among labour market regimes.

The sources of the developments and sentiments summarised in the word "globalization" are not new to our economies. Trade liberalisation has proceeded since World War II and it has always put pressure on firms to increase competitiveness. If the trend of induced productivity growth exceeds the trend of GDP growth, then the expanding sectors cannot absorb the vacant capacities set free by the declining sectors. As a result, we get the threat of unemployment. The US economy reacted to this pressure by opening the wage scale. In Europe, where this path was not feasible, unemployment increased, especially among the less skilled. Europe's answer therefore must be to create conditions leading to a growth that at least equals the productivity growth.

What adversely affects the attitude and sentiments of trade unions about structural shifts is the changing quality of these shifts. Whereas, in the 1960s, we had a shift from low productivity, low paying sectors (agriculture) to higher paying sectors (manufacturing), we have seen—to some extent—the opposite in the 1990s (from manufacturing to low paying services).

Addressing the question of the stabilisation needs, the discussion shows that probably different forms of organisation are needed on different levels.

As far as macro-economic questions are concerned, tripartite solutions are preferable to bilateral solutions, since expectations play a significant role. The formation of "constructive" expectations is more likely in tripartite arrangement and with encompassing organisations, which are to a lesser degree rent-seekers than sectoral associations.

Ludwig Schubert (European Commission, GD II, Brussels), European Macro-economic Policy

What Europe needs is a stable monetary and economic policy framework for growth, since the safeguarding of the European model is closely linked to growth. The workforce in Europe will increase by approximately 33% by 2010. To integrate this increase in the workforce, growth of output has to be increased.

The social systems, which are increasingly getting under pressure, have not become that much more generous over the past 20–25 years. What has changed is the relation of the number of those who contribute to the social security and retirement systems and those who receive transfers. In other words, employment at full time has to increase. If we take for example the number of unemployed in Europe today—around 18 million people, this is not the full story yet. If we compare these figures with the employment rates of the 1960s we should speak of 22 million people unemployed and the comparison with 1970s leaves us with 34 million unemployed if we could achieve the respective employment rates. The output we "let go off", by not having these people employed, runs up to the GDP of France or Germany respectively.

In order to increase employment, a growth rate of output is needed which exceeds the productivity trend. The bottleneck Europe is facing is not qualification, but growth. Investing in the education of the workforce and not offering jobs, is a bad investment. With a given productivity trend of 2%, an output growth of 2 to 2.25% is needed, only to stabilise employment. In order to stimulate the investment needed for this growth, favourable conditions for investment have to be maintained.

And we also know that the full adjustment of relative prices on the labour market (widening of wage structures) is not desirable.

Looking for an environment friendly to growth, we first have to look for the obstacles to growth that Europe is encountering:

(1) The prevailing pessimism that growth could not solve the employment problem is falsified by the Irish experience. (2) Looking at the business cycles, we can see that the sound recovery following the 1973

recession was not repeated in the 1980s and 1990s. This is especially true for 1995, when exchange rate turbulence prevented a stronger recovery. (3) The recession of the early 1990s was—if not induced—at least exacerbated by the conflicting interests of monetary and fiscal policies. (4) As a result of (1), (2), and (3), production capacities remained low due to low real investment. If the investment ratio is low, an increase in demand brings about risks of demand-pull inflation.

The necessary policy mix therefore has to take into account the following elements:

(1) A stability orientated, independent monetary policy can help if a conflict with fiscal policy or income policy is avoided. The macro-economic policy being determined by the Maastricht Treaty, it is less likely that a conflict situation like in the early 1990s will evolve.

(2) As for the wage policy, a moderate real wage increase at a rate a little lower than productivity could be an important contribution to profitability and competitiveness, which in turn should stimulate investment.

(3) Structural policies that are aimed at increasing productivity always have to take into account the growth rates of output that these productivity gains meet.

The EU Treaty addresses macro-economic policy objectives in several connections: The general objectives of Art 2 of the Treaty are also a secondary target for the ECB. So if the target of price stability is not in danger, the growth and employment targets become relevant for monetary policy. Art 102 a and 103 lay the road for co-ordination mechanisms on European level. The Broad Macro-economic Policy Guidelines can be seen as an example for a starting point for co-ordination. The chances are good that the EU-11 Council will find consensus on macro-issues for Euroland.

The co-ordination between the actors of macro-economic policy, in which all of them face different institutional arrangements and constraints, is an additional aspect that has to be considered. Whereas monetary policy is centralised, the only "centralisation" that fiscal policy knows up to now has been the constraint through the Maastricht Treaty and the Pact on Stability and Growth. Income policy is the most decentralised of these policies, lying in the hands of the Social Partners at the national level.

Günther Chaloupek (Austrian Federal Chamber of Labour, Vienna):
The stress and eventual collapse of the social security and retirement system is regularly used as an argument of private insurers to sell their products. Taking a closer look, one can of course not ignore long-term problems of the

changing age structure, but it is still a problem that can be dealt with within the existing institutions and instruments. One of the most important elements of any solution is the employment rate mentioned above.

As for the co-ordination of monetary policy, fiscal policy, Social Partners and the Commission, a few additional aspects should be mentioned:

(1) If the monetary authority does not publish an inflation target, wage bargaining parties will lack a yardstick for negotiating real wages.

(2) When talking about co-ordination between the major players of macro-economic policy, one also has to consider the attitudes of the players towards their counterparts:

– The Commission seems to be willing and committed to accept other players as equal partners.
– The national governments are very heterogeneous in their attitude towards the other players, especially towards the Social Partners.
– The European Central Bank has given rather clear signs that it will not accept the Social Partners as equals in a dialogue.
– The Social Partners are prepared to accept the restrictions *("Sachzwänge")* of monetary policy.

(3) The framework of such a co-ordination does not necessarily have to be formal. Formalisation would require a change in the constitution of the EU. Informal and semi-formal structures have proven to be fairly efficient in many countries.

In the **general discussion** the question is raised of what commitment of the Social Partners could be expected in absence of any access to the ECOFIN or the ECB? Models without formal rules that have worked well for Austria or the Netherlands might thus be inefficient on the European level.

The constraints of fiscal policy within the EEMU do not only stem from the Maastricht Treaty or the Pact on Stability and Growth. What may constrain fiscal policies of the single states even more is the tax erosion caused by unfair tax competition.

A more job intensive growth depends on various factors. The relationship between wage costs and the rate of investment is not sufficiently unequivocal for clear policy recommendations to be based on it. Reductions in working time could create more jobs if these were carried through in a cost-neutral way. Part-time jobs as a solution have to fulfil the condition of being voluntary part-time jobs.

Schubert concludes that the main obstacles to growth in the recent past in Europe have clearly been failures in macro-economic policies.

Subject Area 2: The Traditional and the Future Role of Associations in Politics on the European Level

Ulrich Fritsche, Gustav A. Horn, Wolfgang Scheremet, Rudolf Zwiener (German Institute for Economic Research—DIW, Berlin), Is There a Need for a Co-ordinated European Wage and Labour Market Policy?
With the start of Economic and Monetary Union (or European monetary union) (EMU), Member states will lose their autonomy in monetary policy and fiscal policy will be constrained by the Maastricht criteria and the Dublin Stability Pact. Wage policy will therefore have to bear the main burden of absorbing asymmetrical shocks and of maintaining a member state's competitiveness.

In spite of wide differences in the institutional set-up of wage bargaining systems among EU member countries, the rates of increase of consumer prices and nominal wages are currently very similar across Europe. In many countries, however, this convergence is not the result of a flexible wage bargaining system but had to be enforced by restrictive monetary policy. Consequently unemployment rates are still divergent in the EU.

What are the main features of a European wage policy favourable to economic growth, employment, and convergence towards lower rates of unemployment? What is required is a wage policy of individual countries guided by the inflation target set by the European Central Bank and by the respective country's long-term increase of productivity.

The study by the DIW is based on Keynesian theory stressing the importance of interdependencies among labour markets, product markets, capital and money markets. Its conclusions are at odds with the still dominant neo-classical mainstream claiming that reductions of real wages are required to bring down unemployment in Europe.

Simulations carried out by the DIW (using the basically neo-classical Oxford Economic Forecasting Model) demonstrate that the implementation of the strategy of cutting real wages in all EMU member states would result in higher employment, but would also entail significantly lower growth rates. More people would be holding jobs, but Western Europe as a whole would be a region with a lower income per head.

If, in a group of larger EU member states, real wages were continuously lagging behind the increase of productivity, this would dampen growth in Europe and might even result in a deflationary vicious circle. The simulations by the DIW lend weight to these considerations.

Which institutional arrangements of collective wage bargaining in Western Europe were favourable to productivity orientation? The analysis of the DIW, based on data for the period 1970 to 1996, concludes that pattern-bargaining systems were most responsive to productivity, inflation and unemployment in the required ways. Pattern-bargaining systems combine branch-level collective agreements with a rather decentralised mode of co-ordination.

Due to the risk of deflationary vicious circles, some form of cross-border co-ordination of wage policy within the EMU is needed. How could this be brought about? It is obvious to all observers that aiming for transnational, peak-level co-ordination is unrealistic. Therefore the discussion of possible organisational solutions focuses on network-style forms of co-ordination, based on a mixture of intra-organisational co-ordination by the European sectoral organisations and pattern bargaining.

With respect to the latter, the DIW suggests that wage negotiations at the branch level in a specific EU country take the wage development in the respective sector of the German economy as an anchor. This means, for instance, that wage increases could be higher than in Germany, if productivity in the sector of the country concerned were rising faster, etc. This is what de facto has already been practised by wage bargaining systems in the European bloc of hard currency countries.

Michael Mesch (Federal Chamber of Labour, Vienna) states that the Austrian Social Partners arrive at conclusions similar to those of the analysis by the DIW about the requirements for a European wage policy favourable to economic growth and employment. In a recent study ("Room for Manoeuvring in Economic Policy", Ueberreuter, Vienna 1998) the Advisory Council for Economic and Social Affairs of the Austrian Social Partners evaluated the room for manoeuvring in economic policy in the EMU. In the words of this statement: "On an economy-wide level, a wage policy guided by long-term productivity development is necessary to stabilise purchasing power and growth. If all participant countries of EMU follow such a policy, relative unit labour costs will remain the same. Under such circumstances there would be no need for monetary policy to adopt restrictive measures in case of a surge in demand."

A precondition for this kind of wage policy is co-ordination between the main actors of economic policy. The Advisory Council states: "A mechanism that allows an autonomous ECB and the other actors charged with economic policy especially those actors tasked with wage and income policy is needed to mutually integrate the effects of their respective policies."

The Advisory Council, too, perceives risks looming behind beggar-my-neighbour wage policies: "If real wages persistently lag behind productivity growth, demand (further) suffers. This in turn adversely affects expectations and investment. The issue concerns the national and particularly the European level."

And the Advisory Council sees the up-grading strategy of European countries imperilled: "... the debate about the competitiveness of nations disregards the conditions for quality-based competition. European economies are compelled to continuously 'up-grade', since price competition with less developed economies is neither sensible nor likely to succeed. Furthermore, competition between EU member countries, brought on by the process of liberalisation and the Internal Market, has increasingly motivated national economies to improve their relative position within Europe. To the extent that this results in a beggar-my-neighbour policy in the areas of taxes and (real) exchange rates, the process of 'up-grading' for all of Europe is in peril."

What has actually happened in Western Europe for a number of years, especially since 1993, conforms, however, to a large extent to a scenario of beggar-my-neighbour wage policies: In almost all EU member countries real wage increases have persistently remained behind the advance of productivity!

Intentionally or unintentionally, these countries' wage bargaining systems have followed the macro-economic concepts preferred by the EU Commission. On numerous occasions the Commission has recommended a wage policy in which real wage increases remain one percentage point below the increase of productivity! It would be a very difficult task indeed for the trade unions not only to implement some kind of European co-ordination of wage bargaining at the branch level, but also to attempt this if they face disapproving statements by the official Europe.

Jelle Visser (University of Amsterdam), Societal Support for Social Dialogue. Europe's Trade Unions and Employers' Associations

In the 1990s an invigoration of concertation and policy co-ordination between the Social Partners and the state has been taking place in many EU member states. In a number of countries—notably Ireland, Italy, Portugal,

Spain, Finland and Greece—this has taken the form of social pacts. In other countries, like Austria, Norway and the Netherlands, concertation has been reinvigorated as the standard operating procedure accompanying national wage bargaining and social policymaking. In Belgium and in Germany attempts to negotiate a national pact for employment failed, but new proposals are on the agenda. The possibility of a national employment pact, however, does not appear realistic in France or Britain.

Concertation is most stable if the participating interest groups are sufficiently comprehensive and united. But interest groups must also have the will to compromise, be prepared to seek common solutions and have the capacity to make binding decisions on behalf of their members. The key argument is that concertation depends on, and develops, the strategic capacity of "encompassing" societal interests.

Operationalisation of the latter at the level of peak associations includes four organisational criteria: (1) *representation,* or the proportion of potential members who are actual members; (2) *cohesion,* or the extent to which members are united in a single peak association; (3) *concentration,* or the extent to which members of the peak association(s) are divided over a small number of affiliates; and (4) *centralisation,* or the authority of the leadership of the peak association to take and implement decisions that prove binding on their affiliates or members.

Visser provides an overview of the state of employers' associations and trade unions in the mid-1990s with a view to their participation in social concertation at the national and European level.

Representation: In 1995 almost 41 of the 128 million employed workers in the European Economic Area were members of a trade union. Overall, the union density rate—the proportion of employed workers belonging to trade union—was 32%, nearly ten percentage points lower than in 1980. The variation in trade union membership and density across Europe is very large. Low-unionised countries tend to be located in the south: France, Spain, Portugal and Greece. Eight countries (Sweden, Norway, Finland, Denmark, Ireland, Belgium, Austria, Italy) still have a density rate of 40% or more.

Union density rates not only vary across countries but also across industries and social groups within countries. Data invariably point to lower membership levels for employees in the private sector compared to those in the public sector, for female compared to male employees, for youths in comparison to older age groups, for white-collar workers compared to blue-collar workers, for workers in small firms, and for workers employed under non-standard contracts or on a part-time basis.

In addition to almost 41 million employed members, European unions in 1995 organised approximately 13.5 million unemployed or retired members.

Indirectly, however, union representation affects a much greater proportion of workers. At present, around seventy per cent of European workers employed in the private sector are covered by collective agreements.

A high level of union density tends to be associated with a high coverage rate, but the reverse is not true. A high coverage rate, however, does seem to be associated with a high level of employers' organisations—and vice versa. Ten out of sixteen Western European countries allow the possibility to "extend" collective agreements between unions and employers to non-organised firms by way of public law.

In the mid 1990s, 63% of all private sector workers in Western European countries were employed in member firms of employers' associations.

Cohesion: On average, there are three peak associations representing labour and three representing business interests. Among capitalists, the major cleavages are between large and small firms, between industry and services, and between public and private sector employers. Among workers the most important cleavages are political, between white collar and blue-collar employees, and between public and private sector employees.

On average, the largest union confederation attracts three out of five organised union members; the largest employers' federations attract three out of four employers (if weighted by the number of employees).

Concentration: The organisational landscape of unions is changing rapidly. In all confederations the concentration ratio (based on the four largest unions) increased between 1985 and 1995. This increase was entirely due to amalgamations and the taking over of small unions by large ones. Smaller size and financial revenue, combined with increased demand for protection and high-quality services, has caused a spate of mergers and cost-reduction programmes in trade unions throughout Western Europe. In the second half of the 1990s merger activity has tended to lead to the formation of conglomerate (multi-sectoral) unions.

There are similar attempts at organisational restructuring among employers' associations. The traditional functional division of tasks between employers' and trade associations at the level of peak federations has been abandoned in various countries in recent times. The average number of affiliates is still much higher in the national federations of employers than on the union side, indicating greater heterogeneity, less capacity of control and more problems of internal discipline.

Centralisation: As a rule, authority within unions or employers' associations is closely tied to where (at what level) collective bargaining is conducted. In addition to the level of bargaining, decisions about strikes and lockouts, and the enforceability of higher-level agreements are relevant for the measurement of centralisation.

In Western Europe—unlike Japan and the United States—multi-employer bargaining has, since the 1930s, become the dominant type of wage setting. The major exception in the EU is Britain, where multi-employer bargaining has disappeared in nearly all sectors. In most countries negotiations about wages and conditions of work take place at the branch as well as at the plant level. The relative importance of bargaining at the plant level has increased in recent years. This tendency towards decentralisation of collective bargaining has mainly been driven by employers in the exposed sector of the economy who have been seeking more room to manoeuvre in response to international competition and technological change.

For the effectiveness of multi-level bargaining it is crucial that the different levels (branch and plant level) are integrated so as to prevent them from mutually blocking their respective purpose. The authority of sectoral employers' associations and trade unions over local bargaining and the strength of the mutual obligations enshrined in higher-level agreements (in particular the peace clause and procedures for conflict resolution) are critical conditions in this respect.

There are currently 21 European-level union organisations, and about three times as many European employers' or mixed associations (not counting the 500 or more trade associations). The organisational architecture of the European system of interest representation is very complex. It differs between unions and employers and is incomparable to any national system.

According to **Werner Teufelsbauer (Austrian Federal Economic Chamber, Vienna),** a certain decline of neo-corporatism can only be observed in those countries where the Social Partners hitherto have played a particularly strong and visible role—such as in Germany. But Germany constitutes a special case, still finding itself under the shock of unification: Wage-policy was burdened with absorbing the exchange rate of 1:1 between the DM and the Ostmark. As labour productivity in the Western German economy was three times as high as in Eastern Germany, the Social Partners were unable to cope with this situation.

Different indeed are the various systems of funding: In Britain and the Netherlands employers' associations traditionally financed their activities by means of cartels. This is now no longer possible due to the stricter competition rules within the European Union. This demands new sources of funding, particularly because at the same time more and more services—apart from the lobbying-activities—have to be provided in order to find acceptance among members.

The differentiation between narrow special-interest organisations on the one hand and encompassing associations on the other hand is especially important. Only the latter can assume the role of responsible partners of government. On the European level, any desired strengthening of the Social Partners therefore requires adequate organisational support for encompassing associations with respect to financing, mandates, etc.

Thomas Delapina (Austrian Federal Chamber of Labour, Vienna) seconds the view that a strengthening of the role of European Social Partners is desirable. All recent European success stories have one thing in common: The respective measures were developed and implemented in co-operation with the Social Partners.

On the European level, however, associations suffer from a lack of prerequisites for internal compromise and for binding enforcement among their members. Without public political, administrative, and organisational support this is unlikely to change. Beyond that, the two most important issues are representativity and scope of action. As for representativity, a wide representation of associations of employers and employees seems justified. The inclusion of non-professional organisations, however, would make concertation of interests even more complicated if not impossible. As for the scope of action, European Social Partnership should, as in Austria, not be restricted to classic industrial relations issues. A broader agenda of negotiations would permit trade-offs across several fields of policy.

The following general **discussion** deals with the potential forms of organisational aids. The commonly accepted target seems to be the promotion of clearly defined encompassing, representative and mandated (and thus recognised) European associations. One important tool to get there could be to grant an information-advantage to certain Euro-associations.

Franz Traxler (University of Vienna), Wage-setting Institutions and European Monetary Union

Econometric analysis yields a significant impact of wage bargaining institutions on economic performance (measured by the increase of unit labour costs, which is the criterion most important for EMU requirements) of 18 OECD countries for the period 1970–90:

Economy-wide co-ordination of wage bargaining proves to be effective only if the problem of vertical co-ordination can be overcome. This can be achieved in three ways. The first way is through voluntary co-ordination, which takes place within a rather decentralised framework so that the problems of vertical co-ordination emerge only on a relatively limited scale. The second way is a compliance of the rank-and-file that is enforced by the state. In comparison to voluntary pattern bargaining, the results of this form of co-ordination are less beneficial. In the third way the performance of voluntary, central-level forms of co-ordination (i. e. inter-associational, intra-associational and state-sponsored co-ordination) come close to the performance of pattern bargaining when they are combined with a high degree of bargaining governability. However, voluntary, central-level forms of co-ordination definitely perform worse if bargaining governability is lacking. This contingency is due to the enormous problems of vertical co-ordination that centralised bargaining brings about. Voluntary systems can cope with these problems only if they rely on a supportive (legally-backed) framework that makes bargaining governable. If the problem of vertical co-ordination cannot be solved, uncoordinated bargaining is the (second) best choice.

Overall, the findings of the regression analysis confirm that there is a significant impact of bargaining institutions on performance, which results from a rather complex interplay of horizontal and vertical co-ordination problems.

It is evident that there are significant differences in the structural wage responsiveness of the EMU members. These will place adaptive pressures on those countries that perform particularly poorly, since they combine voluntary peak-level wage co-ordination with low governability.

If transnational co-ordination of wage bargaining is absent, any possible scenario is likely to entail economically and socially suboptimal results for the EMU area as a whole. In the short run, the problem of growing inequality among the member states will prevail since the structural responsiveness of the national bargaining systems differs considerably. Longer-term developments depend on how poorly performing national systems react and how their reactions interact with monetary policy. If adjustment of wage bargaining systems is delayed, manifesting itself in inflationary tendencies in the common currency area, the ECB will presumably tighten monetary policy. If adjustment is fast and tends to overcompensate (e. g. in the wake of massive state intervention in wage policy) in a number of larger EU countries, this may trigger a competitive race for the lowest labour costs. Hence, any kind of longer-term development that fails to establish cross-border co-ordination of wage bargaining runs the risk of getting trapped into "beggar-my-neighbour" policies with self-defeating, deflationary consequences for Western Europe as a whole.

Growing insight into this risk (possibly arising in the course of a trial-and-error process) may pave the way for a *positive* approach to cross-border co-ordination of wage bargaining.

The following lessons from effective patterns of national wage co-ordination are particularly relevant for the co-ordination of wage negotiations in the EMU context:

(1) Economy-wide wage *co-ordination* does not mean *centralisation* of bargaining. This is important for two reasons. In structural respects, a centralised approach to European wage co-ordination would certainly overstretch the limited capacities of the European institutions. In substantive respects, the combination of macro-economic co-ordination and decentralised bargaining is the only way to make two EMU requirements for wage policy compatible: These two requirements are control over aggregate wage increases in line with employment and stability goals and a wage structure that responds in a flexible way to inter-industry and intra-industry restructuring.

(2) Voluntary wage co-ordination across the economy does not necessarily rest on bipartite *negotiations,* as the case of intra-associational co-ordination by the national peak organisations documents. Again, this is essential to the European situation, due to the employers' reluctance to enter bipartite negotiations.

(3) Economy-wide co-ordination does not presuppose encompassing involvement of all groups and sectors of the economy. There is hardly a working national system of bargaining co-ordination that has been able to incorporate all groups. By contrast, it is often a rather small core group that actively contributes to the realisation of economy-wide co-ordination. It follows from this that the large size of the EU is not a structural impediment to European transnational wage co-ordination. The metal industry, which is

highly unionised in most EMU countries, may form the critical mass for Europe-wide co-ordination.

Overall, if there is cross-border wage co-ordination, it can rest only on non-hierarchical, network-style structures, most probably launched by a combination of intra-associational co-ordination at Community level and pattern bargaining. At least in an early stage, this co-ordination may be informal and implicit, resulting from "tacit" intra-associational arrangements rather than from negotiations between the Euro-associations of business and labour.

Since it is very difficult to arrive at agreements on substantive issues (even within the union movement) at the European level, it is reasonable to concentrate Europe-wide co-ordination on procedural issues. This implies devolution of bargaining over substantive issues to lower-level (sectoral) actors in the member states, whereas higher—European—levels confine themselves to defining the guidelines for bargaining. These guidelines may include the precedence of the exposed sector as the pattern setter. Another guideline has to link wage increases to macroeconomic productivity growth in an unequivocal, operational way.

Gerhard Heinrich (Federation of Austrian Industrialists, Salzburg) emphasises the absence of any ideal model. He, too, sees the involvement of the Social Partners in general policy-making, thus sharing responsibilities, as a crucial incentive. Developments in the direction of wage co-ordination will therefore primarily require the shaping of a common general attitude towards wage responsibility. A major obstacle to a co-ordinated European wage policy is the increasing need for greater (rather than smaller) wage differentiation.

In the **discussion** it is widely agreed upon that national bargaining will replaced by European bargaining. On the contrary, the preconditions for a European wage policy must be laid on the national level.

Subject area 3: The European Constitution and the Integration of the Associations

Philippe Schmitter (European University Institute, Florence), Reforming the Channels of Representation for an Eventual Euro-Democracy
Schmitter argues in favour of democratisation of the EU: The EU seems to be evolving towards a novel form of polity that resembles neither a

"supranational state" nor an "intergovernmental organisation". As this incomplete polity tries to cope with its multiple problems of politicisation, enlargement, implementation, and insecurity, it will have to face a growing need for greater legitimacy:

1) Enlargement will render the existing institutions obsolete. 2) With the implementation of the EMU, the dynamic of functional spillover, which up to now has been the driving force of European integration, is exhausted. The manifold consequences of the EMU will necessitate new and political institutions. 3) As there is no consensus on how to constitutionalise the EU, piecemeal adjustments will have to be brought about.

The only solution that seems promising in this situation is the democratisation of EU practices and rules with regard to citizenship, representation, and the decision-making process. Schmitter offers a number of 'modest suggestions for reform' that may not be capable of immediately transforming the EU into a Euro-democracy, but should contribute to unleashing significant changes in the behaviour of political parties, interest associations, and social movements:

– In order to strengthen the autonomy of European parties vis-à-vis national party directorates and to provide incentives for political careers at the EU-level, he proposes giving existing European party formations control over one half of the electoral funds allotted for each member state.

– Moreover he suggests reforms in the official status and funding of European interest associations: 1) the establishment of a semi-public status for truly European interest associations and social movements; 2) the financing of these associations through compulsory contributions (but receipt of these funds would not preclude their also receiving funds from national governments, private organisations or individual persons; 3) the distribution of these funds by means of citizen vouchers: Each Euro-citizen would decide about the distribution of her/his contribution to the Euro-level interest associations with semi-public status.

The latter proposal for reform would not eliminate the current favoured treatment of national and economic interests, but is designed to enlarge the sphere of representation and encourage the opening of new channels of representation.

In his solicited comment on Schmitter's presentation, **Franz Traxler (University of Vienna)** expresses his opinion that democratisation presently constitutes no solution to the EU's lack of legitimacy, as there is no European public and no genuinely European political discourse. Legitimacy may also derive from superior performance: What Euro-citizens expect are solutions for problems (e. g. environmental pollution, unemployment) which exceed the problem-solving capacity of individual member states.

Moreover, democratisation and performance are conflicting with each other to some extent. In the area of representing functional interests, non-competitive, monopoly-like modes of organisation are an essential prerequisite for responsible interest representation and accountable participation in public policy which, in turn, are very important with regard to performance.

The implementation of Schmitter's proposal would institutionalise inter-associational competition for vouchers, and thus would set incentives to adopt populist policy lines. At worst, this might pave the way for some kind of organised populism, which would be the least desirable outcome between neo-liberalism and neo-corporatism.

Melitta Aschauer-Nagl (Austrian Federal Chamber of Labour, Vienna) suspects that for the man in the street the problem with the EU is not a lack of democracy but a lack of recognisable goals. As concerns the discussion about reforms of the system of interest representation in the EU, according to her experience, special interests are already better represented at the EU-level than in the member states.

In the following **discussion,** critical remarks about Schmitter's voucher proposal are prevalent: If the formation of a system of interest associations were left entirely to a spontaneous process, this would result in a fragmented structure of competing associations dominated by special-interest groups with ample financial resources. These special-interest groups would be neither interested in providing public goods nor able to produce them.

With regard to economic performance, social stability etc., a system of encompassing, non-competing interest associations is superior to a fragmented system of competing special-interest groups, as Schmitter himself has pointed out many times. Encompassing associations, however, do not come about spontaneously. Historical evidence suggests that aid from the state is required to establish associations of this kind. Implementation of Schmitter's voucher proposal would push the European system of interest associations in the opposite direction: Encompassing associations in the sphere of economic and social interests able to provide public goods would never result from such a process.

Because of the contradiction between Schmitter's voucher proposal and the required provision of public and merit goods by encompassing interest associations at the EU-level, a combination of the voucher proposal with a system of monopoly organisation of functional interests is suggested: Using their vouchers, Euro-citizens would decide about the representation of various Euro-interest groups within monopolistic functional associations able to provide public goods.

Whether a genuinely European civil society already exists or not, is contested. What Europeans have in common is a certain concept about the organisation of society in general and the social model and the role of associations in particular. The proposed voucher system might destroy one of the few already existing traces of a European civil society, i. e. the European interest associations in the economic and social sphere and the Social Dialogue.

Furthermore it is questionable whether democratisation of the EU by strengthening the European parties is qualitatively superior to democratisation by enhancing the role of associations in the EU-decision-making process. Parties as well as interest associations are to some extent rent-seekers, both are—at least in Europe—publicly subsidised.

In his reply to the discussants, **Schmitter** agrees with Traxler insofar as up to now the legitimacy of the EU has indeed been primarily instrumental and based on performance criteria. But, with the implementation of the EMU, this will no longer be sufficient. The growth of anti-EU political parties in many member states is a clear signal in this respect. Questions of participation and of the decision-making process in the EU will soon become an issue at the national and the European level. Democratisation had better be discussed now, before anti-European movements gain in strength.

One of the most common arguments against democratisation of the EU is the lack of a European 'demos', of a public space. Schmitter dismisses this as ahistorical: A European 'demos' will only come into existence after democratic, i. e. reasonably open and competitive, politics have been practised for some time.

Democratisation by strengthening a pluralist system of interest associations might be preferable to promoting truly European political parties: A pluralist system of interest associations, social movements, etc. is much more open and flexible than the party system, due to the high thresholds for entering the latter.

The EU member states are very diverse in respect of the system of interest associations. There is no single European model of civil society! And certainly Austria is not a typical case, but is instead extremely outlying. What kind of system of interest associations is appropriate for the EU? Though encompassing associations are preferable at the national level, this kind of logic cannot be applied at the EU-level. There is no real possibility of providing public goods through monopolistic interest associations at the European level because any attempt at this—given the diversity of culture, politics, interests etc.—would cause serious, even unsolvable conflicts within these organisations. For the EU-level a pluralist system of interest associations is the only desirable one and the only one that will work.

It is undisputed that the formation of European civil society will need some kind of public funding. The proposed voucher system has the advantage of encouraging pluralism, but ensures at the same time that there is an even base for competition. Furthermore it measures the intensity of preferences. It is not an exclusive system: No association is forced to compete for vouchers and funds deriving from vouchers are not the only source of revenue for associations. Other forms of income, e. g. voluntary private contributions or public subsidies, may compensate for a lack of vouchers. The structure of interest associations arising out of the voucher system is preferable to the one currently in existence, because the latter is not representative and skewed in favour of socio-economic interest associations. For that reason, the voucher system could also be used to determine the distribution of seats in the Economic and Social Committee. Fine-tuning the voucher system to include incentives for encompassing organisations is possible, but not desirable from Schmitter's point of view.

In his contribution (with F. Traxler) to the 1995 Arbeitskreis-volume *"Sozialpartnerschaft und Arbeitsbeziehungen in Europa"* (Verlag MANZ, Vienna), Schmitter noticed a tendency of the EU towards a "variable geometry" of territorial and functional constituencies. Asked whether this assessment is still upheld after the Treaty of Amsterdam and in view of the upcoming realisation of EMU and the Eastern enlargement, Schmitter replies that the "Northern enlargement" (Sweden, Finland, Austria)—surprisingly —did not increase "flexibility" (the *Eurospeak* term nowadays used instead of 'variable geometry'). And the Treaty of Amsterdam clearly diminishes the legal possibilities for "flexibility". The Eastern European first round-applicants will probably not accept all of the present *acquis communautaire*. But presumably all countries that join the EU (or any part of it) will voluntarily agree to submit themselves to a minimum common denominator of obligations and, hence, to the supranational authority of the

Commission and the Court of Justice in these (restricted) matters. The core of obligations will most likely incorporate key aspects of the present *acquis communautaire.*

Justin Greenwood (Robert Gordon University, Aberdeen), The Role of the Associations in a European Constitution

Greenwood assesses the current and future role of interest associations in the EU: Weak Euro groups are no longer the rule. In the late 1990s European interest representation has reached a level of maturity. Given the history of the EU as an economic community, the predominance of producer interests among these associations is not surprising.

While most of the fundamental human and social rights are excluded from the Treaty on European Union, economic rights are the top layers of the constitutional architecture of the EU. Representation and collective defence of interests of workers, including co-determination, are included within the Treaty of Amsterdam, governed, however, by unanimity rules. The Community Charter of fundamental social rights is not binding, is riven with subsidiarity, and leaves the most contentious areas of social policy firmly in the hands of member states. And pay bargaining is explicitly excluded from European social policy. These are difficult circumstances for interest associations to play a leading role in the creation of a European social constitution, or indeed in establishing a European system of industrial relations.

EU collective bargaining is now widely seen within the European trade union movement as a necessity, but there is limited evidence of it emerging at present. The obstacles to European collective bargaining include: the diversity and continued vitality of national industrial relations systems; the failure of an effective European labour market to develop; the weakness of European umbrella organisations; the lack of sectoral employers' associations in many industries. None of the three European Social Partner organisations (UNICE, CEEP, ETUC) enjoy a general bargaining mandate, but rather must seek the agreement of their members afresh each time in order to enter negotiations. While there are seventeen European sectoral trade unions, these often lack sectoral business counterparts willing to act, or capable of acting, on employment related issues.

The annexing of the Social Policy Agreement to the Treaty on European Union did represent a considerable change of gear for the Social Dialogue because it granted the European Social Partners an institutionalised role in European public policy making. To date, however, only two agreements have been concluded under this mechanism. Without the support of employers, the Social Dialogue cannot develop into a system of European collective bargaining! The sheer diversity of UNICE, whose membership spans employers' as well as producers' federations, makes it difficult to reach agreement of any sort on common positions. Given the current situation of European labour markets, it is far easier for employers' associations to get agreement to oppose a legislative proposal than it is to find ground for even a qualified acceptance.

ETUC's principle hope of developing the Social Dialogue into a system of European level collective bargaining lies in three directions: The first of these is an enhanced role for the Social Partners in macro-economic policy with the realisation of the EMU. The second hope is the Commission, an actor whose interests lie in the further development of European level competencies and who, for this reason, continues to be the most proactive force in the development of the Social Dialogue. The third hope lies with the linkage with the employment agenda for Europe. Employment has now become the very top issue on the European policy agenda, with all policies required to contribute to the employment strategy.

For the Social Partners, the key to growth and employment lies in a conducive macro-economic environment, and here there are signs that an enhanced, renewed role for the Social Partners is being sought in a field which is less likely to draw objections from employers.

As an active practitioner, **Bettina Agathonos (Austrian Federation of Trade Unions and ETUC, Brussels)** paints a less pessimistic picture of the future of the Social Dialogue and European social policy. Rather unexpectedly, there has been considerable progress in the field of social policy in recent years: Through the mechanism of Social Dialogue, the European Social Partners received legislative competencies (which in many member states of the EU the national associations of business and labour do not enjoy!). With ratification of the Maastricht Treaty, the area of majority voting in the field of social policy was extended. And since the inclusion of the Employment Chapter in the Amsterdam Treaty the employment goal has been accorded a much more prominent status in EU policy making. It remains to be seen whether progress towards full employment will be supervised with the same stringency as progress towards price stability and sound fiscal policy has been measured.

Furthermore, the Commission now proposes to extend the sectoral Social Dialogue to all sectors. As in the case of European Works Councils, additional financial means will be required for the realisation of this proposal.

With regard to collective bargaining, the first steps towards EU-wide co-ordination of negotiations at the national and regional level have been taken. Trade unions concentrate on trying to foster cross-border co-operation in order to forestall any possible downward pressure on pay and working conditions once the single currency is in place. These attempts are most advanced in the metal industry and in construction. In the metal industry the trade unions have already agreed upon measures to prevent beggar-my-neighbour wage policies.

Gerhard Huemer (Austrian Federal Economic Chamber, Vienna) admonishes not to underestimate the function of mere advisory bodies. Discussions in these bodies are conducive to finding a common understanding of problems and to building relationships of mutual trust. Both affect the actual decisions taken by each of the participants. The decision-making process with regard to the EMU demonstrated this: Support for the EMU by employers' associations and trade unions in the member states was to some extent a result of the Social Partners' dialogue at the European level.

To facilitate future accords of the European Social Partners, Huemer suggests broader agendas for the negotiations. This would permit package deals, which are impossible in the case of an issue-by-issue procedure. Setting up bridges between the Social Dialogue and the macro-economic dialogue would be helpful in this respect.

In the following **discussion** it is pointed out that the established mechanism of Social Dialogue in Brussels is only one of many elements of the entire collective bargaining system in the EU. What might eventually develop is a multi-layered system of European Social Dialogue with a clearly defined division of labour between the negotiating levels.

Under the EMU, there is a need for international co-ordination of national wage policies in order to prevent social dumping and to keep wage increases in line with inflation targets and macro-economic requirements. The only feasible approach towards this kind of co-ordination is building a network-style system of cross-border contacts and negotiations. This co-ordination effort should concentrate on rules. What really matters is a consensus—and not necessarily a formal agreement—on the principles guiding national wage policies. Collective bargaining about wages may continue at the national level, which is far better equipped to cope with this task.

A rather loose network-style system of co-ordination in combination with functioning systems of collective bargaining at the level of member states and with the established mechanism of Social Dialogue in Brussels might eventually form a coherent system of European collective bargaining. This is a concept completely different from strictly centralised European wage negotiations!

Some observers, however, claim that supranational wage co-ordination is unnecessary because monetary discipline enforces wage moderation. It is argued that resorting to restrictive monetary policy is a very costly way—in terms of unemployment—to keep wages in line with inflation targets and macro-economic requirements. Consensus on guiding principles for national wage policies consistent with the latter would avoid these costs.

Analyses of neo-corporatist arrangements in Western Europe suggest that in many cases a relationship of mutual trust between employers' associations and trade unions is of crucial importance. The Social Partners trust each other more than they trust the state! At the European level, however, this kind of high-trust relationship still does not exist.

Evidence from individual countries also suggests that nothing is more conducive to consensus between the Social Partners than attack from outside. External pressure directs the attention of the Social Partners to their common interests, to common tasks, competencies and goals—in other words, to the fact that there is something to be defended. On this account the Social Dialogue, to the extent that it brings about common tasks, competencies and goals, may in the long run cause learning effects and defensive attitudes shared by both sides. It has already changed the employers' attitudes towards the dialogue itself to an astonishing degree.

The Commission is optimistic about the future of the macro-economic Social Dialogue in the EU. For many years this dialogue has been an important forum for exchange of information about the economic situation, the outlook and policy recommendations between the European Social Partners and the Commission. In many instances the dialogue partners have found a common language or even a common understanding. The joint opinions of the European Social Partners and the frequent contacts with the latter have helped the Commission to draft the recommendations on Broad Economic Policy Guidelines.

With regard to the policy-mix under EMU, more discussion about the principles of wage policy between the main actors of economic policy would be helpful. Establishing regular contacts between Ecofin and the European Social Partners will continue to be complicated due to the semi-annual changes in the presidency of the former. As a consequence, attaining a structured dialogue between the European Central Bank and the Social Partners might even turn out to be the less difficult task!

The national political parties should be taken into account with regard to institutional and political changes at the EU-level. The present situation (after the German elections) is extraordinary in so far as 14 out of 15 national governments in the EU are publicly committed to the Social Dialogue as a major component of the European decision-making process.

In his concluding remarks, **Greenwood** states the significant fact that in the discussions nobody has identified the Social Dialogue as embryonic Euro-corporatism! And he reiterates his argument that the attitude of employers will be decisive for the future of the Social Dialogue. Not surprisingly, there are differences of attitude between UNICE and its members. Persons working for UNICE have a vested interest in enhancing UNICE's role in the European decision-making process. It is obvious, however, that some of the members deliberately designed internal rules restricting the umbrella organisation's capacity to act.

Expediency of collective action at the EU-level is very much driven by the need for information in a relatively uncertain environment, when compared to the national level. The costs of non-membership—that is, missing out on essential pieces of information—are potentially very high!

Among the participants of the conference there seems to be agreement on the benefits of a more structured dialogue between the European Social Partners and Ecofin as well as the European Central Bank. At present, however, the macro-economic Social Dialogue is still at an embryonic stage.

10 Conclusions by the *Arbeitskreis für ökonomische und soziologische Studien*

With the creation of Economic and Monetary Union in Europe and with the start of the euro as the common currency for 11 EU member countries in 1999, the framework within which economic policymaking takes place has changed significantly. At the same time, the globalisation of production and the emergence of new competitors have increased competitive pressures not only on the European economy but also on our economic and social system in a much more general sense.

Common Features of the European Family of Economic and Social Models

To define the essential characteristics of this European economic and social model is anything but easy. After more than four decades of European integration, and despite the remarkable degree of convergence achieved among EU member states not only with respect to per capita incomes, important differences and distinctions remain, so that within Western Europe several sub-species of the European model can be distinguished. On the other hand, in comparison with North America and Japan, it becomes easier to establish certain common features of the European economic and social order: orientation towards high productivity growth, a lower degree of income inequality, an elaborated system of social security and also a more important role of interest associations in economic and social policy.

These and other features of the European system constitute strengths and weaknesses in the process of global competition. European integration and the creation of EMU in particular must be seen as responses to international challenges. Given Europe's diversity concerning national policies and institutions, each member state of the EU will have to look for "best practices" in order to meet the challenges of competition. With respect to the EU, it will be necessary to develop a genuinely European approach to those matters of policy that are to be dealt with at the supranational level.

Balanced Policy Mix

To regain full employment in the European Union, a balanced policy mix is required that takes into account supply-side conditions as well as the growth of demand. This macro-economic policy mix is all the more conducive to growth and employment the more the stability-oriented monetary policy is supported by appropriate budgetary policies and wage developments.

Policy Co-ordination

To achieve this kind of coherent policy mix, adequate co-ordination between monetary, fiscal and wage policy is necessary.

Monetary policy is the only area that can rely on a single, central, and independent institution, the European Central Bank (ECB). A mechanism is needed that allows the autonomous ECB and the other main actors of economic policy—the Ministers for Economic, for Financial and for Social Affairs, and the Social Partners—to mutually integrate the effects of their respective policies. It should in particular be examined whether it is possible to find operational modalities for building bridges between these major players determining the macro-economic policy-mix in Economic and Monetary Union (EMU) in the framework of the strengthened economic policy co-ordination called for by the European Council in Amsterdam.

Mechanisms of consultation are processes in which actors inform each other about their intentions and capacities, elaborate information provided to them by experts, and clarify and explain their assumptions and expectations. Participants are likely to become better informed about each other's intentions and more respectful of each other's capabilities. This, in turn, may help them to trust each other's commitments.

The Social Partners are already integrated in the decision-making process about social and employment policy and the discussion process about macro-economic policy guidelines at the EU-level:

Macro-economic policy: Formal Social Partner input to macro-economic policy of the EU is channelled through the Economic and Social Committee; the Standing Committee on Employment (for dialogue between the Council, the Commission, and the Social Partners); and the Social Dialogue itself, through the Macro-economic Group. All of these institutional structures have advisory powers only. As concerns the Broad Economic Policy Guidelines, the Commission is discussing the draft of these with the Social Partners in the organisational framework of the Macro-economic Group of the Social Dialogue.

Formal meetings of the Social Partners with the Chair of the ECOFIN Council, the key macro-economic decision-making body, were initiated in May 1998. Contacts with the European Central Bank and with the EURO 11 Council have so far been informal.

Social policy: The Amsterdam Treaty concluded in 1997 has provided for advances in the areas of social affairs and employment policy mainly through the incorporation of the Agreement on Social Policy into the main body of the Treaty and the establishment of the new Employment Title. It has substantially increased the role of the European Social Dialogue and has given considerable powers and responsibilities to the Social Partners as key actors in the shaping of social Europe and the establishment of a European industrial relations system.

The new text of the Chapter on Social Policy has several important implications for the Social Partners and the Social Dialogue: firstly, the further development of a new legislative approach where the Social Partners can conclude agreements at the European level which can serve as the basis for legislation on social matters directly under the Treaty. Secondly, the Social Partners have to be consulted on any legislative proposal in the social field and may initiate a suspension of the legislative process by entering into negotiations aiming at the conclusion of a European agreement.

Employment policy: The new Employment Title lays down a yearly process to establish a co-ordinated strategy for employment policies, the Employment Guidelines. The Social Partners are involved in all stages of this process and contribute to the implementation of the Employment Guidelines: The Employment and Labour Market Committee, which prepares and discusses the reports drawn up by the Commission, invites representatives of the Social Partners to its meetings. Twice a year, before the two European Councils, the Social Partners meet with a troika of heads of member states and of governments and with the Commission.

European Cross-border Co-ordination of National Wage Policies

Under the conditions of the EMU the bargaining parties of individual countries might be tempted to achieve a short-term competitive advantage by keeping the rate of increase of money wages below those of the main trading partners within the EU. This is nothing but an attempt at beggar-my-neighbour policy: Domestic unemployment is reduced by gaining additional market shares in neighbouring countries. But these attempts to succeed by real depreciations are ultimately in vain: In order to maintain competitiveness, other EU member countries will be forced to emulate these measures. If a number of larger countries followed such a strategy, this would dampen economic growth in Europe and might even result in a deflationary vicious circle.

Empirical data about wage developments suggest that the scenario outlined above conforms to a large extent to what has actually happened in the EU for a number of years, especially since 1993: In almost all EU member countries real wage increases have persistently remained behind the advance of labour productivity.

In order to avoid beggar-my-neighbour wage policies potentially inducing deflationary spirals, some form of co-ordination of national wage policies in the EMU is required. This would not imply transnational wage bargaining by European peak or sectoral associations. Attempts to co-ordinate would focus on very general "rules of the game". Sectoral wage negotiations would still take place at the national level. Discussion about possible organisational solutions for the cross-border co-ordination of these bargaining processes concentrates on network-style forms of co-ordination, based on a mixture of intra-organisational co-ordination by the European umbrella organisations and pattern bargaining.

First steps towards cross-border co-ordination of sectoral wage negotiations have already been taken by trade unions, especially those of the metalworking industries. National unions from this sector have been discussing general guidelines for wage bargaining and ways to implement transnational co-ordination of actual negotiations.

These co-ordination attempts on the unions' side of a few sectors might then lead to informal consultations between the respective European sectoral employers' associations and trade unions about economic circumstances and their interpretation, the actors' objectives and capabilities, etc.

Orientation of European Wage Policy

Coherent with a policy-mix favourable to economic growth, increasing employment and economic convergence would be wage policies of sectoral bargaining partners at the national level guided by the inflation target set by the European Central Bank and the long-term increase of labour productivity of the respective economy.

Such an orientation would give fast-growing economies, whose productivity level has been "catching up", the scope for relatively high wage increases. And this orientation would prevent the onset of inflationary pressures, since average unit labour costs would remain unchanged.

Sectoral wage negotiations at the national level, furthermore, have to take into account the sector-specific circumstances and the maintenance of conditions favourable for job-creating investment.

Invigoration of Neo-corporatism

The 1990s have seen, in many countries, an invigoration of neo-corporatism, which a few years ago many authors regarded as defunct. The resurgence of concertation, of central co-ordination, and of social pacts concluded by the Social Partners and the government substantiates this.

Concertation is not to be confused with bargaining; it provides a setting for more efficient bargaining by helping to separate negotiations over 'the state of the world' from negotiations over the division of costs and benefits. Negotiators over welfare state reform, labour market regulation or wage setting practices must, first, identify a course of action which is superior to the status quo, and, second, reach agreement over the distribution of costs and benefits of the action they choose. Concertation can help to solve the first problem, spelling out "win-win" solutions before engaging in hard bargaining over distributional aspects.

Due to better information about each other's intentions and capabilities, trade unions and employers' associations engaged in enduring Social Dialogue are more likely to develop a relationship based on mutual trust about each other's commitments. Trust is essential for a long-term perspective, making it possible for interest groups to accept concessions in the short run because they know that the other side will not exploit the situation and abuse one's temporary weaknesses. Trust, a long-term perspective and the possibility to discuss and influence a broad range of policies (issue-linking), helps to institutionalise a reform process in many small steps and avoid veto-positions.

A sustained and effective practice of concertation and central negotiations about social pacts depends upon, first, the capacity and willingness of the state to share regulatory authority with interest associations which it does not administratively control. The institutionalisation of concertation requires that state actors not merely create and maintain a framework for political exchange, but also develop a certain minimal steering capacity to guide societal bargaining in the direction of the "public good".

Secondly, trade unions and employers' associations need to be able and willing to engage in a practice of concertation and bargaining over social pacts. Concertation and central co-ordination are most stable if the participating interest groups are sufficiently comprehensive and united. But interest groups must also be willing to compromise, be prepared to seek common solutions and have the capacity to make binding decisions on behalf of their members. The key argument is that concertation, central co-ordination and social pacts depend on, and develop, the strategic capacity of "encompassing" interest associations.

Explanations brought forward for the persistence and indeed the invigoration of central co-ordination and concertation in Europe are multi-dimensional. A first element of explanation is the impact of the Maastricht convergence criteria. Economy-wide control of labour costs assumes added urgency. Second, the persistence of long-term, structural mass unemployment, with the associated dangers of social exclusion, polarisation of incomes etc. has prompted national responses, e. g. tripartite pacts on employment policies. Third, the reform of welfare and social security systems has come to the top of the political agenda as governments attempt to meet the criteria for EMU in a context of rising demands on the social system by wide-scale unemployment, an ageing workforce etc. Concertation with the Social Partners is in such circumstances a means of facilitating implementation. Fourth, a shift from redistributive demand-side to regulative supply-side corporatism reflects the need to maintain or enhance the competitiveness of national economies. Public goods provided by encompassing Social Partner organisations are of crucial importance in this context.

Constraints for Euro-associations

The existing Euro-associations of employers and employees are confronted with many obstacles: the diversity and continuing vitality of national industrial relations-cultures; lack of financial resources; weakness vis-à-vis national member associations. None of the three European Social Partner organisations (UNICE, CEEP, ETUC) enjoy a general bargaining mandate. Each must seek the agreement of its members afresh each time in order to enter negotiations.

The diversity of UNICE, whose membership spans employers' as well as producers' federations, makes it difficult to reach agreement on a common position. Representatives from all member federations of the fifteen member states are present during the negotiations in the framework of the Social Protocol. The agreements reached on this expert level have to be approved by each of the member organisations in order to reach unanimity. Due to these circumstances, the procedures until agreements under the Social Protocol have been reached and signed are quite lengthy. But up to now all agreements on the expert level have been signed by the three negotiating partners.

Other constraints for European organisations are the topics dealt within the Social Dialogue on European level: Usually it is the European Commission, who chooses a subject and prepares the consultation of the Social Partners. The fact that only one subject is on the table and the fact that the respective subjects are quite limited makes it difficult to find trade-offs in the bargaining process. But these trade-offs guarantee for a "win-win" situation, the precondition for the Social Partners' willingness to start negotiations.

The main institutional challenge for European interest associations in the near future will be the development from pure lobbying-organisations, defending only the particular interests of their members, towards organisations that are able to assume full responsibility for the common welfare. Given that development, agreements between the Social Partners on European level cannot only be reached more easily but can also be implemented at the national level.